# Understanding Community Care

0333675924

Also by Ann McDonald

*Challenging Local Authority Decisions: Practitioners' Guide*

# Understanding Community Care

## A Guide for Social Workers

Ann McDonald

palgrave

Published by
PALGRAVE
Houndmills, Basingstoke, Hampshire RG21 6XS and
175 Fifth Avenue, New York, N. Y. 10010
Companies and representatives throughout the world

PALGRAVE is the new global academic imprint of
St. Martin's Press LLC Scholarly and Reference Division and
Palgrave Publishers Ltd (formerly Macmillan Press Ltd).

ISBN 0–333–67592–4

This book is printed on paper suitable for recycling and made from fully managed and sustained forest sources.

A catalogue record for this book is available from the British Library.

10   9   8   7   6   5   4   3   2
09   08   07   06   05   04   03   02   01

Copy-edited and typeset  by Povey–Edmondson
Tavistock and Rochdale, England

Printed in Malaysia

*To Felicity, with love*

# Contents

## CHAPTER TEN

## CHAPTER ELEVEN

# Acknowledgements

I would like to acknowledge, with thanks, the encouragement and help that I have always received from colleagues in the School of Social Work at the University of East Anglia, Norwich. Many friends, colleagues, practice teachers and students on the Dip. SW programme at UEA have contributed ideas and practical examples of their experiences of community care. I would particularly like to thank Kay Shail and Bill Wivell for their interest and support throughout the writing of this book. Undertaking such a substantial piece of work and seeing it through to its conclusion would have been impossible without the computer skills of Denys McDonald and the practical help of Georgina Henry-Routledge. Finally, I would like to thank my editor Catherine Gray for her encouragement and persistence.

ANN MCDONALD

# Introduction

The advent of community care has had a profound effect upon the practice of social work in all sectors and in all specialisms. Though the statutory sector might appear to have been most obviously affected by legislative changes and the introduction of care management, the ramifications of the purchaser/provider split with incentives to develop the independent sector have meant a fundamental reappraisal of the skills and competences needed by beginning social workers in the statutory, the voluntary and the private sectors. The changes are relevant not only to those employed in adult care but also to those employed in the criminal justice system and in community work; parallel opportunities for change have also developed in work with children and families.

This book seeks to explain the essential nature of community care in its historical, political and economic context. It surveys changes not only within social services but also in health, education, housing, social security and the criminal justice system. Care management, as a new role or task, is set against more traditional models of social work practice. Care management, like any other method of social work must be evaluated for its ability to innovate and for its effectiveness in targeting sources of need and suggesting means by which they might be resolved. Since the book is predominantly aimed at a student social work audience, reference is made throughout to competencies at qualifying level and to the values requirement contained in CCETSW's revised Paper 30 (1995). It is hoped, however, that experienced social workers will also find it a useful exposition of some basic concepts in community care policy and practice.

Considerable emphasis is placed upon legalism and due process, acknowledging the importance of a correct understanding of the legislative framework which supports community care policy and the critical nature of procedural rights where there is competition for resources. Helping users of a service to understand what is available, by what means and at what cost is fundamental to a user-centred model of practice. These are also principles of good administration which the system of community care is designed to uphold. This is not to imply that the care management process of assessment, care planning, monitoring and review can be mechanistic; the challenge to the reflective practitioner is to integrate new models of working with the traditional social work agendas of care, protection, support and advocacy.

What is controversial is the extent to which community care has changed not only the context and style, but also the meaning, of social work practice. By emphasising efficiency in the allocation of resources and the rationality of competition, business skills have been incorporated into the job that social workers do. Providing support and advocacy for vulnerable and disadvantaged people will necessarily involve values and choices which fit uneasily into this framework. Community care is a system based on needs, not on rights. The social worker's role in assessing need means that he or she acts as a gatekeeper for potential users of services. How many people are allowed to enter the system, and according to what criteria, will vary in relation to the amount of resources the agency has at its disposal, its policy decisions concerning competing demands on those resources, and its interpretation of its legal obligations towards different individuals and groups. Arguably this compromises professionalism by the constraints that it imposes on the breadth of an assessment or the range of choices that can subsequently be offered. Tensions may exist between economic and social objectives, managing the budget and advocacy for the best deal possible for an individual who is seeking a service.

These sort of dilemmas mean that social work cannot be atheoretical. Community care policy is based upon a consensus model of society within which change is seen as incremental and based upon rational principles. This is overlaid by a belief in personal responsibility and family values. Thus the means-testing of payment for services and the emphasis on informal, or family-based, care may be seen to reflect a system based on unequal opportunities and traditional roles. The role of the social worker is therefore to work within the system basically to support it, though with some scope to ameliorate its harshness with respect to some groups or individuals seen as deserving or unfortunate. Radical perspectives would, by contrast, emphasise the importance of challenging the system rather than working within it. Anti-oppressive practice highlights structural and individual aspects of oppression based on race, gender, sexuality, disability and social class. The theoretical orientation of the worker will in turn determine the method of intervention which is favoured as well as the outcome that is sought. Despite its prescribed emphasis on procedures and process the need for reflective and analytical practice is thus enhanced rather than undermined by community care.

Even though social work within community care has become closely identified with care management, other methods of working cannot thereby be discounted. If it is accepted that the relevant assessment is not simply that of individuals but of social relationships in families and groups then social casework remains a relevant method of intervention. Most people will have a pre-existing social network of family and friends and involved professionals around which a package of care can be built. Maintaining and adjusting these relationships is the stuff of social casework. Given that formal services are inadequate to compensate for informal care, a focus on the needs of carers and other family members is an essential part of maintaining people in the community. Harnessing the resources of the community itself to support its members or incorporate new ones, will involve skills in community social work as well as in networking.

Evidence-based practice increasingly emphasises the importance of evaluation, monitoring and review. It is important therefore that criteria for progress and achievement are fixed at the outset. The terms 'quality assurance' and 'quality control' show a concern that quality should be built into systems for delivering service. The important question then is: whose quality is that which is being determined and assessed? That of the provider, or that of the consumer? Systems of regulation such as that for residential and nursing home care have always had to juggle these, sometimes competing, notions of quality. It is important not only to give people a right of 'exit' from a system with which they are unhappy, but also the best systems allow for the consumer's voice to be heard in the design of services.

Having accessible and independent means of challenging decision-makers is particularly important when resources are scarce. Procedural rights – to be assessed according to a fair procedure, and to have an opportunity of stating one's case against known priorities – assume greater significance when substantive rights are limited. Policy makers also need to know where deficiencies in services are perceived to lie. Adams (1998) sees social work as moving towards proceduralism and away from theory-based and value-driven aspects of critically reflective practice. Empty proceduralism, in the sense of accumulating paperwork to serve only bureaucratic ends, is of course to be resisted. But proceduralism which is part of due process is itself driven by values of fairness and distributive justice. Certainly the Department of Health's policy guidance on community care (DoH, 1990a) emphasises the partnership aspects of sharing written care plans and reviewing such plans in a holistic way rather than service by service. Thus proceduralism can serve higher order ends by emphasising the sovereignity of the service user.

For the practice learner in social work, to whom this book is primarily addressed, the student's learning needs in any organisation need to be balanced against standards of service that the agency has to guarantee. A trend noted by the Social Services Inspectorate in its preliminary assessment of the effect of community care on Social Services Departments (1993) was that professional leadership (from team managers as qualified social workers) was being replaced by managerial accountability, especially for budget holders. Issues of professional and personal development therefore may have been pushed further down the agenda of managers. This is bound to have an effect upon the practice learner's experience of the agency as a learning environment.

Another area in which the development of a professional identity has perhaps become more difficult is that of multi-disciplinary working. Griffiths (1988) certainly saw care management as a role which could be performed by people with backgrounds other than social work, and although some authorities have appointed only qualified social workers to care assessor posts, others have recruited people from a variety of backgrounds. Finding a distinct identity for social work has thus become more difficult. Petch (1997) draws a distinction between role and task. The role of the assessor or care manager may be open to people from different professional groupings, but the task of the social worker is prescribed by a distinctive set of values and skills which focus on respect for persons and skills in negotiating social and personal relationships. The long-term nature of care management, particularly for people with chronic needs, should not be under-estimated. Case management had its roots in the United States (Raiff and Shore, 1993) and was conceived essentially as long-term. The recent popularity of short-term, task-centred work should not be allowed to detract from the long-term, but dynamically changing needs of people with disabilities or chronic ill health. For them, the emphasis will be on enablement and support and their needs are unlikely to be amenable to short-term, curative solutions.

The knowledge base of beginning social workers, even within the parameters only of adult care, is increasing large. Since only a minority of the population (less than 10 per cent) will ever come into contact with a social worker, a knowledge, for example, of mainstream services in housing, health and the social security system is obviously of importance. Even people with significant social needs will be catered for by mainstream services, and as ideas of normalisation and community presence take root, numbers of vulnerable people in mainstream provision will increase. The voluntary and private sectors will also be taking large numbers of people whose needs are similar to those being maintained by the statutory sector. What users of services want more than anything else is information upon which to base decisions and make choices. Therefore this book contains a considerable amount of information about what services are available, to whom and at what cost. It is designed to enable different systems to be fitted together more smoothly by taking a holistic view of the meaning of community care services and the task of putting them together in a package of care. It seeks to explain the language of community care in a way that fits the experience of social workers and the tasks that they face.

# 1

# Social Work within Community Care

Although the National Health Service and Community Care Act 1990 is rightly seen as a watershed in the reorganisation of the delivery of services within local government, the effects of such changes on professional development are only just beginning to be seen. Not for nothing was the 1989 White Paper entitled 'Community Care in the Next Decade and Beyond'. Systems, organisations and professions take time to adapt to fundamental changes in philosophy about how services should be delivered, to whom and at what cost. One of the fundamental questions is the extent to which social work has been required to adapt, and has adapted, to such changes. This book is intended as a guide for social workers, particularly student social workers, who are located within the system of community care. It seeks to give a realistic but a positive view of the demands that are made upon them by new ways of working, but also seeks opportunities for rethinking the knowledge base of social work, its skills and values which are appropriate to an era of change.

Although the focus of this book is on changes in the delivery of social services, such developments as the purchaser/provider split, the growth of managerialism and the devolution of services are paralleled by changes in other systems within the welfare field. The interconnectedness of services, including health, education, social security, housing and criminal justice is not a creation of community care, but is something which is a necessary premise of the holistic assessment of need upon which service delivery is based. Detailed consideration therefore needs to be given to similarities and differences in the organisation and delivery of these services and upon their value base. Only in such a way can opportunities for, and barriers to, interdisciplinary working be highlighted.

## Policy development

The historical development of community care will be traced in Chapter 2, and has been well-documented elsewhere (Bornat *et al.*, 1993; Malin, 1994). What is not so commonly discerned is that historically there have been two separate strands of policy development, the one 'top down' and the other 'bottom up' which are brought together into one system of community care. The first development was the movement to close the large institutions which had housed patients who were chronically mentally ill or had learning disabilities. This strand of social policy (the 'top down') was formalised in the Hospital Plan of 1962 – which means it began more than a generation ago. Patients thus discharged were then to be recipients of 'care in the community'. The development of policies designed primarily to retain people in the community, and to prevent, or at least delay, their movement into residential or hospital care (the 'bottom up') came more than two decades later in the mid-eighties and was given the name 'community care'.

It is the latter meaning of the term community care that this book adopts, insofar as it looks at day-to-day practice on the ground designed to maintain people within their existing communities. The provision of aftercare services for people discharged from psychiatric hospital care is included in this definition, given that hospitalisation is now likely to be a temporary episode within an individual's history.

## Social policy perspectives

The social policy perspectives examined here are relevant to all adult services, i.e. services for older people, people with mental health

CARE IN THE COMMUNITY

COMMUNITY CARE

Figure 1   *Policy development*

problems, those with physical disabilities or learning disabilities, and recipients of drug and alcohol services. Means and Smith (1994) recount the long history of neglect which is common to these groups, both in the unsatisfactory nature of institutional provision, and in the persistent failure to develop adequate community-based systems of support. An analysis of the reasons why past provision has been inadequate can illuminate the motivations behind current policy. Means and Smith (1994) use the perspectives of political economy, institutions and service neglect, informal care and service neglect, and cultural stereotypes to explain both inertia in policy change and marginalisation of these groups.

The political economy perspective focuses on changes in the mode of production and the shift from a communal agrarian to an urban economy based on individual waged labour. Those who were seen as unproductive – the old, the sick – were necessarily marginalised within such a system. By the provision of pension and welfare benefits they were moved into structured dependency upon the state (Townsend, 1981). Minimal provision for older people, no longer valued as workers, could also be used to socialise a younger generation into the virtues of family responsibility, thrift, and saving for the future (Thompson and Thompson, 1993). The current debate around funding continuing care for older people draws heavily upon the political economy perspective. Ageism and disablism are thus seen as structurally entrenched in social and economic policy. Welfare legislation for those groups conceals such structural inequality by presenting old age or disability as 'personal tragedy', thus shifting the focus to the individual. The claims of these groups are not then acknowledged as rights of citizenship, but are granted as privileges or concessions. Equal opportunities legislation, such as the Disability Discrimination Act 1996, is used to deflect dissent by the granting of concessions, not rights.

For people dependent upon public welfare, Means and Smith identify a frequent theme in the literature on institutions: that many were designed to impose stigma upon residents, and to serve as a warning to others. Institutions, typically in remote locations, isolated residents from the community as a whole. Institutional provision, however, is not cheap; hence the attractiveness of arrangements to support people in the community, possibly at a lower cost, and certainly with greater control over access to expensive resources. There will inevitably be a difficult transitional period when institutions close before community resources have developed sufficiently to meet this new demand.

Reliance on informal care giving by family and friends is not of course a creation of community care policy, but a background to much service neglect in the past. Fear of undermining the family as an institution, as well as increasing public expenditure, may serve as a justification for placing limits on the availability of domiciliary care, and of emphasising personal and familial responsibility. This, of course, places an enormous burden on informal carers, the majority of whom are women. Reaction has come from feminist writings (Finch, 1989; Dalley, 1988) who see the exploitation of women's labour as inevitable without heavy state investment in care, including residential care. This feminist critique of community care is based on research into carers' domestic, family and work commitments. Whether it creates unhelpful divisions between disabled people who receive help and those who provide it, is an issue raised by Jenny Morris (1993a). The role of informal carers within community care is further discussed in Chapter Seven.

Cultural stereotypes about ageing and disability have informed service provision. Negative stereotypes of old age emphasise physical and mental decline, and dependency. Old age is presented not as a developmental stage, but as a 'problem' for policy makers to address. The 'Rising Tide' initiative in the 1980s with its references to a 'demographic timebomb' (Health Advisory Service 1983; Bernard, 1987) is an example of this. Disability, conversely, has been presented in legislation and in social policy as personal tragedy (Oliver, 1996) in avoidance of a collective need to adapt the assumptions and arrangements of non-disabled people which act as barriers in the fields of education, housing and employment among others. An unsympathetic legislative framework has inhibited the development of anti-discriminatory practice with this group of people.

**The social policy of community care**

The analysis of social policy may conveniently be presented in a Social Democratic, Marxist, Feminist or New Right framework (Thompson and Thompson, 1993). The Social Democratic view is that change is incremental, based upon consensus and a humanitarian reaction to objectively-verifiable 'facts' such as demographic change or increased prosperity. The introduction of old age pensions may be presented in this way as facilitated by greater prosperity and a desire to compensate in old age those who had contributed to the common good. A Marxist analysis (Guillemard, 1983) of the same pensions provision would be that it placated workers no longer productive at a time of threatened high unemployment. In this way, the collective power of the working class would be weakened. Similarly, excluding 'unproductive' people such as those with learning disabilities from mainstream education and employment would support the major aim of efficiency in production. The role of women would be to provide domestic services at no extra cost. The feminist perspective on 'care' similarly sees the interests of women as submerged under the demands of the other members of the family or community, which is in the interests of neither. Women provide free labour under such a system, and enable the state to continue to play a residual role. The emphasis on personal and family responsibility is a theme taken up by the New Right: it informs much of community care policy, particularly in its emphasis on the residual nature of public provision.

The New Right approach of course is not confined to the provision of social welfare services. Common themes have been developed through-out the period of the last Conservative government of 1979 onwards, for the following public services:

- education
- health
- housing
- social services
- social security
- criminal justice

The common themes are:

- the purchaser/provider split
- the mixed economy of care
- targeting
- consumerism
- quality mechanisms

The split between purchasers and providers of services was not an innovation as such, since those functions had often been divided administratively within the same organisation. What was new was the concept of the enabling state whose role was to encourage the development of service provision within the independent sector, not through direct provision. The services to be provided were not necessarily universal in character, but were to be targeted on those in greatest need. Who defines what need is, and according to what outcome measures, therefore becomes crucial. Entitlement to benefits and/or services on the basis simply of citizenship was to be further undermined by the spread of means testing to pay for services and by the notion of consumerism; greater freedom of choice for users of services was an important theme together with better complaints mechanisms for those who were dissatisfied with standards of service. Concern for quality led to greater emphasis on standard-setting and inspection, covering public as well as private provision. This greater concern with regulation was somewhat ironic, given the overall belief in the effectiveness of market forces in increasing efficiency by increasing competition in quasi-markets. A whole new language had to be learned.

The National Health Service and Community Care Act 1990 places upon local authorities a duty to assess those who appear to be in need of community care services. A common framework is thus provided within which a range of people with different individual needs are to be assessed and have their needs met. However, within this common framework, different patterns of provision have developed and are likely to continue to develop according to age and type of disability. Some groups which have historically been marginalised within social services departments may take advantage of new administrative arrangements and ways of working to transform service provision. For other groups, such as older people, the community care changes may have led to reduced levels of provision, and an obligation to pay for the care that is received. A brief overview of service developments within community care for different service user groups is given in Chapter Twelve.

## The social work task

CCETSW's revised paper 30 (CCETSW, 1995) describes competence in social work practice as a combination of knowledge, values and skills: 'it is only practice which is founded on values, carried out in a skilled manner and informed by knowledge, critical analysis and reflection, which is competent practice.' (p. 3) All of these elements are integral to practice with whatever client group in whatever setting. Their particular appropriateness to social work in community care will be highlighted in the ensuing chapters. Note that the emphasis is on social work practice, and not on care management. Whether or not care management has taken over from social work as the professional role within community care is discussed further in Chapter Seven. Certainly, the skills and methods of social work practice are appropriate for use in a care management role (Sheppard, 1995). The skills of social work, it is argued, extend beyond this role to the provision of therapeutic interventions and support not necessarily contained within the brief of a care manager seen as predominantly a commissioner of services. Yet the importance of skills to meet the psychological and emotional needs of vulnerable adults must constantly be emphasised. This is true at the point of assessment as well as at subsequent stages. This means that it exists independently of the purchaser/provider split, which (artificially) seeks to separate out assessment and provider functions.

Care management is the preferred means by which the assessment of needs, planning, monitoring and review is to be carried out (DoH, 1990a). Practice guidance is officially formulated in the Managers' Guide to the implementation of the National Health Service and Community Care Act 1990 (SSI/DoH, 1991b) and in the Practitioners' Guide (SSI/DoH, 1991a). Care management as described in the Practitioners' Guide is a process comprising seven stages:

Stage 1: Publishing information
Stage 2: Determining the level of assessment
Stage 3: Assessing need
Stage 4: Care planning
Stage 5: Implementing the care plan
Stage 6: Monitoring
Stage 7: Reviewing

The guidance encourages practitioners to view the process in cyclical terms with review of unmet need informing the assessment process, both on an individual level and in terms of planning services at the macro level.

Social workers will be most commonly employed within this process on the 'purchaser' side. They also have a role within the provision of services in day care or residential units, or in specialist roles, in resource teams. They will not necessarily operate in this provider role within the statutory sector. Social workers may be employed within the voluntary sector or the private sector in any of these provider roles, or,

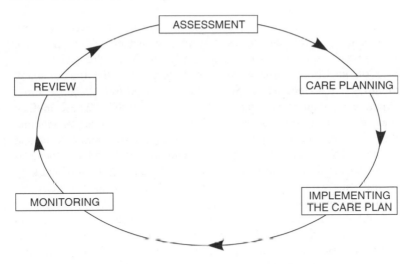

Figure 2    *The cycle of care management*

indeed, in an assessor role, where the provision of public funding is not an issue. Any description of what social work is in community care has to take these variations into account.

The dichotomy of role within the purchaser/provider split in some ways reflects the social care planner/counsellor divide inherent in social work and set out for consideration in the report of the Barclay Committee: *Social Workers, their Role and Tasks* (1982). Thus social work has always had to struggle with these two aspects of its role. Community care has not created the dichotomy, but it has emphasised it. The challenge now is to retain the dialogue between the two roles and not set up barriers, whether organisational or intellectual, which prevent the skills of one being used for the benefit of the other.

**Parallels with the Children Act 1989**

Child care services have not, on the whole, had to deal with this dilemma. Working with children and families is seen legitimately to combine care planning and helping roles; within social services departments the provider functions of adoption and fostering have a long-established and valued role. Change within child care services has been driven by a desire for a clear and more efficient legal framework as well as by a professional desire to work in partnership and influence from research on the importance of family life for children. The value-base of the Children Act 1989 is made explicit in the first of many volumes of guidance on the Act, *The Care of Children: Principles and Practice in Regulations and Guidance* (DoH, 1989b). These include both principles in relation to individual children and young people and their families and principles in relation to agency responsibilities and systems. The values upon which the guidance is based are those of respect for individual needs and potential, the development of working partnerships with parents and families, and the avoidance of discrimination or stigma.

Corporate responsibilities stress the importance of co-operation between authorities in planning and in ensuring the proper use of available resources. This officially sanctioned and professionally agreed value base is absent from community care legislation, even though there are similarities in structure and concerns between child care and community care legislation.

Macdonald (1991) draws useful parallels between the provisions of the Children Act 1989 and of the National Health Service and Community Care Act. The philosophy underlying both Acts is seen as one of providing services within the 'community' or family' home according to individual needs. The specific issues which are paralleled in both pieces of legislation are:

- assessments of need with regular reviews
- clear and explicit planning
- published information on services and eligibility criteria
- complaints procedures and user representation
- minimum intervention
- practical support to carers/parents
- service agreements and charges
- inter-agency working
- provision of day/respite/preventative services
- registers of potential users
- registration and inspection
- quality control and quality assurance

As Macdonald says 'The fundamental difference between the two Acts primarily rests on the arrangements for funding and the client group that they endeavour to serve. Clearly an Act targeted at children and their families has a somewhat more paternalistic role than one where the State tries to act as facilitator and enabler' (Macdonald, 1991, p. 12). Some authorities have however adopted a care management role within children's services. Benefits have been perceived to be: work is more clearly focused and time limited; there is a stronger emphasis on outcomes; the development of provider services in the independent sector is more clearly emphasised. Care management as *method* can thus span organisational divisions.


## The legal framework of community care

The Community Care Act does not offer a comprehensive legislative framework for the practice of social work in adult care. In this it differs from the Children Act 1989 which, with the exception of adoption, replaces previous legislation and applies the same principles to voluntary and to compulsory intervention. The legislative framework for working with adults cannot be understood from a reading of the Community Care Act alone; reference needs constantly to be made to previous legislation relevant to the provision of services, and important pieces of legislation are to be found outside the framework of the Act; this is the legislation on disability and mental health.

Lewis and Glennerster (1996) see the history of the Community Care Act as almost wholly driven by financial considerations; in particular, by the need to redress the 'perverse incentive' for the growth of the adult residential sector which was based on unlimited access to social security funding. Devolving gate-keeping powers to local authorities gave them lead agency status in the provision of services in the community; nevertheless, the limits of their discretion could be controlled by central government through the funding process. Central government could limit the amount of money available within which services could be rationed. Allocation of these scarce resources could therefore proceed on the basis of 'need', with the professionals as intermediaries in defining and assessing need. It would still be possible, under this sort of regime, for the state to act as a 'facilitator and enabler', but this would be far from a policy of open access to services.

Fundamentals of the new system such as the purchaser/provider split and care management are, however, not statutory; they are a creation of policy and of practice. The policy guidance is set out in 'Community Care in the Next Decade and Beyond' (DoH, 1990a) and describes *what* social services departments should be doing in terms of reorganisation. *How* it should be done, by managers and practitioners on the ground, is set out in 'Care Management and Assessment: Managers' Guide' (SSI/DoH 1991b) and 'Care Management and Assessment: Practitioners' Guide' (SSI/DoH, 1991a). The absence of legal imperatives has meant that the pattern and pace of change has been different in different parts of the country; different models of care management have been developed to meet different organisational objectives, and also different views on, for example, professional autonomy and user involvement. An issue then arises as to the status of this guidance: is it binding, or is it merely advisory; what might happen if there is a conflict in any particular case between what the guidance says, and a different interpretation of the authority's legal powers (McDonald, 1997). The answer to this question is explored in Chapter Two.

It is paradoxical that such uncertainties should exist within an administrative system which emphasises legalism. Both the Children Act 1989 and the National Health Service and Community Care Act 1990 provide for complaints procedures which offer redress for individuals aggrieved by the decisions of local authorities and those for whom they are legally responsible (through contract specifications). Quality assurance – building quality into systems through the registration of services and by inspection and review – is based upon an assumption that there is common agreement on standards and objective ways of measuring them. Legalism, however, does not necessarily extend to support for entitlement to services as a matter of legal right. There may be an expressed duty upon social services departments to provide services of a particular sort such as domiciliary care or residential care, but access to such services is not expressed in terms of universal entitlement; it is mediated through the concept of 'need'. An assessment of need, whether for social services, medical care, housing or any other type of benefit, is the classic tool of social policy in rationing scarce resources. Nor does legislation specify how much of a certain type of benefit should be made available to meet the demands placed upon it; it may be very little, or it may be a good deal. Much emphasis is then placed on devising procedures for a 'fair' allocation of services, and a due process model for dealing with potential disputes. Local authorities will devise procedures manuals for their staff to seek to encourage conformity with this due process model, and will reserve some decisions with greater-than-average resources implications to senior managers to deal with strategically.

## Clients, service users and consumers

The public relations task of making potential users aware of what services are available and how they can be accessed is crucial to a consensual model of practice. Despite official encouragement to focus on ways of disseminating information, the evidence is that local authorities are not good at letting people know what services are available (Age Concern, 1994; Mencap, 1995). At practitioner level, an exchange model of assessment (Smale and Tuson, 1993) which sees the potential user as at least an equal partner in the process of assessing needs, is dependent upon that person having sufficient knowledge and information about what is available in order to make an informed choice. A new use of language is emerging which in itself changes expectations of role. The trend is away from the use of the term 'client' (which implies a passive recipient of a professionally determined service) towards the term 'service user' or 'consumer' which connotes a more active and discriminating role. As service users are increasingly likely to be contributing financially to the cost of the services they receive, they will seek wider choice and value for money in the services on offer.

Whilst consumer sovereignty may be in the ascendancy for those people who are able to exercise choice, there is, at the same time, a dilemma for social workers in community care in balancing the rights of vulnerable, and often very ill, people against pressure from a wider society to deal with threats to safety and public order. This is most clearly manifest in social work with people who are mentally ill, where there has recently been rapid legislative change designed to secure greater monitoring of, and control over, people in the community. There are however similar dilemmas in work with people who are vulnerable to exploitation by others, or at risk of self-neglect in the community, and who may lack the mental capacity to consent to the provision of services designed for their protection. Fundamental issues of citizenship and civil rights are at stake here, and the claims of social work to speak for those who are oppressed or marginalised in society (Jordan, 1996) are being put to the test. Issues of anti-oppressive and

anti-discriminatory practice often focus in practice upon risk assessment and risk management in work in adult services. Community care
can never therefore be seen as the atheoretical application of services to
willing and informed consumers.

## Knowledge, skills and values

The relationship between theory and practice hinges on the question
'How do knowledge and thought influence or inform our actions?'
(Thompson, 1995). But this combination of knowledge and action is
insufficient without the integration of social work values. Formal
knowledge may come from the social sciences, from psychology or
from an understanding of legislation; practice will give us experience in
observation and application. Reflection and analysis link theory and
practice, so that by the application of theory we can better understand
why we do what we do at more than an intuitive or learning-by-rote
level. This process, which leads on to hypothesis-testing and new forms
of experimentation, does not end with the emergence of the 'reflective
practitioner'. The process is more likely to be a cyclical one in an
attempt to bridge the gap between 'the high ground of academic rigour
and the swampy lowlands of practice' (Schön, 1993).

Payne (1998) emphasises the importance of reflexivity in social
work, in the sense of gaining evidence about the consequences and
effectiveness of our actions which in turn modifies our approach to
practice in the future. This approach to the production and nurturing of
a reflective practitioner is the aim of any professional training. Social
work cannot be divorced from its value base. Ability to integrate values
into practice means that Dip.SW students must (CCETSW, 1995)
identify and question their own values and prejudices, and the
implications of those for practice. The complexities of this sort of
exhortation at both a theoretical and a practical level are discussed in
Chapter Eight.

## The functions of social work

What is the function of social work within this system of community
care? Is it there to serve the system, or to ameliorate it? This is, of
course, not a new debate. Social work has never resolved the dilemma

of whether it is a service to the state in the pursuit of social policy through the enforcement of legislation and the rationing of scarce resources, or whether it is a means by which marginalised and disadvantaged groups can have their needs drawn to the attention of service providers.

Griffiths (1988) saw the role of care manager as one potentially open to people from a variety of backgrounds, not explicitly limited to social work. Sheppard (1996), however, has argued that social workers' knowledge, values and skills equip them particularly well to act as lead professionals in a care management role. Though there is separate guidance on particular pathways for children's and adults' services, relating to evidence indicators, no distinction is drawn between the competences required in child care and in adult care; a unity of interests across the profession is assumed and transferability of skills is placed at a premium.

To what extent is the development of community care as an administrative system a threat to the profession of social work? The threat may be twofold. Firstly, the distinctive feature of a profession is the possession of a distinctive body of knowledge and skills: if other types of people can become care managers, where does this leave social work? Secondly, the growth of managerialism may pose a threat to the autonomy of social workers insofar as a narrow administrative defini-tion of tasks may reduce the scope for professional discretion.

Lewis and Glennerster (1996) found that one of the authorities they surveyed had differentiated between the job of care manager and that of a social worker; they had done this by retaining social work-staffed 'field work' teams as a resource available to the front-line assessors of need who were care managers. The system led however to much confusion and some duplication of tasks, and worked imperfectly where specialist social work services such as ASWs in mental health were needed from the outset. A rigid purchaser/provider split may give rise to an administrative model of care management whereby tradi-tional social work skills such as counselling are labelled as the prerogative of providers and are squeezed out (Lewis and Glennerster, 1996). This is despite Challis' early assertion (1992) that social work skills are important in assessment in engaging the client, forming a relationship and giving advice. To relegate social work to a secondary provider function thus diminishes the assessment process which is logically prior to it, and which sets the agenda for future goal-setting and planning.

Petch (1996) perceives a distinction between role and task. Care management may be the job description of individuals appointed as care managers, or it may be carried out by social workers alongside other social work tasks, which include the provision of therapy. Whether role or task, however, the skills context of social work with vulnerable people in the community is an important input into the process of care management. Designing, putting into place, and supporting a package of care for a person in the community, is not just putting together a basket of goods and services, it is the creation and management of a complex set of human relationships (Smale and Tuson, 1993). It involves skills in negotiation and planning which are based on a sound understanding of the social and psychological development of human beings. It also involves practice skills such as interviewing, communicating, assessing, recording, counselling and mobilising of resources, all of which are central skills in social work training (Coulshed and Orme, 1998).

**Models of practice**

While theories, both political and economic, may explain why new organisational systems emerge, and how inputs can be related to outcomes in terms of increasing welfare, the real focus of our interest is what happens on the ground. Social work in community care has evolved important new models of practice. Different ways of working in adult services across the range of work with older people, people with physical disabilities and learning disabilities and those with mental health problems are examined in Chapter Twelve. Community care has developed differently for each of those groups. There are different ways of organising services, different mixes of professional expertise, e.g. in community mental health teams or community mental handicap teams, and different approaches to user involvement in the design and delivery of services. Community care has also expanded to include new services for people with HIV/AIDS and drug or alcohol problems. The history of community care, and an examination of the legal context within which it operates, are the subject matter of Chapter Two. The legal paradigm of rights, duties, powers and remedies is an essential framework within which individual authorities' interpretation of their obligations to citizens may be judged. Changing roles and values in Chapters Seven and Eight explore the impact of community care upon these aspects of the profession of social work. Careful attention is given to the process of care management through the stages of assessment, care planning, monitoring and review in Chapters Three to Five. The substantive areas of health care provision, housing and finance, are examined in Chapters Nine, Ten and Eleven for how they interlock in a holistic way. The emphasis throughout is on the practicalities of working within this new system, and of seizing opportunities for innovation that it presents as well as noting its limitations.

## Social work training

The revised requirements for the Diploma in Social Work enable students either to be generalists or to follow a particular pathway to the award. Attainment of the Dip.SW is expressed in terms of the achievement of core competences, each of which is divided into separate practice requirements for which there are evidence indicators in the sense of particular types of work which may be undertaken on placement in order to illustrate the knowledge, skills and values which constitute the practice requirements. Particular pathways through the Dip.SW may also be offered for which the evidence provided will vary according to the pathway followed. Some programmes may have a particular pathway in community care, or in adult care, generically defined; others may have particular pathways which are specific to mental health, disability, or social work with older people.

There are six core competences:

- communicate and engage
- promote and enable
- assess and plan
- intervene and provide
- work in organisations
- develop professional competence

These, and the practice indicators, give a contemporary account of the nature of professional social work. CCETSW has issued guidance on particular pathways to the Diploma in Social Work; and the guidance on adult services will be referred to here. Because students choose to follow a particular pathway, this does not mean that their employment opportunities must or should be confined to work with that service user group. Though some skills and more knowledge will be specific to a particular pathway, the concept of transferable skills and the fundamental core of values continues to be emphasised within the Dip. SW. The sixth core competence 'Develop Professional Competence' is in fact an amalgam of the other five, insofar as evidence from the other competences can be used to illustrate the achievement of an ability to manage and evaluate one's own capability to develop professional competence as a beginning social worker.

Within community care, the distinctive contribution of social work is sharpened by the multidisciplinary nature of care management; rights, needs and resources are often in conflict; economic principles of efficiency and value for money may appear to overshadow welfare or care considerations. This book aims to address these issues for students of community care, for whom the practice requirement 'contribute to the resolution of professional dilemmas and conflicts, balancing rights, needs and perspectives' is particularly apposite. A small number of exercises and case studies are included for students to undertake their own research or develop their own knowledge, skills and values in this challenging new area of practice.

# 2

# The History of Community Care

This chapter will examine the history of community care and its implications for social work practice. Changes in other areas of social policy, notably health, education, housing, social security and the criminal justice system are also charted, insofar as they show a consistency of approach. The new legal framework within which social welfare policies are defined and delivered is described. This change to the statutory framework inevitably has had an impact on social work, perhaps changing its very nature, insofar as social work exists (Davies, 1994) as a statutorily sanctioned activity.

The impetus for change to a system of community care was not professionally driven, it came from the policies of a Conservative government committed to free market principles and a reduction in public spending. Social work in the mid-1980s was predominantly generic, rooted in casework as a method of intervention, and unconcerned with economics. Social work was largely the prerogative of statutory agencies, the effectiveness of which was not, on the whole, subject to an analysis in terms of value for money. During the latter part of the 1980s, however, there were a number of reports published which disclosed inefficiencies within the existing system and proposed changes which more transparently linked resources to outcomes. The concentration was on process rather than skills and on systems rather than human relationships. Not surprisingly, the social work position in all this was a reactive one, and social work today is still engaged in the struggle to re-establish its role in the new order which emerged. The Dip. SW, however, assumes that knowledge of the origins and purposes of the major tenets of community care policy is an essential foundation for the core competence 'intervene and provide services to achieve, change, through provision or purchase of appropriate levels of support, care, protection and control'. Thus some knowledge of history is fundamental to operating creatively as a social worker within the new system.

There were three strands to community care policy in the 1980s:

- the ideological
- the outcomes of research
- the economic

These will be separately explained below.

## The ideological

The ideological stance was promulgated by Norman Fowler, then Secretary of State for Social Services, in his speech in Buxton, Derbyshire in 1986 which talked about 'rolling back the boundaries of the state', envisaging a fundamental shift from the role of the state as provider, to that of enabler. In December 1986, Norman Fowler asked Sir Roy Griffiths, who had previously been instrumental in reviewing management in the NHS, to conduct a review of community care policy and, in particular, in his terms of reference: 'to review the way in which public funds are used to support community care policy and to advise on the options for action that would improve the use of those funds.' The Griffiths review was prompted by two earlier reports which highlighted deficiencies and contradictions in policy. The House of Commons Select Committee Report on Community Care in 1984–5 had been critical of the inadequate care provided to patients discharged from long-stay psychiatric hospitals into the community. The Audit Commission report 'Making a Reality of Community Care', published in 1986, had also drawn attention to the 'perverse incentive' provided to (mainly elderly) people to enter residential care by the direct payment of fees from the DHSS without proper assessment of need. Griffiths, reporting in 1988, recommended that local authorities should take the lead role in planning, according to local priorities, and that responsibility for funding residential care should be transferred to local authorities from the DHSS. Private enterprise and voluntary agencies would be encouraged to act as providers of care. The system would be managed for individuals through a process of case (later care) management, possibly involving a number of different professional groups.

Initially, the Griffiths Report was not well received by central government because of the greater discretion it appeared to give to local government – which could be of a different political complexion from the centre. Ultimately, however, the opportunity to stem a bill for private residential care that had grown from £10 million in 1979 to £1000 million in 1989 proved irresistible, and the Griffiths recommendations were largely replicated in the 1989 White Paper 'Caring for People: Community Care in the Next Decade and Beyond' (DoH, 1989c). The objectives of the White Paper were stated to be:

1. to promote the development of domiciliary, day and respite services to enable people to live in their own homes wherever feasible and sensible;
2. to ensure that service providers make practical support for carers a high priority;
3. to make proper assessment of need and good care management the cornerstone of high quality care;
4. to promote the development of a flourishing independent sector alongside good quality public services;
5. to clarify the responsibilities of agencies and so make it easier to hold them to account for their performance;
6. to secure better value for taxpayers' money by introducing a new funding structure for social care.

**The outcomes of research**

Research published by the Personal Social Services Research Unit at the University of Kent and commissioned by the DHSS (Davies and Challis, 1986) also appeared to confirm the value of targeting scarce resources upon those most vulnerable to admission to expensive residential care. The research concentrates chiefly on frail elderly people (Phillips, 1996), but findings derived from it have been extrapolated to other client groups. The American experience of case management (Raiff and Shore, 1993) also highlighted the value of this method in bringing together diverse providers within a 'package of care'.

Two major themes in the history of community care have been: deinstitutionalisation, and increased support for vulnerable people in the community. Community care is fundamentally a system for delivering services to people in need, and its success is measured not only in terms of effectiveness in achieving these outcomes, but also in its efficiency in terms of process and procedure. The 'production of welfare' approach adopted by the PSSRU at the University of Kent adapts what is basically an economic model by evaluating inputs (staff time, physical resources, and money) against outputs (length of time remaining in the community, improvement in carer stress). The process which most efficiently achieves these outcomes was presented as that of care management – as a system which mediates needs, resources and interpersonal relationships.

Pilling (1992) usefully summarises the different projects undertaken and their major findings. The Kent (Thanet) project (1985–9) examined the effectiveness of care in the community for frail elderly people when managed by care managers with limited caseloads and access to community resources, including local volunteers who were paid a minimal wage. The Darlington Project (Challis *et al.*, 1995) by contrast targeted potential continuing care hospital patients in order to demonstrate that care in the community could be equally cost effective. Multipurpose workers were used who were able to work across the health care/social care divide.

Parallel to these community care projects were 28 Care in the Community Projects which looked at the resettlement of former long-stay patients into the community. It was a condition of funding that these projects incorporated a system of care management. The reports subsequently produced on all these projects are, from a social work perspective, curiously unsatisfying. Care management as a system is divorced from any sense of the established social work role in settling people into communities or providing support services for them to remain there. Few examples are given of direct interventions between care managers, service users and their families, which means that the potency of skills in building relationships rather than organising resources is not visible. The health/social care divide is also presented as unproblematic when this clearly was not the case, especially in the Darlington project (Challis *et al.*, 1995) where there are instances of hospital consultants re-admitting patients on their own analysis of risk without consultation with the project team.

**The economic**

The development of ideas about community care in the 1980s was fundamentally based on free market principles. It was one manifestation of the move towards the enabling state; the state as commissioner of services rather than a direct provider. This concept of the enabling state is seen also in the development during the same period of new patterns in the provision of other fundamental services such as health, education and housing. This was a fundamental ideological shift towards the importation of market principles into social care. The system divides neatly into purchasers of care and providers of care. Thus, for social services, the local authority purchases services from a range of voluntary and private sector providers as well as, or instead of, making available its own in-house services such as domiciliary care or day care. Under health service reorganisation, health authorities and GP fundholders purchased services from NHS hospitals and community trusts. In education, the local education authority will assess a child as having special educational needs, but may have to purchase educational services from grant-maintained schools outside of the LEA system. Local authority housing departments are now less likely to build their own housing stock than to nominate tenants to housing associations for social housing.

In all of this, certain trends are discernible:

1. public sector direct provision of services is becoming the exception rather than the norm;
2. a multiplicity of care services are, potentially at least, able to develop;
3. the user of services is treated as a consumer, rather than as a client;
4. accountability for quality of service is divided between organisations in the public and private sectors.

An outline of the key economic concepts within community care is discussed below.

**Quasi-markets**

The services that the purchaser/provider split creates are known as quasi-markets (Le Grand and Bartlett, 1993). They are 'markets' (in the economic sense of the term) because they replace monopolistic state providers with competitive independent suppliers. However, in contrast to conventional markets, all of these organisations are not necessarily out to maximise profits and they are not necessarily privately owned. On the demand side, consumer purchasing power is not directly expressed in money terms by the ultimate user of the service. Instead agents for the user (care managers) are the people who exercise choice and purchasing power from an agency budget set aside for that purchase. Quasi-markets are often not based on free competition in terms of standards or quality of service; residential care for example remains highly regulated by local authorities according to national legislation.

## The mixed economy of care

One of the assumptions made in the development of a mixed economy of care is that the public/private and voluntary sectors are qualitatively different from each other. Taylor *et al.* (1995) in their research reject this notion by pointing out similarities as well as differences. Many organisations which were in the independent sector nevertheless had a strong 'statutory' flavour; many of their staff were ex-employees of statutory organisations or statutory organisations were strongly repre-sented on their management groups. Funding and contract arrange-ments also meant that the interests of the statutory sector had a strong stake in the survival of the organisation. The private sector itself was also found to be very diverse, ranging from small family firms and partnerships to large corporate concerns with shareholders. The volun-tary sector (traditionally concerned with doing on behalf of others) had also been joined by a diverse group of 'not-for-profit' organisations, such as housing associations and floated-off trusts and companies. Taylor *et al.* break down these not-for-profit organisations into three groups:

- community (run for and by people from a particular neighbourhood or (possibly ethnic) community);
- user (run by service users or ex-users, or by carers for carers);
- donor organisations (where people give their time or money to help others).

They see the most important qualitative difference as being between organisations run by and for users, and organisations run on more paternalistic lines. What distinguishes private organisations from the rest is a lack of mutuality and sense of collective empowerment, as well as an absence of a campaigning stance on behalf of service users.

The replacement of grant aid by a contract culture to fund the voluntary sector has had major effects (Russell, 1995). One effect has been to 'professionalise' what were previously volunteer roles by the employment of people who understand legal and financial issues; the scope for user involvement is also diminished. The transaction costs of prolonged contract negotiations are disproportionately large, and funding is highly volatile. Statutory organisations are unsure how to treat voluntary organisations; are they partners (to be involved in strategic decisions) or are they merely agents. From the voluntary sector's perspective, a common concern is that tight contract specifications and responding to the statutory sector's priorities should not undermine their autonomy and capacity for innovation.

**The economics of community care**

Concern over the rising cost of residential provision, particularly for older people, was a major incentive for introducing a system of community care. Free access to public funding through the social security system was to be replaced by the gate-keeping function of needs-led assessment. Community resources could be further developed by this freeing up of funds. If the government was seeking a cheaper option, however, community care never promised that it would cost less money overall than expanding residential care. The Audit Commission report of 1986 (para. 13) made it quite clear from the outset that the total (though not the unit cost) of community care, would be 'comparable with the cost of institutional care'.

Devolution of budgets from central government to local authorities necessitated amendments to the Standard Spending Assessment for local authority Personal Social Services. The total amount available to be shared between the 137 local authorities that have social services functions was £7392 millions for the financial year 1997–8 and £8792 millions in 1999–00. The distribution formula used is based on demographic profiles in each area with an older population attracting proportionally more funding. This formula was the conventional way of allocating social services funding. The new system introduced in 1993, however, incorporated two distinct new elements:

- the Special Transitional Grant, and
- a number of Specific and Special Grants for particular purposes.

Special Transitional Grant money was intended to meet some of the additional start-up costs of community care; it also contained a transfer element of funding which would otherwise have been used by the Department of Social Security on funding residential care. It was originally planned that the Special Transitional Grant would come to an end in 1996, but political pressure for some ringfenced money ensured its continuance into 1997/8. The amount in 1997/8 was comparatively small: £325 million. Also, local authorities were required to spend 85 per cent of the transfer element of the grant in purchasing services from the independent sector. Special Transitional Grant was regressive in that each year a greater proportion of the money became absorbed into the Standard Spending Assessment and thus became available for non-community care purposes such as housing and education. The Special Transitional Grant has been phased out altogether for 1999–2000. In addition to the Special Transitional Grant, small special grants were paid to local authorities for services for unaccompanied refugee children and for guardian *ad litem* services. Specific grants were also payable for mental illness, alcohol and drug services and HIV/AIDS. Seventy per cent is provided centrally, and local authorities have to match this with a 30 per cent contribution themselves. Many local initiatives have been supported with such money and, on the whole, it has been used for innovative projects rather than the propping-up of existing resources. The Mental Illness Specific Grant ceases at the end of 1998–9 and is replaced by a (larger) mental health grant. The aim of the grant is to modernise and improve social services for adults with severe mental illness who need specialist psychiatric care but who are living in the community.

As political change has happened, so this has been reflected in the amount and type of money made available from central government. Clearly funding interventions are an important way in which local government can be encouraged to support policy directives from the centre. A review of Personal Social Services Funding in 1998 (LASSL (98)18) brought the system of Special Transitional Grants to an end, and also introduced a new allocation formula for *children's* services. The Mental Illness Specific Grant was replaced by a Mental Health Grant, increased by £46.4 million pounds against signed undertakings by local authorities to use the funding to secure additional and improved services. A prerequisite of the funding will be an assessment, jointly with health authorities, of the mental health needs of their local populations. A Social Services Modernisation Fund worth £1.3 billion pounds and guaranteed for three years was created to seek best value in the provision of services, a better qualified workforce and improved protection and inspection services. Some refocusing of priorities and spending allocations has thus been undertaken by the Blair government since 1997; however, the basic framework of community care and its funding base remains intact.


## From policy to legislation

Putting political and economic aspirations into legislative form has however, proved difficult. A lack of professional consensus on meanings and interpretation meant that a finely crafted piece of legislation like the Children Act 1989 would not be replicated in community care. The National Health Service and Community Care Act 1990 is in itself a minimalist piece of legislation, which transforms the organisation of social services departments in just nine sections of the Act (ss. 42–50). Section 46(1) of the Act requires each local authority to prepare and publish a plan for the provision of community care services in their area, and in so doing to consult with representatives of the private and voluntary sector as well as with housing and health authorities. There is also a duty to consult representatives of users of services and to consult private carers. Section 42 of the Act enables local authorities for the first time to contract with the private sector, and to make placements in nursing homes (subject to agreement from the Health Authority in individual cases) as well as in residential care homes. The duty upon the local authority to charge for such accommodation is reiterated.

Section 47 is a central section of the Act insofar as it contains a duty to asses the need for community care services (as defined in s. 46 of the Act) and subsequently to make a decision as to what services should be provided. Finally, s. 50 requires local authorities to set up representation and complaints procedures and amends the Local Authority Social Services Act 1970 so as to allow the Secretary of State to issue directions to local authorities in the performance of their social services functions. The main themes of the Act are described below.


## Community care plans

The first community care plans were produced in April 1992 in accordance with the Community Care Plans Direction 1990; they therefore preceded by one year the implementation of community care 'on the ground' in April 1993. Local authorities are required to publish modifications to the current plan at intervals of not more than one year. Concern that providers of services were being insufficiently consulted led to a requirement being placed by the Community Care Plans (Consultation) Direction 1993 to consult any organisation representative of providers in the area which notifies the local authority of its wish to be consulted.

Community care plans are public documents and blueprints for the authority's strategy for the coming year. They also contain a wealth of information on eligibility for services, assessment criteria and local authority procedures. Joint plans with health authorities may be produced to reflect local resolutions of the boundaries between social care and health care and to seek to provide a seamless service. Local authorities are now also required to produce Childrens' Services Plans which will need to be consistent with community care plans particularly for services young carers and for young people with disabilities.

**Community care services**

Section 47, the assessment section of the National Health Service and Community Care Act 1990, refers to an assessment for 'community care services'. The term 'community care services' is in itself a term of art with a literal legal meaning. It does not mean *any* services that may be available to a person living in the community; strictly speaking it means only those services which are defined as community care services in s. 46(3) of the Act. This means services provided under:

- Part III of the National Assistance Act 1948
- Section 45 of the Health Services and Public Health Act 1968
- Section 21 of and Schedule 8 to the National Health Service Act 1977
- Section 117 of the Mental Health Act 1983

Part III of the National Assistance Act 1948 refers in s. 21 to the duty to provide residential accommodation for those 'in need of care and attention not otherwise available to them' and in s. 29, to the power to provide services for people who are substantially and permanently disabled. Section 45 of the Health Services and Public Health Act 1968 gives a power (but not a duty) to local authorities to provide support for elderly people.

The National Health Service Act 1977 again empowers a local authority to provide services to those suffering from or recovering from any type of illness, and also a duty to provide a home help service for their area. Section 117 of the Mental Health Act 1983 imposes aftercare duties in respect of those people detained under s. 3 of that Act, and some other sections. This definition thus brings together a hotchpotch of existing pieces of legislation covering different aspects of the provision of welfare services. The important point to note is that the 1990 Act imposes no new substantive duties upon local authorities to provide services that they were not already providing under existing legislation. There is some scope for innovation; for example, drug and alcohol services and services to people with HIV/AIDS may be provided under s. 21 and Schedule 8 of the National Health Service Act 1977. However, any expectation that the National Health Service and Community Care Act 1990 would of itself give an entitlement to a whole new range of services has proved to be illusory.

The complexity of the current law, and the failure in 1990 to review and modernise the relevant legislation, is criticised by Clements (1996). Entitlement to service remains clouded by the distinction between powers and duties. Some services the local authority has a duty to provide (such as residential care); other services are discretionary insofar as the local authority has only a power to provide them (meals on wheels, for example, or day care for elderly people). The position is further complicated by the use of local authority eligibility criteria; these seek to limit access to services to people at a certain level of need. Are such criteria lawful? The answer depends upon the proper interpretation of s. 47; the central section of the Act, and the section most familiar to social workers in the framing of their statutory duty to assess for and to provide services.

## Assessment and provision of services

Section 47(1)(a) of the National Health Service and Community Care Act 1990 provides that the local authority has a duty to carry out an assessment where it appears to the local authority that any person for whom they may provide or arrange for the provision of community care services may be in need of such services. The appearance of need therefore triggers the duty to assess – not any request for assessment as such. Section 47(1)(b) goes on to say that the local authority, having regard to the results of that assessment, shall then decide whether those needs call for the provision by them of any such service. As subsections (a) and (b) are conceptually distinct, it is clear that the process is a two-stage one: first the assessment of need and, second a decision on the provision of services to meet that need. Needs-led assessment, however, is not the same as user-led assessment; in other words, what people say they want or would like may not be the service that the local authority will provide. The Managers' Guide to the Interpretation of the Act (paras 12 and 13) emphasises the relativity of need:

> Need is a dynamic concept, the definition of which will vary over time in accordance with
>
> • changes in national legislation
> • changes in local policy
> • the availability of resources
> • the patterns of local demand

The application of this definition in effect means that need may be defined as non-existent in circumstances where there are no resources to meet that need. So local authorities may restrict resources to people who present the greatest risks, who are the most vulnerable, or the least well supported by informal carers. The legality of this sort of policy was challenged in the *Gloucestershire* case (*R.* v. *Gloucestershire County Council, ex parte Barry* [1997] 2 WLR 459), and resolved in favour of the local authority. The political background to this case was the decision by Gloucestershire County Council to withdraw (by letter) domestic cleaning and laundry facilities from 1500 disabled people in their area. Though withdrawal of services across the board without formal reassessment in individual cases was held to be unlawful, the principle that services could be redistributed according to changing eligibility criteria at the assessment stage as well as at the service provision stage was upheld. This is not to deny the necessity for assessment per se; it is clear that there are a number of factors to be taken into account by the local authority in reaching its decision:

• the nature and extent of the person's disability;
• the manner in which and the extent to which his quality of life would be improved by the service;
• the cost of the service, taking into account any financial assessment.

The local authority must also carry out its functions in a responsible manner; it cannot set eligibility criteria so unreasonably high that obviously needy people would be left without a service. Relativism, however, is the order of the day.

Because the National Health Service and Community Care Act 1990 provides only a framework for the assessment of need and the provision of services, the 'what' and 'how' of administering the system remains to be specified. This is done by means of Directions and Guidance from the Secretary of State; the extent to which such powers are used is indicative of a greater or lesser desire for conformity between authorities, and thus the balance between central and local government. Though the Secretary of State has not used his power to issue directions on how assessments should be carried out under the National Health Service and Community Care Act 1990, the Policy Guidance 'Community Care in the Next Decade and Beyond' (1990), and both the Managers' Guide and the Practitioners' Guide (1991) are explicit about processes and preferred outcomes. The Policy Guidance addresses the question of what is to be achieved, or the objectives of community care policy in terms of support for people to remain in their own homes, and the help for carers. The Practice Guidance says how this is to be achieved – through the process of care management.

Guidance is also issued on specific issues such as the relationship between health authorities and social services authorities in continuing care as well as on the respective and joint responsibilities of social services and the housing departments on meeting the needs of homeless people. Guidance will state whether or not it is issued under the authority of section 7(1) of the Local Authority Social Services Act 1970. If guidance is issued under this section it carries more authority than if it is not.

Section 7(1) says that: 'Local authorities shall, in the exercise of their social services functions, including the exercise of any direction conferred by any relevant enactment, act under the general guidance of the Secretary of State.' The Policy Guidance 'Community Care in the Next Century and Beyond' (1990) is issued under s. 7(1); this means that local authorities are bound to follow the advice contained within it, unless acting differently is a considered and objectively justifiable decision.

In the case of practice guidance, not issued under s. 7(1), there is a presumption that local authorities will have regard to such guidance, and failure to take such guidance into account will be good grounds for challenging decisions made in disregard of it. For further discussion see McDonald, 1997. The London Borough Council of Islington was criticised in the Rixon case (Cragg, 1996) for failing to follow the policy guidance. Its deficit was in producing an inadequate care plan which did not properly address the social and educational needs of Mr Rixon, a young man with severe disabilities. The care plan produced had also not followed the format laid down in the Practitioners' Guide, and although such practice guidance was not formally binding there was an assumption that it would be 'conscientiously' taken into account. This qualitative dichotomy between policy guidance and practice guidance is replicated in the Guidance on the Carers Act 1995 and the Community Care Act (Direct Payments) Act 1996 (see below).

Directions have greater legal force than guidance. The difference is that whilst local authorities must act 'under' guidance (with some scope for deviation) they must act in accordance with directions and have no choice but to follow them. Directions therefore are mandatory, and in community care have been used sparingly. Relevant examples are the Complaints Procedures Direction 1990 (requiring local authorities to establish complaints procedures to a given format), and the National Assistance Act (Choice of Accommodation) Directions 1992, requiring choice in accommodation arranged by the local authority. Social workers should certainly be made aware of such Directions by their managers.

Local authorities' procedures manuals are a management tool to regularise decision-making throughout an organisation. Adherence to procedures also acts as a quality assurance mechanism. Lipsky (1986) calls people who are responsible for day-to-day decisions – such as social workers – 'street-level bureaucrats'. Such people need to respond rapidly, often with insufficient information, to requests for service. There will inevitably therefore be a tension between the demands of rapid throughput and procedural requirements and policy imperatives expressed in guidance and legislation. This makes quality assurance mechanisms to monitor how systems are actually working even more important. Parallel to the bureaucratic system, and on occasions in conflict with it, are professional expectations and value systems which are intrinsic to the performance of the care management task by the social worker.

## Health service changes

Bureaucratic and professional tensions have also arisen within other public welfare systems during the era of community care. The National Health Service has undergone profound changes over the past two decades which parallel those within Social Services Departments. Changes in the NHS have however had a longer genesis. Change began in the mid-1980s with what was called 'the move to general management'. This sought to replace executive control of the NHS by clinicians with administration by professional managers, appointed for their management skills rather than their knowledge of patient care. The basic principles of the NHS from its inception in 1948 however remained intact; health services were to continue to be funded out of general taxation (as opposed to, say, an insurance system), and services would remain, on the whole, free at the point of delivery. The major divide within the system was between hospital services and community services; the latter provided by pharmacists, community nurse and general practitioners. The idea of a purchaser/provider split in health care stemmed from the White Paper 'Working for Patients' published in 1989 (DoH, 1989a). Though contemporaneous with the White Papers on Community Care, relationships between the two systems, particularly in relation to the nursing needs of elderly people, those with disabilities and those with mental health problems living in the community, were not defined (Means and Smith, 1994). As Social Services Departments became the lead authority for social care, the particular contribution of health care services to community care was not explored. This history of separate development has meant that the whole of the subsequent history of health care and social care has necessarily been one of the need for collaboration and consultation.

The National Health Service and Community Care Act 1990 did however bring in two major changes in respect of health care: the creation of NHS trusts and the opportunity for fund-holding GP practices. Though the public nature of the NHS remained, an internal market was thereby created within which NHS hospital and community trusts would provide services to be commissioned by Health Authorities undertaking a strategic planning role for their region. Services for individual patients would then be bought by GPs who, if they were fundholders, could choose their own providers, rather than having them chosen by the health authority. Contracts within the internal market were subject to a legal regime which is entirely their own. There is no real evidence that they increase patient power (Harden, 1992). The transformation of the NHS is discussed in greater detail in Chapter Ten.

The basic statute under which health care is provided is still the National Health Service Act 1977. Section 1 of this Act states that it is the duty of the Secretary of State:

> to continue the promotion in England and Wales of a comprehensive health service designed to secure improvement:
>
> a) in the physical and mental health of the people of those countries, and
> b) in the prevention, diagnosis and treatment of illness.

*How* this is to be achieved is not specified. The duty in section 1 of the 1977 Act is what is known as a 'target' duty; owed to the public at large, and not enforceable in individual cases. Attempts by patients to enforce s. 1 to forestall the closing of NHS facilities have not been successful because of the public law nature of the this duty (see Chapter Six).

General Practitioners are the most obvious point of contact in the community. They have the status of independent contractors and are obliged by their terms of service to provide a service 24 hours a day for 365 days of the year. A patient cannot demand that his general practitioner refer him to any particular hospital or consultant for specialist treatment, but once a patient is referred, decisions on the extent of treatment to be provided are for the hospital consultant, not the general practitioner. GPs have particular terms of service obligations to people over the age of 75 to offer consultation to them at least once every year. There is no obligation to make monitoring visits to any patient unless proper medical practice demands it for any particular medical condition. Though NHS responsibilities might appear wide ranging, their practical operation is thus subject to both market forces and considerable clinical discretion. Aggrieved patients are best advised to use NHS complaints procedures to seek redress but despite the complexity of service provision there is no inter-linking between these and social services departments complaints procedures.

Co-operation between social services departments and health authorities may take the form of jointly funded projects, multi-professional teams such as Community Mental Health and Mental Handicap Teams, or individual collaboration to put together a package of care. Dimond

(1997) explores some of the limits of this co-operation, in terms of legal liability. Though decision-making may be shared through informal case-discussions, or more formally through the calling of case conferences or on ward rounds, there is in no sense a collective responsibility for actions taken. Each employing agency is responsible ultimately only for the actions of its own staff. This is most evident when discharge from hospital is an issue; it is the consultant responsible for the patient's treatment as a whole who makes the decision, notwithstanding consultation with other staff. In the mental health field the Care Programme Approach, to which supervision and supervised discharge may be allied (see p. 194) makes the lead role to be taken by health even clearer.


**Education changes**

The provision of state-funded education has also been subject to the purchaser/provider split. The Education Act 1988 introduced Local Management of Schools (LMS) and enabled individual schools to apply for grant maintained status in order to control their own budgets independently of the local education authority. Schools are also enabled to compete with each other to attract pupils and their success in public examinations is published in the form of league tables. Parents (if not pupils) have become consumers who can make choices between available schools.

The purchaser/provider split in education is particularly relevant to pupils who have been recognised as having special educational needs and who have been 'statemented' as needing special educational provision. The LEA as purchaser will then 'own' the statement, but will have to find a school which is willing to provide the special education to meet the child's needs (and the parent's preferences). Part III of the statement enables other services to be specified; physiotherapy for example, or speech therapy, which will support the special educational provision. If funding for this is not made available by the health authority, the LEA will have to seek to purchase such services on the open market. Disputes between the LEA and parents are no longer a matter for internal resolution; appeal lies to the Special Educational Needs Tribunal against a refusal to make a statement, as well as to challenge the content of the statement itself. This again is an instance of increasing legalism within administrative systems.

Education, however, is not confined to schooling. The Practitioners' Guide (1991) makes it clear that assessment of educational needs, broadly defined, is an essential element of a comprehensive assessment. As the Rixon case (p. 36) shows, social workers as assessors have an obligation to be proactive in referring on to appropriate agencies for educational needs to be met even though there are no current resources.

## Housing

Good quality housing is a necessary but not sufficient condition for effective community care. Many people would choose to remain in their own homes if necessary adaptations could be made for acquired disabilities, and the idea of 'life-time homes' has become an important issue in building design. Movement out of institutions also depends on suitable accommodation being available; but suitable in this context will include the availability of good support services as well as bricks and mortar. The contribution of housing to community care is further discussed in Chapter Eleven.

In social policy terms, the movement has been away from direct local authority provision of housing stock towards the development of housing associations as providers of care. Public subsidy has come to be provided in the form of means-tested housing benefit. The Housing Act 1996 has addressed the problem of homelessness by placing more emphasis on personal responsibility; the legal definition of local authorities duties towards homeless people now excludes those who have a reasonable chance of securing accommodation for themselves on the open market, and local authority responsibility, once accepted, is not to secure permanent housing, but to make housing available only for a period of two years (subject to review). Local authorities are also empowered to use 'introductory tenancies' for up to one year so as to test out people's suitability for permanent housing. Advocating on behalf of homeless and vulnerable people will therefore become a more complex task for social workers as they strike a balance between stressing the need for accommodation without over-emphasising potential problems that the resident may pose in housing management terms. Housing authorities for their part will legitimately be looking to community care assessments to meet support needs.

Social Services Departments are themselves sources of accommodation under Part III National Assistance Act 1948. Section 21 of that Act imposes a duty to provide residential accommodation 'to persons in need of care and attention not otherwise available to them'. The Public Assistance Institutions inherited from the old Poor Law formed the core of such accommodation; these evolved into homes chiefly for elderly people. There has recently, however, been an upsurge of interest in the reinterpretation of the National Assistance Act 1948 as a potential source of support for people who might more generally be described as 'in need of care and attention not otherwise available to them'. Asylum seekers, excluded from the public housing sector and from social security benefits by the Asylum and Immigration Act 1996, have successfully used the National Assistance Act 1948 to secure support. This has led Clements (1996) to see social services departments as performing the function of a residual welfare net to fill the gaps left by other agencies or by government policy.

**The social security system**

The Department of Social Security administers the benefits system through the Benefits Agency. Though the system is administered according to national rules laid down in legislation and guidance, some parts of the system, for example the Social Fund (see p. 172) contain a significant element of local discretion. There is little co-ordination between the Benefits Agency and community care systems, even though many recipients of community care services have social security benefits as their sole source of income, and some benefits such as disability living allowance, are based on medical and social need. The introduction of charges for domiciliary care and direct payments (in some areas) has begun to fudge the boundaries between money and the care that it will buy. Though social workers have acknowledged the importance of welfare rights advice to maximise income, they have generally shown a reluctance to become enmeshed in financial issues. Yet financial issues raise fundamental questions around the basic values of confidentiality, family responsibility and personal autonomy which raise real dilemmas for social workers (Bradley and Manthorpe, 1995). Some of these dilemmas will be further addressed in Chapter Nine.

## The criminal justice system

Since the Criminal Justice Act 1991, the emphasis within the criminal justice system has been increasingly offence-based. There is less emphasis on the personal characteristics of the offender or on welfare -issues. Community care assessments are of relevance however at a number of points in the process. In some parts of the country diversionary schemes exist to interview people arrested by the police who may appear to be dealt with more appropriately by Social Services Departments. Social workers or Community Psychiatric nurses may also attend Magistrates' Courts to identify individuals going through the criminal justice process. The identification of drug and alcohol problems associated with offending behaviour has become an important part of the work of the Probation Service which may work with voluntary agencies in providing individual or groupwork programmes. Prisoners anticipating release are also entitled if they appear to be in need of community care services to an appropriate assessment. This is an important link because the outcome of a parole hearing may depend upon support being available in the community.

## The challenge for social work

Sheppard (1995) regards community care as 'the greatest challenge to social work for at least 20 years' (p. vii). He identifies elements both of continuity and change. The change is in the threat to professionalism with the bureaucratisation of social care and the inclusion of market principles. The continuity lies in the relevance of core social work approaches: interpersonal skills; working with social networks and social supports; and task centred practice. What is likely to be diminished is 'sentimental work' (Strauss, 1964) such as counselling, in which the client sets the agenda, and the traditional casework approach in which the relationship is seen as the major factor in therapeutic work.

The focused nature of care management is however a development to be welcomed. As long ago as 1979, Goldberg and Warburton ('Ends and Means in Social Work') were critical of long-term and often aimless casework and surveillance, especially with children and families but also with physically disabled and elderly people. Inter- mittent long-term support, punctuated by hectic activity in times of crisis, rarely results in any change of behaviour for personal growth. If the focus is to be on personal change, a sustained but time-limited relationship within which clients feel safe enough to confront emotional problems can lead to a less crisis-ridden existence and in some cases to behavioural changes (Mattison and Sinclair, 1979). Similarly, with older people, Goldberg and Warburton found that monitoring and review visiting was the predominant social work activity with elderly people allocated to long-term teams. Yet in over two-thirds of the cases surveyed, unanticipated events occurred before the next planned review. This could be an illness leading to admission to hospital, or increasing frailty leading to a loss of coping skills. In these circumstances, maintaining contact through provider services, or developing community networks for support or early warning of deterioration, would be more effective than periodic but sustained social worker visits. Community care policies by enabling such networks to develop and focusing the involvement of care management on strategic issues, are less likely therefore to allow such drift to happen.

# 3

# Needs-Led Assessment

Good quality assessment is the cornerstone of effective social work practice, whatever the setting; this was true prior to the coming into force of the National Health Service and Community Care Act 1990, and it is even more true today. For social workers, the major impact of the 1990 Act is to place assessment for community care services on a statutory basis, so that what social workers may legitimately claim to be doing when they are carrying out an assessment now is statutory work; work which demands the highest priority and the greatest degree of expertise. One consequence of doing statutory work is of course that it is the legal interpretation of the assessment process which is all important; it is more compelling than departmental policy and procedures, which are at best interpretations of legal powers and duties. Assessments may not only be of individual needs, but also of organisational systems (Coulshed and Orme, 1998). 'Work in accordance with statutory, and legal requirements' is thus necessarily a practice requirement within the core competence 'assess and plan'.

This chapter considers the new statutory framework within which assessment takes place and examines the dilemmas inherent in assessing need within the context of increasingly scarce resources. The reader is reminded that community care assessment may become relevant in contexts other than in adult care; for example, within work with children and families where there are mental health problems or disability issues, or in a criminal justice context. The generic nature of assessment work is therefore emphasised. Skills needed in assessment are explained both according to a due process model and for the development of partnership in practice between the agency and the service user. Assessment of carers' needs is also included here. The fundamental question throughout is what is a need and who legitimately defines it as such. Examining the statutory framework is a good place to begin to try to answer this question.

## The statutory framework

Section 47(1) of the 1990 Act is the key section. It introduces, for the first time, a duty to assess. Section 47(1) says:

> where it appears to a local authority that any person for whom they may provide or arrange for the provision of community care services may be in need of any such services, the authority –
> a) shall carry out an assessment of his needs for those services; and
> b) having regard to the results of that assessment, shall then decide whether his needs call for the provision by them of any such services.

It is worth noting here that sub-sections (a) and (b) are quite distinct; the assessment of a need for services is separate from the decision whether or not services should be provided. This distinction emphasises that assessment is in itself a 'service' in its own right that the local authority is under a duty to provide, irrespective of whether services are available or indeed asked for. It is also clear that the local authority should itself take the initiative in providing assessments. The duty to assess is not dependent upon a request being made, but upon the local authority deciding that it appears to them that a person may be in need of services. This is important at the initial screening or referral stage where an individual will often phrase his request in terms of an ineligible service, for example, help with domestic cleaning. This does not disentitle that person to an assessment of his need for other services (which further investigation may reveal). Disseminating information, the first task within care management (see p. 12), thus shades into assessment at this point.

Community care assessments may also become relevant in contexts other than adult care. Child care workers working with parents with disabilities should be able to refer on for community care assessments. So should workers in the criminal justice system with offenders who are mentally ill, or drug or alcohol dependent. A community care assessment can secure access to whole other groups of services for these people.

### *What is assessment?*

Veronica Coulshed (1991, p. 30) gives a succinct definition of what assessment is: 'an assessment is a perceptual/analytical process of selecting, categorising, organising and synthesising data.' In other words, assessment is an intellectual process which seeks to make sense of the world by gathering together, interpreting and processing information relevant to the issue or problem under scrutiny.

The emphasis on assessment as ongoing stresses the dynamic nature of the process; as new information is gathered, or situations change, so the assessment will change. An assessment therefore is basically a working hypothesis for action. It is not a process which is confined to individuals. Specht and Vickery (1977) introduce the idea of a unified assessment which may be applied to individuals, to groups, to neighbourhoods, to organisations and to the wider environment. This sort of approach is particularly suited to a care management model of social work, as it seeks to address, in the round, the answers to all the following questions:

- what is the problem?
- who is the client?
- what are the goals?
- who or what has to be changed or influenced, in order to meet the goals?
- what are the tasks and roles of the social worker?

Of course, the answers to these questions can never be objectively determined. They all to a greater or lesser extent depend upon: the theoretical orientation of the worker, their professional perspective, their degree of knowledge about this and comparable situations, their value system, and the synthesis of the relationship between worker and client. Macdonald (1991) stresses the importance in assessment of emphasising strengths, rather than problems. To begin with a deficit model may act as a powerful interpreter of all subsequent actions negatively in the light of that model.

### The assessment process

Source materials for the putting together of an assessment may be diverse. They may come from: agency files, other professionals, interviews with clients, interviews with carers. The Managers' Guide to the Implementation of the Act (1991, p. 46) is explicit about the administrative knowledge base required. In order to undertake an assessment of need, staff have to know:

- the needs for which the agency accepts responsibility;
- the needs for which other care agencies accept responsibility;
- the needs of carers which qualify for assistance;
- the agency's priorities in responding to need;
- the financial assessment criteria for determining user's contributions;
- the agency's policy on risk to the user and to the community;
- the legal requirements.

This emphasis in assessment on the dichotomies between need/risk; strengths/resources; and users/carers is something taken up by Hughes (1993), and she describes a framework for the assessment of older people which utilises these categories to map out all the different elements of a situation and the perspectives of the participants within it. The particular knowledge that the social worker will bring to the situation is not simply knowledge of legislation and guidance, but knowledge of sources of risk and harm, whether individual or structural, and knowledge of the impact of change, loss or gain on people and relationships.

Emphasis is on needs-led rather than resources-led assessment, that is, on an assessment which is based on individual interpretations of need rather than the matching of people to resources. This is not, however, the same as user-led assessment where the individual defines his or her own care needs without professional interpretation. The Practitioners' Guide (para. 3.35) makes it clear that assessment in community care is professionally determined. 'Ultimately, however, having weighed the views of all parties, including his/her own observation, the assessing practitioner is responsible for defining the user's needs.' A due process model is however acknowledged insofar as practitioners must ensure that users understand:

- what is involved in the assessment procedures
- the likely timescale
- what authority the practitioner holds
- their entitlement to information. participation and representation
                                 (Practitioners' Guide, para. 3.16)

It is the responsibility of the worker therefore to guide people through the assessment process. This requires a range of interpersonal skills to encourage people to explore often difficult areas of their lives and relationships under circumstances of stress.

**Skills in assessment**

A study of users, perceptions of helping skills, 'The Standards we Expect' (Harding and Beresford, 1996), emphasised the importance of the following skills:

- listening and communicating
- counselling and understanding
- knowledge about local services
- enabling and negotiating
- a sense of judgement about risks

All of these are basic and enduring social work skills. Particular skills may be needed in interviewing people with different needs; for example, people whose language of choice is not English, or people with sensory impairments. The core competence 'communicate and engage' stresses the importance of understanding both verbal and non-verbal communication skills, and blocks to communication due to language differences, differences in values and perceptions of need and risk. The worker will need to be aware of their own value base and assumptions, which may not reflect the experiences of people who live with poverty or racism as part of their daily lives (Cameron *et al.*, 1996). In interviewing older people, the complex relationship between age, poverty and the use of language – 'I'm just managing' – is explored by Barrett (1996). How language is used as a coping or defence mechanism needs to be understood not only in a historical context of avoiding 'the welfare' or 'the workhouse', but for its continuing relevance to the marginalisation of older people through poverty and ageism when scarce resources are to be allocated. The research evidence (Robertson, 1995) is that older people are themselves acutely aware that they are expected to demand little and be content with less.

The interaction between assessors and service users is seen by Smale and Tuson (1993) as fitting one of three models:

1. the questioning model where the assessor sets the agenda and is perceived as the 'expert';
2. the administrative model where pro formas are drawn up by managers to constrain both users and professionals;
3. the exchange model, where the assessment process is embarked upon as a shared enterprise, and where the user is respected as the expert on himself or herself.

The exchange model, where both parties together construct their own agenda is clearly the means by which stereotypical assumptions may be avoided, and strengths as well as deficits acknowledged.

Genuineness, empathy and warmth on the part of the interviewer are fundamental personal attributes, constantly emphasised in the literature and supported by research studies of what users want. These qualities are associated with the work of Carl Rogers (1967) in developing skills specifically in counselling: 'the Rogerian approach'. They are fundamental, however, to any type of interview which is based upon respect for persons. Genuineness involves not only personal authenticity – not putting on a 'show' of interest where really there is none – it is also about acknowledging one's own role, including the bounds of one's authority as an employee of an agency (Davies, 1994). Empathy is an ability to put oneself in the shoes of the interviewee and a willingness to see things from their perspective; it is not dependent upon having had similar life experiences oneself, and is different from 'approval'. Warmth is an intensely personal quality, and will not be shown by the interviewer whose first concern is to complete his own agenda. It must be able to transcend overt expressions of hostility or rejection by the interviewee; its expression will better allow the interviewer to respond to expressions of emotional as well as material need.

There are many books available which deal with skills in interviewing: for example, Egan (1990); Burnard (1989). All can help with the task of structuring the interview so that it has a beginning, a middle and an end. Other relevant skills concern working with people who are angry and upset, or who may say too little or too much. An important technique is that of active listening. The active listener uses open questions requiring more than a single word answer, reflects what is said back to the interviewee to 'check it out', points out ambiguities or contradictions in what people say, and reframes issues with the intention of inviting the speaker to change their perspective on the problem.

All these skills are different from ordinary conversational skills, and to an extent have to be learnt. They are best learned by practice, perhaps by role playing interviews based on real-life scenarios, in advance of them actually taking place. Just as useful as playing the interviewer is playing the interviewee to see at first hand the impact of language and demeanour upon the experience of genuineness, empathy and warmth.

**Assessment and working in partnership**

Smale and Tuson's (1993) exchange model of assessment fits well with
Marsh and Fisher's (1992) agenda for developing partnership in
practice between the agency and the client. Marsh and Fisher's
principles of partnership are that:

1.  Investigations of problems must be with the explicit consent of the
    potential user(s) and client(s). Where there is no consent, investi-
    gations should be kept to the minimum consistent with statutory
    responsibilities.
2.  User agreement or a clear statutory mandate are the only bases of
    partnership-based intervention.
3.  Intervention must be based on the values of all relevant family
    members and carers.
4.  Services must be based on negotiated agreement, rather than
    assumptions or prejudices concerning the behaviour and wishes
    of users.
5.  Users must have the greatest possible degree of choice in the
    services that they are offered.

Working in partnership thus demands openness and honesty about the
purpose of the intervention and its legal basis. Though developed in
relation to work with children and families, it is equally relevant to
working with people with mental health problems, including elderly
people with dementia. This is because it requires as a prerequisite for
involvement either a clear legal mandate, or consent. Arguably the
National Health Service and Community Care Act 1990 by imposing a
duty to assess where there is the *appearance* of a need for community
care services, is such a mandate. The scope of the assessment will,
however, be a matter for negotiation. The approach is respectful of
persons insofar as it protects them from intrusive questioning about
personal issues which are not strictly necessary for the fulfilment of the
legal mandate. The emphasis on negotiated agreement seeks to avoid,
or at least clarify, assumptions that may be brought to the assessment
concerning, for example, the obligations of carers, the culture of the
family or the allocation of gender roles. Agreement need not necessarily be explicit; it can be inferred from behaviour, for example, in a
positive response given by a person with dementia to a first introduction to a day centre. The fifth requirement, that potential users should
have the greatest possible degree of choice is allied to openness about

why particular services might not be available. Giving people a written care plan which includes unmet need is part of this process of enabling people to measure what they believe to have been agreed against the actual service provided. The desire and the ability to work in partnership is taken for granted in the practice requirement 'work in partnership to review people's needs, risks, strengths, responsibilities and resources' within the core competence assess and plan.

---

*CASE STUDY* ▰▰▰▰▰▰▰▰▰▰▰▰▰▰▰▰▰▰▰▰▰▰▰▰▰▰▰▰

Mrs Daisy Cotton is 75 years old and lives with her daughter Rose, aged 40, who has Down's syndrome. They are not in receipt of any services from the Social Services Department.

Mrs Cotton has been informed that she needs to be admitted to hospital for a hysterectomy within the next four weeks. She says that she will not go unless proper arrangements can be made for Rose. Mrs Cotton's GP makes the referral, and the case is allocated to you as social worker.

How would you approach the assessment? With whom would you speak? What would be the short-term and long-term goals of assessment?

---

## A due process model

Skills in assessment, though central, must be supplemented by knowledge of what a due process model requires. Because assessment is a legal process, under a statutory duty, it will attract legal requirements of fairness. This means that a assessment must:

1.  Take all relevant matters into account, but not irrelevant matters into account, e.g. the service user's ability to purchase services elsewhere.
2.  Address all the relevant issues on which the final decision must be based. This places a responsibility on the assessor to lead the interview to ensure that all essential information is included.
3.  Meet the service user's legitimate expectations, e.g. if the local authority has published (in its Community Care Plan, or otherwise) an account of the procedure to be followed in making an assessment, then this must be followed.

The National Health Service and Community Care Act itself recognises that in some circumstances appropriate assessment may not be possible prior to service provision. Section 47(5) accordingly allows community care services to be provided to an individual without prior assessment of need 'if, in the opinion of the authority, the condition of that person is such that he requires those services as matter of urgency'. However, 'as soon as practicable thereafter, an assessment of his needs shall be made in accordance with the preceding provisions of this section' (s. 47(6)).

## Determining the level of assessment

Determining the level of assessment, i.e. differentiating between straightforward requests for services and requests which need more complex assessment, is seen as a management task and is the second stage of the care management process. The Managers' Guide to the Implementation of the Act (1991) differentiates between six different levels of assessment ranging from simple (single service) to comprehensive. Specialist assessments may be provided by other people within or outside the social work team, such as occupational therapists. Comprehensive assessments cover all potential areas of need and are multi-disciplinary in nature.

Preliminary findings by the SSI (1993a) were that this process was not working smoothly, and qualified staff were being inappropriately burdened with too many simple assessments. Best use was thus not being made of the range of staff available. On the other hand, the Ombudsman (Commissioner for Local Administration) has, in a number of cases, been critical of local authorities, for applying over-rigid criteria in determining the level – and the priority – of assessment.

The Managers' Guide gives detailed guidance only on the content of a comprehensive assessment (level 6). A comprehensive assessment should cover all of the following:

- personal/social care
- health care
- accommodation
- finance
- education/employment/leisure needs
- transport/access

Assessment of health care needs and housing needs (so far as they are relevant) will necessitate referral on to the appropriate Area Health

Authority or Housing Authority inviting them to assist 'to such extent as is reasonable in the circumstances, in the making of the assessment' (s. 47(3) National Health Service and Community Care Act 1990). This is obviously an important provision for determining the viability of inter-professional assessments, when the complementary provision of services is often crucial for the putting together of a package of care. Attempts to compel co-operation by legal action have however proved unsuccessful. As each authority is charged by statute with its own sphere of action, so they are competent to set their own internal priorities for service. This has been seen most clearly in disputes between social services departments and housing departments in respect of provision for homeless families and asylum seekers. The inter-relationships between social care and housing, health and financial matters are dealt with in the later chapters of this book.

Service users who are disabled will find it advantageous to stress the disability aspect of their situation when approaching assessment. This is because para. 3.9 of the Practitioners' Guide (1991) advises that all those considered to be disabled should be entitled to a comprehensive (i.e. level 6) assessment. The definition of 'disabled' used here is that contained in s. 29 National Assistance Act 1948 which covers all those 'substantially and permanently disabled' whether by a physical disability, learning disability or mental disorder – potentially a wide, and diverse, group of service users.

Furthermore, if at any time during the assessment under s. 47(1) of the 1990 Act it appears to the local authority that the person being assessed is a disabled person, s. 47(2) requires the local authority to make a decision as to the services he requires as mentioned in s. 4 of the Disabled Persons (Services, Consultation and Representation) Act 1986. This seems a very complicated provision; bringing in a different assessment regime for people who are disabled which diverges from the mainstream assessment under s. 47. Why should it be beneficial for people to be dealt with under the Disabled Persons Act 1986? The answer is that the Disabled Persons Act 1986 is the way into a list of services for disabled people including the provision of aids and adaptations, day care, domiciliary care and holiday provision, which is set out in s. 2 of the Chronically Sick and Disabled Persons Act 1970. The 1970 Act, which in its day pioneered the idea of rights for disabled people, has been criticised for its 'shopping list' approach to services compared to the needs-led approach of the 1990 Act. However, as the needs-led approach has become constrained by resource limitations and strict eligibility criteria, the rights-based approach of the 1970 Act has again been in the ascendant. This appeared to give applicants a much surer foundation on which to advocate their needs. However, following the *Gloucestershire* case (see p. 34) it now appears that services under the CSDPA are also subject to local authority eligibility criteria. The advantage of linking such services and of requiring local authorities to publicise them still remains.

**What are needs**

The crucial question then becomes: what is a need, and who legitimately defines it as such?

Doyal and Gough (1990) point to the absence of a clear and detailed theory of human need upon which accurate needs assessment can be based. There is no metalegal right of citizenship which contains within it a catalogue of those needs which must be satisfied in order to enable optimal social participation; indeed, shifting political and economic circumstances make a consensus on need controversial. What assessment systems are about are procedural models of need; how to get what is available. Braye and Preston-Shoot (1995) in this context see needs, rights and resources as a triangulation, the invocation of any one of which can be countered by the tensions arising between the other two. Thus talk of rights is inevitably undermined by the perceived conflict between needs and resources.

The Practitioners' Guide (1991, para. 11) defines needs as the shorthand for: 'the requirements of individuals to enable them to achieve, maintain or restore an acceptable level of social independence or quality of life, as defined by the particular care agency or authority'. Needs then are by their definition never absolute, and thereby within the realm not of rights, but of privilege. 'Need is thus as a relative concept. In the context of community care, need has to be defined at the local level. That definition sets limits to the discretion of practitioners in accessing resources' (Practitioners' Guide (1991, para. 13).

In other words the assessment process is seen to reflect Smale and Tuson's managerial typology, within which conformity to pre-set eligibility criteria triggers 'need', and professional discretion is at a minimum. This definition of need was, however, accepted as the proper interpretation of the local authority's legal duty under s. 47 National Health Service and Community Care Act and under s. 2 CSDPA by the House of Lords in the *Gloucestershire* case. The right of the local authority to take into account resources at the assessment stage as well as at the service provision stage was upheld. The local authority would only be deemed to be acting illegally if it set the criteria so high that even very disabled people would not qualify, or if it always applied a blanket policy and failed to take individual differences into account.

Is this a satisfactory analysis of what s. 47 was intended to achieve? Arguably not, insofar as it implies that the right to assessment can be constrained by a shortage of resources, or by a localised increase in demand for a particular service. A resource-led definition of need at the assessment stage compromises professionalism; is the occupational therapist constrained never to assess a need for a bathroom adaptation, because all that is available is bath boards and bath seats? If so, there would be no concept of unmet need for local authorities to be cautious of recording. The Laming letter to SSDs (CI(92)34) advised local authorities to aggregate unmet 'preferences' rather than unmet need in such a way that individuals could not be identified, so as to avoid legal challenges. Such an approach is unacceptable to service users. The Wiltshire User Network, responding to the NISW survey The Standards We Expect (1996) stated it thus: 'not recording unmet need is a disservice to us service users. Armed with information, we can have the evidence to complain.' Without some means of recording unmet need, the cyclical process within care management of using information on unmet need to inform service planning cannot be achieved. Certainly the *Practice* guidance makes it clear that a care plan should contain details of 'any unmet needs with reasons – to be separately notified to the service planning system' (1991, para. 4.32). Within the Dip. SW also there is a professional brief to 'report on any shortfalls in resources and gaps in provision to assist in the development of appropriate services, including the gap between assessed need and provision'. This evidence indicator comes within the practice requirement 'work in partnership to negotiate and plan responses to assessed need' and is, I would argue, essential to it.

## Recording and record keeping

How, and by whom, contacts, assessments and care plans are recorded gives a powerful message about the status accorded respectively to professionals and service users. Shared records which contain evidence of positive contributions from the interviewee indicate an approach to working which is one of partnership. Signing and receiving a copy of the care plan enables services actually received to be checked against assessed needs and legal requirements. Recording should distinguish fact from opinion. For example, a comment that someone's house is unclean, or that they are aggressive is simply an opinion. The actual state of the house or description of their behaviour, though it may be chosen selectively, is more readily accepted as an objective statement of fact. The practice requirement 'exchange, process and report information' within the core competence 'develop professional competence', however, contains no commitment to shared records. Emphasis is on recording, evaluating and storing information in accordance with agency policies and procedures, and the production of 'clear, precise and understandable correspondence and documentation for service users, carers and other professionals'. Recording is thus treated as a bureaucratic task, rather than an opportunity for dialogue and development. For people with a fragmented life-history agency records are an important storehouse of their past. Great care therefore should be taken that the material contained therein is accurate and contains positive as well as negative information.

Inter-professional working necessitates a new approach to assessment. Shared records may facilitate work by different professionals within the same agency. Different line management systems and different interpretations of statutory responsibility may however mean that recording has to incorporate the referral-on of information between systems. Issues of confidentiality then come into play. Medical personnel in particular may be reluctant to pass on information without the consent of the patient, except where there is an obvious risk to the patient himself or to some identifiable other person (BMA/Law Society 1995). This approach is also apparent in the protection from disclosure without consent of third party information in the legislation relating to client access to files; the Data Protection Act 1984 and the Access to Personal Files Act 1990 (see Shemmings, 1991). Certainly all agency records should now be written and organised with the possibility in mind of future access by the service user.

## Assessment of carers

Providing proper support for carers was stated to be one of the cornerstones of community care policy as outlined in the White Paper of 1989. Pressure from the carers' movement has endeavoured to formalise this commitment. The coming into force of the Carers (Recognition and Services) Act 1995 has entitled all those who provide a 'substantial' amount of care on a 'regular' basis (both undefined) to a separate *assessment* of their needs as a carer. However, this is dependent upon the person for whom they care going through the process of being assessed for community care services. Both adult and child carers are included in the legislation. However, even carers providing a lesser amount of care who are outside the scope of this legislation have the right to be involved in the user's assessment as the Policy Guidance (1990) makes clear. Arguably, a consideration of the needs of carers should be part of any assessment. Certainly, one of the evidence indicators for the core competence 'promote and enable' is the promotion of the rights of children and adults while balancing these with those of the wider community, *which includes the rights of carers*.

The Department of Health has published both Policy Guidance and Practice Guidance (DoH, 1996) on the interpretation of the 1995 Carers Act. The Policy Guidance (para. 20) asks local authorities to ensure that it becomes part of routine assessment practice to inform any carer who appears to be eligible under the 1995 Act, of their right to request an assessment. That the result of the assessment should also be recorded and users and carers should also be informed about complaints procedures (para. 34). Access to the local authority's complaints procedure is given directly to carers by this Act. The statutory definition of carer includes parents of disabled children. 'Young carers' of adults undergoing community care assessments are also included within the Act.

The Act however contains no promise of services directly for the carer; instead their ability to provide care is a factor to be taken into account in the provision of services to the user. An assessment may however be prospective where a carer 'intends' to provide care on a regular basis, thus allowing informed decisions about giving up work, or offering a home for example, to be made. 'Paid' carers are excluded from the definition of carer; the Act is therefore clearly intended to support the informal provision of care by friends or relatives in the community. The Practice Guidance makes this clear in its preamble of 'Practice Aims and Objectives': the type of practice being advocated is 'an integrated family based approach which does not see either the service user or carer in isolation' and which does not destroy 'existing informal support networks'.

Model guidelines are given of what a carer's assessment might cover:

- their perception of the situation;
- the nature of their relationship with the user;
- the tasks undertaken and consequent impact;
- tasks carers would like help with;
- their social contacts and support received from family, friends and neighbours;
- their emotional, mental and physical health;
- their willingness and/or ability to continue to provide care; and the options available to the carer, particularly carers who are in employment;
- their understanding of the illness or disability of the patient and its likely possible development;
- other responsibilities e.g. work, education, family, child care commitments;
- carers strengths and ways of coping, and any particular stress factors and/or aspects of the caring task which the carer finds particularly difficult.

The guidance does not explore the ramifications of Twigg's (1989) typology of how social workers view carers, which may highlight the ambivalences in their relationship; are they co-workers, or are they a resource? are they clients in their own right? The Practice Guide does, however, recognise the potential for conflicts of interest between users and carers (para. 11.1) 'Illness and disability often create stress in family relationships and may give rise to significant tension and conflict between users and carers. Care managers may be working with complex relationships. Assessment, in such cases, is a skilful process the aim of which is to support family and other caring relationships and to assist individuals in finding their own solutions.' The value, in such circumstances, of social work skills is acknowledged also in the Practice Guide (para. 9.4): 'Some situations will require skilful counselling and mediation, using core social work skills.' One such situation might be the user's refusal of an assessment, upon which the carer's rights to an assessment depends. Confusingly, the Practice Guide and the Policy Guidance give different answers to this dilemma; the Practice Guide states quite baldly (para. 2.11), 'If a user refuses an assessment, their carer does not have the right to request an assessment,' whereas the Policy Guidance (para. 5) reminds local authorities of their *duty* to carry out an assessment where a need is perceived, under s. 47 Community Care Act and s. 17 Children Act 1989 (relating to disabled children as children in need).' Where the user refuses services, the Practice Guide (para. 11.1) suggests various tactics:

- the use of two workers within a multidisciplinary team to negotiate a solution
- the keeping of separate records
- protecting the confidentiality of information gleaned from either source

*EXERCISES*

1. Consider issues in the assessment of carers using a carer's diary
2. Consider how employers should respond to the needs of carers.

The part of the Practice Guidance concerned with young carers, reminds the practitioner that the appropriate legislative framework for the provision of services to children is the Children Act 1989. However, the provision of community care services to the adult (para. 15.2) 'should ensure that young carers are not expected to carry inappropriate levels of caring responsibilities'. Social workers will need to take a family perspective when considering the needs of carers. Lack of generic training should not result in a narrow view of responsibility for either 'the child' or 'the adult'. Instead the views of both should be considered, and there should be a readiness to refer adults on to services appropriate to their needs. The contribution of mental health, disability or drug and alcohol services to the welfare of children in a household through the targeting of adults should not be underestimated. There may be situations in which individual casework or counselling is appropriate and those in which only structural or organisational change can offer any solution. For carers, this organisational view may lead to the development of carers groups or new services, such as night sitting. Working with carers therefore challenges social workers to explore a range of methods of intervention.

# 4
# Care Planning

The putting together of a care plan is a delicate and crucial task as it may set the agenda for services and support for years to come. Formulating the care plan is the fourth stage of care management, the aim of which is: 'to identify the most appropriate ways of achieving the objectives identified by the assessment of need and incorporate them into an individual care plan.' (Practitioners' Guide, 1991 p. 61)

## A 'blueprint for action'

Care planning will be looked at here in terms of the allocation of resources and costs. Particular attention will be paid to policy and practice guidance and its usefulness in addressing the dilemmas that social workers face in the implementation of the care plan. A care plan is a blueprint for action designed by the social worker and service user which follows on from assessment and which, according to the Practitioners' Guide (para. 4.2), may usefully be approached as a series of linked activities which are to:

- determine the type of plan
- explore the resources of users and carers
- establish preferences
- cost the care plan
- agree service objectives
- co-ordinate the plan
- identify unmet need, and
- record the care plan

The meaning and content of each of these activities will be explored in this and subsequent chapters.

Though this listing of activities is a template answer to the basic question of what should go into the care plan, it falls short of locating the care planning function within the parameters of social work. Social work intervention will focus on issues of risk, protection, support, therapy and empowerment; these are the major agendas to which social workers work, and of which care planning is derivative. Basic agreement first needs to be reached on the goals of intervention, and the outcome-measures which are to be used to determine whether or not those goals, for example, maintaining independence, or providing support for carers, are being achieved. The values upon which the care plan is based must also be explicit in promoting self-determination, and working actively with individuals and groups to counter discrimination. A care plan is not simply a 'basket of goods and services'; it is a complex set of human relationships (Smale and Tuson, 1993), the achievement and maintenance of which require skills both in negotiation and in the management of change.

## Determine the type of plan

All users in receipt of a continuing service should have a care plan (Practitioners' Guide para. 4.3), even if the assessment of need is a simple one which can be met by a single service. Without a definition of objectives, even for a single service, the functions of monitoring and review become meaningless. Comprehensive, multi-disciplinary assessments of need are likely to result in complex care plans. One of the fundamental objectives of care management is to clarify the responsibilities of agencies (DoH, 1989c) and the care plan is an essential tool in locating this responsibility for the benefit of the service user and also for other agencies. Who should receive a copy of the care plan? Clearly, all users and carers and significant service providers. Research however has shown (Mencap, 1995) that a minority of users received copies of the care plan, and that the format was unhelpful. In particular, there was little scope for recording differences of opinion and emphasis between care managers, users of services and carers.

## Explore the resources of users and carers

Consensus often appears to be assumed, where in reality there is none. The Practitioners' Guide (p. 67) recommends that points of difference between the user, carer, care planning practitioner or other agency should be contained in the care plan, but in the major part of the text the Guide assumes that agreement can be reached on priorities, and the definition of service requirements. There is no exploration of how these fit with eligibility criteria or agencies' definitions of acceptable risk and need, in particular in work with involuntary clients in mental health and the criminal justice system.

'Care planning should not be seen as matching needs with services 'off the shelf' but as an opportunity to rethink service provision for a particular individual' (Practitioners' Guide, para. 4.12) This statement lies at the heart of individualised care planning. Separating the purchaser and providing functions ought in theory to free purchasers from conventional service provision and enable budgets to be used in creative ways. Early models of care management where care managers were provided with sums of money to maintain people in the community equivalent to the cost of residential care, were based on this premise. Indications from the SSI inspections, however, are that there is in practice little creativity around. The conservatism may be compounded by the inability of care managers to purchase outside lists of approved providers. The Practitioners' Guide recommends (para. 4.15) that 'where a practitioner is unable to accede to their preferences, users should receive a full explanation and be reminded of the complaints procedure' Similarly, where there is conflict in reconciling preferences and resources 'users may wish to avail themselves of independent representatives to promote their interests': Practitioners' Guide (para. 4.5).

## Establish preferences

The assessment of need and the provision of services are mediated not only by user choice, professional judgement and practical availability, but by the operation of eligibility criteria, as a means of prioritising who does and who does not have allocated to them a particular service. The Policy Guidance (1990, para. 3.24) lists service options in order of preference for 'preserving or restoring normal living' (as it is put). These are:

- support for the user in his or her own home
- a move to more suitable accommodation
- a move to another private household, e.g. to live with family
- residential care
- nursing home care
- long-stay care in hospital

Arguably, desiderata such as user choice were, from the inception of the new system of community care, never designed to take precedence within care planning. Price Waterhouse in their (1991) report for the Department of Health entitled 'Implementing Community care: Purchaser, Commissioner and Provider Roles' placed 'client choice' first on their list (para. 2) of reasons for favouring a purchaser provider split. The purchaser/provider split would 'facilitate increased client choice through the empowerment of care managers' (*not* the empowerment of users) (para. 10). They went on to say: 'It is important to remember that the empowerment of care managers on behalf of clients does not mean absolute client choice. Professional views, departmental policy, budgetary constraints and availability will all have a major impact on the package of care provided.' Operational and strategic imperatives may thus overcome both user choice and professional judgement. For example, cost efficiency in the provision of in-house day care may make that a preferred option over use of the independent sector. Departmental policy may determine who gets what type of resources within those available.

Eligibility criteria are used to target resources onto those deemed to be most in need of them, 'need' being seen as a cost-benefit concept. The question of who should be in the target groups is based on the valuation of outputs, for example keeping people out of residential care. Prioritising need in this way has led to a reduction or non-availability of services for some people. As resources become more limited, so people with lesser needs may find that they no longer qualify for a service, or a service previously provided such as domestic help, is no longer available. Discretion also remains in how to meet needs. For example, the provision of residential care for someone who would otherwise need 24-hour care at home, would be a proper use of discretion in the allocation of resources. However, rigid adherence to a policy that no more than a certain number of hours of home care would be provided at home, would be an unlawful fettering of discretion. Given the individualised nature of assessments, each case would still have to be dealt with on its merits.

The care plan itself is operational through the system of commissioning or contracting for care. It is one of the paradoxes of community care that where local authorities purchase care on behalf of service users, it is the local authority who is the customer or consumer with purchasing power, and not the service user himself or herself. An inevitable tension is thus created between the economic and social objectives of care management: managing the budget versus advocacy for the best interests of the service user. Mares (1996) identifies a new range of business skills needed by care managers. These are handling contracts, costing care packages, negotiating prices with providers, monitoring the quality of service and sourcing suppliers. In addition, care managers should be aware of the 'cost' of their own time involved in such activities, as well as that or other professional colleagues such as occupational therapists or home care managers whose skills and resources they may wish to include in the assessment.

Care management fits in with the purchasing of services at the strategic level through the use of standardised service specifications and model contracts, so that the front-line worker negotiates only the details of the individual service to be provided to the user, based on the care plan. Thus the local authority may have a list of approved providers of, say, residential care or day care who are already contracted to provide a certain number of places for local authority nominees according to pre-set quality standards concerning, for example, staffing levels, size of accommodation and activities provided. Fine-tuning may then take place around the choice of particular room lay outs or activities to be provided.

There are three main types of contract that local authorities employ (DoH, 1993b):

- block contracts, where the purchaser buys access to a part of the whole of a service or facility for a specified price
- cost or volume contracts, where a volume of service and a total cost is agreed and any additional service is provided on an individual price basis
- individual or spot contracts where the purchaser contracts for a service for an individual user for a specified time at an agreed price

Each of these types of contract combines different risks for the provider, and varying degrees of flexibility for the user. Care managers need to know what type of contract is favoured by their local authority in what sort of circumstances.

Most local authorities have not devolved budgets down to the level of the individual care manager; the possibility of strategic planning is usually preserved by some centralisation of budgets at team manager level or above. Nevertheless, decisions made by individual care managers to choose a particular care provider will influence the pattern of future supply. Transaction costs involved in negotiating with a range of different providers may militate against variety in provision and bulk purchasing of resources.

Mares (1996) sees purchasing decisions as being based upon the notion of 'best value' – a balance between quality and cost. Care managers remain accountable, in purchasing decisions, as elsewhere, for their professional judgement in making placements or providing services. Best value may not mean selecting the cheapest service, but balancing cost against quality of service provided. It is also useful for contracts to contain a degree of flexibility on such matters as, for example, the timing of visits in a contract for domiciliary care. This means that detail can be agreed between the provider and service user without having to involve the purchaser. It is good practice to append a copy of the care plan to the contract.

It was indeed one of the hopes of community care policy that innovative services would be developed, and Community Care Plans have to specify how independent providers have been linked in to planning for service development. Mares (1996) identifies a key task of care management as 'sourcing suppliers' where 'sourcing' is a business term which means identifying sources of supply. Thus a key difference between traditional social work and care management is seen as the activity of seeking out potential new resources and working out which will provide the best solution for the individual user within the budget available. Traditional social work, by contrast, involves co-ordinating existing services and liaising with other agencies.

*EXERCISE*

Find out what services are available locally for supporting service users in their own home. Relevant sources may be the statutory sector, voluntary sector or private providers. Services may include domiciliary care, befriending schemes or recreational activities. You may wish to focus on one particular group of people such as older people, carers or people recently discharged from hospital. Information thus gathered could be put together in the form of a reference book to assist in care planning.

## A critique of the applicability of accounting practices within community care

Lapsley (1996) considers this new visibility for accounting measures and models as part of a much larger phenomenon within the public services – the 'new managerialism'. However, as an accountant, he is sceptical not only about the transportability or portability of private sector accounting practices into public service organisations, but also about its compatibility with the values of social care.

This new public management has a number of general features which are echoed in the organisation of community care. They are:

- hands-on professional management
- explicit standards and measures of performance
- greater emphasis on output
- the shift to disaggregation (splitting) of financial units
- the shift to greater competition
- stress on private sector styles of management practice
- stress on greater discipline and parsimony in resource use

In all of these components accounting has a role to play (Lapsley, 1996); however, seeing the use of budgets as dealing in objective facts is a mistake. Purist notions such as 'efficiency' and 'accountability' are hard to sustain when political pressures undermine financial discipline, and there is more emphasis on procedure than outcome because outcomes are not well known. Despite this, the rhetoric of financial accountability has the potential for assuming a primacy over, or at least equating to, the traditional values of social service staff in terms of client choice, confidentiality, dignity and so on (Lapsley, 1996). Early research (Stalker, 1994; Lapsley *et al.*, 1994) looked respectively at the operation of devolved budgets within individual social work teams, and the monitoring of contract specifications by those responsible for contract-setting in social work departments in the Scottish regions. Contract specifications were found not to be rigorous in accounting terms. For example, they did not question the (relatively) high cost of local authority care in relation to private care, but accepted this as part of the necessary background to client choice. Provider costs were not much examined either in terms of efficiency, since reliance was placed on the legitimacy of the registration first and foremost as measure of 'quality', and reference to levels of Department of Social Security support was used as a measure of 'value'. Thus accepted social work measures replaced objective analysis of efficiency and effectiveness. Certainty, in any case, would be hard to achieve when it is so difficult to forecast in advance what demands for care will be made, when 'member thresholds' within Social Services committees may operate to underwrite budget deficits for particularly popular services, and when the boundaries with informal care are flexible enough to move costs. Lapsley (1996) sees this cautious approach in the face of pressures to give a new, high profile visibility to accounting as entirely appropriate, given the realities of achieving organisational change in public services where there exists a dominant, embedded set of values.

## Cost the care plan

The Guidance is clear that assessment and exploration of resources are stages in care management that should precede any assessment of the financial position of the service user. Thus the local authority should respond in an equitable way to need irrespective of any contribution which may be sought to the cost of the services. For the service user, however, the comparative cost of different options may be essential information in deciding whether they will, for example, opt for an intensive package of domiciliary care rather than a day care option. 'Users should always know the estimated cost to themselves of any options under active consideration' Practitioners' Guide (para. 4.16) and 'no user should agree a care plan before they have been advised in writing of any charges involved' Practitioners' Guide (para. 4.18)

Maximising the uptake of benefits (though not explicitly mentioned in the guidance) will be an important part of making informed financial choices, as will knowledge of the comparative costs of different funding regimes, for example for funding sheltered accommodation from housing benefit, or private residential care through the income support system. Details of benefits entitlements, and charging policies are contained in Chapter Nine.

## Agree service objectives

The principal contractors for the provision of care may be the local authority and the social service provider, with the individual service user a mere beneficiary. So what is the status of the care plan once it has been devised? The Practitioners' Guide (para. 4.38) puts forward the view that 'the care plan does not have a legal standing as a contract', though 'to reinforce the sense of commitment', contributors (including the user) may be asked to signify their agreement by signing. For the local authority's part, 'a care plan may be used as evidence in the consideration of a complaint.' Though it should be used to clarify service objectives a care plan is not a document fixed in time, and should contain within itself a date for its own review (often six or eight weeks hence depending upon administrative practice), or a statement of the contingency factors which would trigger an earlier review.

The basic question to ask is whether the service has been effective in the sense of achieving its objectives, The objectives of the service are the goals which the service seeks to achieve, such as retention in the community or a problem-free discharge from hospital. Describing social care services in terms of inputs, process, outputs and outcomes is an approach which has been adapted from business management. The advantage of specifying services in these terms is that it enables service planners to analyse more closely the way in which particular services achieve results (Mares, 1996). Review enables authorities to check that objectives are still relevant and are being achieved.

The personnel involved in the review may be different from those involved in the assessment. Some local authorities have appointed people specifically to work as 'reviewers', particularly of residential care, whilst others have delegated review functions to provider staff. There are practical difficulties, of course, in breaking continuity by allocating different functions to different personnel, particularly where review staff may be less well qualified than assessors, and where providers may have a financial interest in continuing services. More fundamental, however, is the presumption (or so it seems) in favour of short-term rather than long-term involvement by assessors and purchasers of service. Some of the dynamic nature of assessments (Coulshed, 1991) must inevitably be lost in this process, and the opportunity for methods of intervention such as the psychodynamic, which are based on a continuing and evolving relationship with the client, are lost. The problem has been particularly noted in mental health services (Huxley, 1993).

### Co-ordinate the plan

The co-ordination and implementation of the care plan is the fifth stage of care management; 'the guiding principle of implementation should be to achieve the stated objectives of the care plan with the minimum intervention possible' (Practitioners' Guide, para. 5.1) Minimum intervention is defined however not in terms of values, such as self determination and empowerment, but in utilitarian terms minimising the number of service providers involved. The example given is of introducing 'generic care workers who perform a range of tasks that have traditionally been divided between home care and auxiliary nursing staff'. (Practitioners' Guide, para. 5.1) This certainly has been a feature of some care management projects, most notably Darlington (Challis *et al.*, 1995) but is in itself not uncontentious, given that health care is that which is provided free at the point of delivery, although social care has to be paid for by financial assessment.

Implementation is viewed solely in terms of securing necessary resources or services, not in terms of targeting change within systems. The radical perspective on personal issues as consequences of structural deficits cannot be accommodated within this definition of implementation. The care plan is viewed as a closed system, individualistic in nature. The preferred role for the practitioner is that of social care planner, not service broker. The task is then to garner together the available services, within the limitations of a budget, during which process 'the practitioner is accountable to both the user and the agency'. (Practitioners' Guide para. 5.3)

The possibility of conflict between user and agency is not addressed. What the user seeks, the agency may not be able to give, or may disallow on the grounds of policy or cost. Alternatively the agency may be seeking to impose a service that the user does not want but which is deemed necessary for his or her protection, or to monitor her or his progress; supervised discharge from psychiatric care, is a case in point. Where legislation imposes protective duties upon the local authority, tension will inevitably exist between client empowerment and professional accountability.

Services contributing to a package of care may be nothing more than a listing of conventional service provision. Kathryn Ellis in her (1993) research into user and carer participation in needs assessment 'Squaring the Circle':

> was continually struck by how marginal the support provided by social services or any other community-based services was to most people's lives; those needs which had not been addressed or even on the agenda were frequently the most significant. The fact that several people with disabilities were unable to get jobs, that a man with a progressive illness could not find suitable transport to get him to school where he had wanted for many years to do voluntary work, that several older people were isolated and housebound, that a

woman with learning disabilities did not have the support to live more independently, that many people were struggling to manage on low incomes, that several carers had to juggle work and caring to maintain the household income – these were priority issues. (Ellis, 1993, p. 41)

It is arguable that only a minority of these issues are the responsibility of social services departments as statutorily defined and thus within the proper purview of any system of care planning (Davies, 1994). However, by framing people's experience solely in terms of the limited context of community care, their aspirations about overall life-style are not considered, and an opportunity has been lost for the definitions of need used in assessment to be used to encompass a broader slice of people's lives (Ellis, 1993, p. 41). This should be what 'negotiating the scope of assessment' (Practitioners' Guide 1991, para. 3.3) really means, if as the guidance says, 'the individual's needs are to seen in their proper social context'. Certainly, for a comprehensive assessment (to which people with disabilities are entitled), the Practitioners' Guide (1991, p. 58) suggests that all of the following issues are covered: self-perceived needs, abilities attitudes and life-style, race and culture, social network and support, housing, finance, transport and risk. One would expect then that care plans would mirror such agendas.

   In the provision of resources to meet needs identified in the care plan, authorities should be free to use a variety of providers and should not be constrained by conventional patterns of service organisation. This is what needs led assessment really means. So a need for social stimulation will not necessarily be met by a day centre place; it may be met differently by the provision of transport and a facilitator to enable someone to visit family or friends. Prior to the introduction of community care, there used to be difficulties with 'out of authority' placements that local authorities would not fund. With the opening up of markets in social care, this should no longer be a barrier; however, a report from the local government Ombudsman (94/C/3690) into a complaint against Trafford Metropolitan Borough Council shows that this is not necessarily so. The case concerned the provision of day services for a young physically disabled man who had just left college; the only day centre for physically disabled people within the borough was unsuitable because it catered chiefly for older recently disabled people with better social skills. It was only when the man's parents took the initiative themselves that he was allocated a place at another centre outside the borough. The local authority was criticised for not having a policy on how and when it would find services outside Trafford. Failure to consider provision elsewhere was maladministration.

## Identify unmet need

Care management was conceived as a cyclical process (see Figure 2 p. 13) in which feedback from the user of services was incorporated back into the planning stage. Important for the success of this process is how to identify and what to about unmet need. The Practitioners' Guide (para. 4.35) acknowledges that need may remain unmet for a number of reasons:

• resources are unable to meet demand
• the quality and type of service is irrelevant to need, or unacceptable to users
• the conditions of service are inappropriate to need, for example, no weekend cover.

'There will continue to be situations in which there is a mismatch between the solutions provided by the existing services and the solutions identified by users, carers and practitioners. Care planning has a contribution to make in minimising this mismatch by defining the disparity and promoting the appropriate changes in service' (Practitioners' Guide, para. 4.36). Para. 4.33 of the Practitioners' Guide sees a benefit in differentiating between types of unmet need, including those that are:

• statutory obligations, for example, those included in the Disabled Persons Act 1986
• defined as entitlements under local policies, for example, failure to provide services within defined timescales
• current policies or criteria, for example, the emerging needs of those with HIV/AIDS.

There should also be a ready means of prioritising these unmet needs (para. 4.34). Certainly, the consequences of failing to meet these categories of need will be different. The identification of new needs is an issue to be raised for consideration when community care plans are revised. Failure to achieve internal targets, or those devised externally, for example by the Citizen's Charter, will attract the attention of local authorities' own Inspection Units, but failure to fulfil *statutory* obligations is both a major cause for concern at an organisational level, as well as being open to challenge by individuals through litigation (see Chapter Six).

## Record the care plan

Fine-tuning the care plan against standard service specifications is thus one aspect of quality assurance. The translation of care plans drawn up by care managers in the community into care plans within day care and residential care has not been much considered. Even before the purchaser/provider split, the worlds of community and day/residential care were largely separate spheres of influence. The consequences of such demarcation is that evaluation of progress against goals set becomes more difficult. It is desirable therefore that the two systems are brought together with the care manager from the community being involved in the drawing up and review of the care plan in residential and day care.

When people move, as they frequently do, between the community and the hospital and residential care, it is essential that information travels with them: this may be biographical information, information on medical needs, or the care preferences of the individual – the food they like to eat, the time they like to get up in the morning. Recording of the care plan is an important final step in clarifying agreement between the care manager, service user and service providers on the objectives of the care plan and the means of achieving those objectives. Doel and Shardlow (1998) identify four specific purposes behind recording information. These are: procedural, investigative and speculative, personal, and providing continuity. As far as care plans are concerned the procedural aspect – the providing of an accessible account of past processes and agreements – is uppermost. The investigative and speculative function of recording will be important when complex situations are being explored, as in cases of suspected abuse. The personal aspect of recording underlines the value of life history and is linked to client access to files. Both this and the function of records in ensuring continuity of care are important in long-term work.

The local government Ombudsman has stressed the importance of operational policy for adult residential care, for which individual care plans are an important element. In investigating an allegation of neglect in residential care (investigation 94/A/3636 against Lambeth London Borough Council) the Ombudsman said, referring to care plans in residential care: 'they are a necessary part of ensuring that each individual's needs are not lost once they are admitted to an establishment. They are vital for preventing institutionalisation . . . care plans are a continuous process'. It was also seen as important that problems should not be allowed to drift, and that any issues should be discussed at an early stage with residents and relatives. A care plan should facilitate an episode of residential care becoming a positive experience. Accordingly: 'An important factor in a care plan is to establish the resident's potential and areas of vulnerability so that full potential can be realised during their stay.' It goes without saying that any incidents (in this case, falls) should be recorded, and that a management system should be in place to allocate responsibility for asking for medical assistance.

## Social work interventions: risk and protection; support and care

The social worker as care manager will, by virtue of his or her professional role, be involved in the social work agendas of risk and protection as well as support and care. The care plan will be an important tool in risk assessment and risk management. Organisational constraints on purchasers may limit opportunities for further direct work to be undertaken with individuals once tasks have been identified for action within the care plan. Longer term therapeutic involvement may be seen as a provider service to be bought in, rather than as part of a holistic process. The relevance of both risk assessment and protection, and support and care, to the process of care planning are discussed below.

### Risk and protection

Care planning around issues of risk involves matters of judgement which are informed by cultural values and norms, as well as by professional accountability within a statutory framework. The Children Act 1989 quantifies risk in terms of significant harm as the threshold for statutory involvement, but there is no exact equivalent in adult care. Nor are there complex procedural arrangements for assessing risk,

allocating responsibility and monitoring risk and authorising intervention such as exist in child protection procedures. The only exception to
this in adult care is the introduction of supervision registers and
supervised discharge arrangements under mental health legislation
(see Chapter Ten). This has the effect of leaving individual practitioners exposed, and individual clients without formal means of
involvement in decision-making.

'Is he at risk?' is a question often posed in a range of different
circumstances. It may be asked, for example, in relation to people with
dementia who forget to light their gas fire when they turn it on, so
'running the risk' of explosion and of hypothermia. It may also be used,
say, of a person with learning disabilities living alone, who is finding it
difficult to say no to local people who want to borrow and use his or her
home for their convenience. The risks for each must be particularised,
but the general issues are the same ones of risk assessment and risk
management. Doel and Shardlow (1998) analyse risk in social work
practice as an amalgam of the perceived dangerousness of the situation,
and the social worker's willingness to intervene. It cannot be assumed
that the former necessarily leads to the latter. Mediating factors for the
social worker may be: attitudes to taking control, cultural views about
acceptable behaviour, fear of making mistakes, fears about one's own
safety, beliefs about the role of social work in society, confidence about
one's professional judgement and knowledge about the legal context of
social work practice.

Risk assessment involves both the estimation and evaluation of risk.
Estimation includes statistical incidence (it is known for example that 1
in 5 of the population over the age of 80 will suffer from dementia), and
the application of general knowledge to particular situations (the
combustible qualities of domestic gas). The evaluation of risk is,
however, a balancing process in which the application of judgement
is bought to bear. The factors to be taken into account are:

- the *likelihood* of a particular event happening;
- the reasonably foreseeable *consequences* of that event happening;
- the interests of the people affected by the consequences of the event
  happening;
- the *cost* of taking precautions against the happening of the event or
  its consequences;
- duties owed by other people.

Thus, in the first example of the person with dementia who forgets to light the gas fire, the likelihood of an explosion happening is high, but the likelihood of the person suffering damage from the cold would depend upon the time of year. The consequences of an explosion would be grave not only for the person himself but also for his neighbours (point three, above). However, if the risk were only one of hypothermia, the consequences would affect only the individual himself and might well be dependent upon his general state of health. The cost in practical terms of taking precautions against the event happening could involve a change in the form of heating in the house to a safer central heating system, or disconnection of the gas supply whilst the householder was alone in the house. No doubt there would be some discussion of whether the individual was safe to remain at home or whether residential care should be considered.

A forgotten element in the equation is often the *emotional* cost of leaving a familiar environment for residential care, but it is one which should certainly be weighed in the balance. The assessment of risk is often an exercise which is undertaken with the object of avoiding criticism if something goes wrong which public authorities know about. Is this sufficient reason for overriding self-determination? The answer depends on whether or not there is a duty to intervene; the only duty under s. 47 National Health Service and Community Care Act 1990 is to assess for community care services, not a duty to 'make safe'; outside of the Mental Health Act 1983 and s. 47 National Assistance Act 1947 there are no grounds for intervention if services are refused. As in the case of the person with learning disabilities, the client's perception of the risk is important; are they able to evaluate what is happening, and make an informed decision if it is a situation they wish to continue to live with. Is the social worker comfortable or not with the use of authority?

Much will then depend upon the management of the risk. Interventions may be devised to manage the risk by introducing assistance into the home, or providing other forms of support. Advocacy services may be helpful in monitoring satisfaction with the intervention. Above all, in risk management administrative systems are necessary to provide a forum for decision-making and to enable review to happen. Preferably these should be inter-agency; as with care management generally unintended conflicts can arise if there are different agency strategies for dealing with the risks associated with vulnerable clients.

## Support and care

Sheppard (1995) sees social workers' abilities to offer a range of interventions as particularly appropriate for the professional role of care manager. Prior to the implementation of the National Health Service and Community Care Act 1990 there was disquiet that the social work contribution was being overloaded with the process of care planning. Concentration on the purchasing function is acknowledged to have had this effect (DoH, 1991, para. 47). 'The provision of advice and on-going support for clients by social workers is very important in professional terms. However, the language of care management can lead to this function being under emphasised as compared to brokering for the provision of services by third parties.' The assumption that the difficulties of very vulnerable people can be resolved within a very brief timescale is clearly false. If continuing support is not given then re-referral is inevitable for at least a proportion of these cases.

The American system of case management, upon which care management is based, was never seen as a short-term solution; it was always seen as a procedure for dealing with long-term cases, within which a combination of practical assistance, therapy and support could be offered. The prominence of the task-centred method of social work within care management may have been misconstrued to favour involvement that was only short-term, and based upon only practical concerns. Yet there is clearly a place for the task-centred approach within long-term work in which issues may be dealt with sequentially; and it is a misrepresentation of the term 'task-centred' to see it as not relevant to emotional or relationship problems.

Nor is the offering of 'advice and support' to be seen purely as a provider function; there is an acknowledgement that a purist separation of purchaser and provider roles is inappropriate here: 'To this extent, advice and support can be viewed as entirely appropriate to the purchaser side of the department. Equally there are occasions where the provision of advice and support may be a discrete activity' (DoH, 1993, para. 47). What is important, however, is an end to vagueness about ends and means; insufficient clarity about ends to be achieved works against the operation of clear criteria in selecting means. The role of the social worker can be as confidant, therapist, broker or advocate.

This focusing on ends and means is not new; it was addressed by Goldberg and Warburton in 'Ends and Means in Social Work' (1979).

They then saw that a variety of ends could be pursued falling into the following general categories:

- no change intended
- major environmental change needed
- changes needed in the personal/social environment
- changes in social role
- changes in behaviour/attitudes/relationships

Clearly these different ends will attract different strategies. Major environmental change may require negotiation with other agencies such as housing, to physically relocate an individual. But even in such a situation, this skill as negotiator will not be *all* that is needed; sensitivity to a feeling of loss for the old environment may invoke the use of counselling skills until the adaptation is made. Changes in the personal/social environment may need the use of groupwork skills to integrate people into a new social environment such as a day centre. Changes in social role will involve people in transitions; to worker, to parent, to carer, for example. Changes in behaviour and attitude, including offending, may be amenable to a behaviourist or a cognitive approach, and work with relationships may involve family counselling, family work or family therapy. The orientation of the worker and his or her reading of the situation will influence the choice of method, but the range of interventions available illustrates the complexities within the care planning role.

The role played by the social work practitioner itself will need to be adapted for different organisational contexts. Hughes (1995), adapting Øvretveit (1993), describes four different roles which practitioners may undertake in different situations:

- the care profession – specific role;
- the role as member of the care package team;
- the care manager role;
- the role of the developer of services.

The care profession – specific role, describes the situation in which the practitioner is caseworker, having responsibility for assessment and the provision of professional help, with the role and function *vis-à-vis* other professionals being one of liaison rather than co-ordination. The member of the care package team will provide profession-specific services but in the context of a multidisciplinary network of service providers directly accountable to the care manager for their own role within a package of care. The care manager may or may not be providing a profession-specific service but is responsible as manager for orchestrating, maintaining, monitoring and reviewing the effectiveness of the care package (Renshaw, 1988). The practitioner as developer of services has a role to play in stimulating agencies through the commissioning process to provide what is in short supply or lacking. These then are the tasks that have to be performed in order effectively to deliver services. How can they be achieved by practitioners?

An example of the professional-specific role might be a social worker in a hospital setting; whereas the social worker as member of a care-package team may be working within a community mental health team or community mental handicap team. So far, so good. In relation to the third category of care manager, however, will it in fact be possible to divorce that role from the professional qualification of the post-holder? Arguably the skills, knowledge and values of the social work practitioner will not stand alone, but will become enmeshed, as described above, in the role of care manager (Reigate, 1995; Sheppard, 1995). The practitioner as developer of services is an interesting role. Certainly in that role, as described, there will be a responsibility to use information on unmet need to stimulate new services, and this could apply to in-house services, such as domiciliary care, in equal measure. There will also be a need to explore community networks proactively: 'Entrepreneurial case management requires the mobilisation, indeed the creation of informal networks, not merely their support or revival.' (Davies and Challis, 1986, p. 47) This is akin to a community development role. There is also another developmental role to be undertaken; with the concentration of qualified workers on the purchasing side, provider side workers may need additional support and input in dealing with more complex cases; a consultative function may thus arise and may need to be incorporated into the care plan.

## Abuse issues

The greater concentration of vulnerable people in the community has awakened awareness of the potential for abuse and a desire to explore means of protection from exploitation and neglect. Within the competence 'assess and plan', working in partnership to identify and analyse risk of harm, abuse, neglect or failure to protect is detailed as a practice requirement. The identification of potential harm, abuse, neglect or failure to protect adults is an evidence indicator for this requirement within the guidance on the Particular Pathway in adult services. The focus of such concern has been the abuse of elderly people, but not exclusively so (ADSS, 1991); the abuse, particularly sexual abuse, of people with learning disabilities is of increasing concern (Turk and Brown, 1993). Parallels may be drawn with experience of domestic violence and with child abuse in four areas in particular (Stevenson, 1996):

- the nature and definition of the phenomenon
- incidence and prevalence
- social and professional attitudes
- service responses

**The nature and definition of the problem**

Adult abuse is a socially constructed phenomenon insofar as various aspects of behaviour and their consequences are defined by others as constituting or not constituting a category which is given the title 'abuse'. Various definitions may exist which focus upon the legality of the action, the intention with which it was performed or its consequence. The definition adopted by Action on Elder Abuse, an organisation prominent in this field, locates abuse within the context of caring relationships, and defines as abusive actions which may not be illegal; it also covers inaction (or neglect) as well as action. 'Elder abuse is a single or repeated act or lack of appropriate action occurring within any relationship where there is an expectation of trust which causes harm or distress to an older person' (Action on Elder Abuse, 1996). Five main types of abuse are detailed:

- physical – for example, hitting, slapping, burning, pushing, restraining or giving too much medication or the wrong medication;
- psychological – for example, shouting, swearing, frightening, blaming, ignoring or humiliating a person;
- financial – for example, the illegal or unauthorised use of a person's property, money, pension book or other valuables;
- sexual – for example, forcing a person to take part in sexual activity without consent. This can occur in any relationship;
- neglect – for example, where a person is deprived of food, heat, clothing, comfort or essential medication.

These types of abuse may be distinct; or may be experienced at the same time. Mutually abusive situations, for example between an older person and their spouse or child, may well exist and it is accepted that older people may themselves abuse people who care for them.

## Prevalence and incidence

The hidden nature of abuse makes reporting highly variable, and is bound up with social awareness generally and definitions and categories of abuse. The only study of prevalence in the UK was undertaken by Ogg and Bennett (1992) using the OPCS survey; it produced figures of a prevalence of 15.2 for physical abuse per 1000 population and 53.9 for verbal abuse. Financial abuse also had a prevalence of 15.2. Surveys amongst more vulnerable groups of people have given much higher numbers; the best known of these is Homer and Gilleard's (1990) study of 51 carers of patients receiving respite care in hospital; 45 of these admitted to some form of abuse.

Although victims of abuse are found across the whole age spectrum, and irrespective of social class, gender or ethnic origin, there is evidence that they are disproportionately in the older age groups, and more likely to be female. Cultural factors may also have an influence on the type and nature of abuse (since physical abuse is more highly correlated with living in the same household and male abusers). Financial abuse is spread across the income range to a greater extent than physical or psychological abuse, and people living on their own are at greater risk of financial abuse and neglect by others (McCreadie, 1996).

## Social and professional abuse

Stevenson (1996) sees public concern over the abuse of older people as increasing. One of the aims of Action on Elder Abuse, which was founded in 1992, is to promote awareness of the issue of abuse amongst the public and professionals. There have, however, been critics of the adoption of this campaign by professionals (Biggs, 1997); given that there is little direct evidence that older people themselves see abuse by carers as a major concern. Their concern is about standards of care in domiciliary and residential services, and lack of the basic necessities of life in terms of adequate income and responsive services (Robertson, 1995). Re-focusing attention on abuse within a domestic setting may paradoxically assist the redefinition of abuse in residential care as an issue of 'quality' or service neglect, rather than a matter for the criminal law or disciplinary procedures. Seeing abuse as an aspect of inter-personal relationships also excludes abuse which is rooted in ageism, racism or sexism, and thus makes these issues more difficult to challenge directly.

## The service response

Service responses need to be set in the context of an assessment of the need for community care services as a whole; within which abuse is one particular issue (ADSS, 1995). Stevenson (1996) expresses concern about the proceduralisation of adult abuse in the same way that procedures have come to dominate child protection, though she sees some proceduralisation as necessary to ensure inter-agency co-operation. The Association of Directors of Social Services (1995) has recommended that local authorities devise procedures, and a majority have in fact done so. No procedures however can compensate for professional awareness of the nature of abuse and of appropriate responses. The response chosen will depend upon the analysis of the causes of abuse. It is clear that not all of these analyses fit the dependent victim/stressed carer model, and nor should they. Biggs (1997) in particular is critical of an attempt to use social policy in this way to monitor informal care.

Homer and Gilleard (1990) indicated that different types of abuse could be ascribed to different causes and there was no one correct approach to interpretation or intervention: 'Physical abuse is perpetrated by people with disturbed and disorganised personalities irrespective of the physical and mental state of the abused . . . Verbal abuse and neglect were both significantly related to poor pre-morbid relationships, an association not seen for physical abuse . . . neglect was associated with socially dysfunctional carers' (Homer and Gilleard, 1990, cited in McCreadie, 1996, p. 34).

Glendenning (1997) proposes a number of models for understanding abuse which can be free of professional bias and which can be the basis upon which crisis intervention and prevention techniques are developed.

1.  The situational model: based upon an amalgam of structural factors such as low income and isolation; factors personal to the abused person such as poor health and physical dependency, and carer stress or burn-out.
2.  Social exchange theory: based upon the idea that social interaction involves a balance of rewards and punishments which are upset by the dependency of the elderly person and the greater powerfulness of the care-giver.
3.  Symbolic interactionism: referring to the adoption over time of familiar roles and expectations. These may be upset when one person unexpectedly becomes a carer, or where a strong parent declines in cognitive ability because of dementia.
4.  Personal characteristics of abusers and victims: emphasis here is laid upon the psychopathology of the abuser (related to mental health, drug or alcohol dependency), and their social isolation. A history of violence may also be a factor, as may the quality of the relationship between the abuser and the abused.

Any of the above may be considered to be risk factors of abuse, but there is insufficient evidence from research to suggest that any of them are of predictive value. What is important is that the individual worker is aware of his/her own perspective on the situation and where it comes from. Interviewing skills are of primary importance: 'Familiarity with interviewing people in a non-directive fashion about sensitive issues, being able to tolerate ambiguity and use counselling skills are necessary prerequisites to assessment and intervention in this area, as is an awareness of how our own personal values and beliefs about ageing and abuse can affect our judgement – not always in the best interests of the abused, client or patient.' (Goudie and Alcott, 1994, p. 235)

Action on Elder Abuse have produced a leaflet 'The Abuse of Older People at Home: Information for Workers' (1996) which gives supportive advice on action to be taken when abuse is suspected. It also covers financial protection, liaison with the police, legal interventions, and advice on decision-making when people are mentally incapacitated. It reiterates that where someone has the mental capacity to make decisions, interventions can normally only be made with that person's consent. Discussion of the need for training, the development of inter-agency working, and developing supportive and empowering services is included by McCreadie (1996). Though most of the discussion and research has concerned older people, it should not be forgotten that other adult groups considered to be at-risk vulnerable groups were defined by the Association of Directors of Social Services as early as (1991) to include people:

- who suffer from mental illness including dementia;
- have a physical or sensory disability;
- have a learning disability;
- suffer from severe physical illness.

The law provides an insufficient framework to allow for intervention (Law Commission, 1995; McDonald, 1993). There is in adult care no equivalent to the emergency protection order or child assessment order under the Children Act 1989, nor is there any power (outside of the Mental Health Act 1983) to secure entry to premises, if entry is refused. Section 47 of the National Assistance Act 1948 is an anachronistic piece of legislation which provides for the compulsory removal from home of people who are chronically sick or aged and living in insanitary conditions who are not in receipt of proper care. It may be used in cases of neglect (including self neglect), but has been much criticised as draconian and procedurally deficient (application is made to the magistrates' court and no legal aid is available).

Reform of the law is long overdue, despite the recommendation of the Law Commission (1995) that 'a new jurisdiction' (or court, akin to the Court of Protection) is needed to deal both with personal issues and financial protection (see Chapter Nine). This new jurisdiction would apply to people who were mentally incapacitated, that is unable to make decisions for themselves because of mental disorder or learning disabilities and would provide a forum in which conflicts over care or access could be decided. An expansion of the scope of powers of attorney is also proposed to enable people to appoint attorneys to take decisions on their behalf concerning, for example, admission to residential care or medical treatment. This would clarify and formalise the position of family and carers who are often called upon to make such decisions without legal authority for so doing.

Utilising the concept of significant harm, borrowed from the Children Act 1989, as a threshold of intervention would enable multi-disciplinary assessments of physical, psychological and emotional harm to be made. (McDonald, 1994). Some proceduralisation, perhaps on the case conference model, is necessary to bring people together to take responsibility for decisions (Stevenson, 1996) The criteria for inter-vention should follow the 'essential powers' approach of guardianship under the Mental Health Act 1983 (Hoggett, 1989); that is the minimum necessary intervention. Such intervention would be the 'legislative mandate' that Marsh and Fisher (1992) look for as a basis for partnership where consent cannot be given. If guardianship is the model to be followed then these essential powers would specify where that person was required to live, medical attendance to be given, and monitoring visits to be permitted. Within the core competence 'intervene and provide services', the practice requirement 'contribute to the care, protection and control of people who are at risk to themselves or others' presupposes a strong monitoring element to identify signs of deterioration, and also to challenge behaviour that causes risk. At the same time, the agency must have a legal mandate to provide the amount and type of support and care needed to maintain people safely within the community, or to assist their transition from it.

Equally, there is no right (strictly defined) to community care services to provide practical support. In the United States mandatory reporting laws exist which compel professionals, under penalty, to report suspected incidents of abuse. In the United Kingdom there are no similar provisions. This means that the true extent of abuse may be concealed. In child protection it has also been shown (Stevenson, 1996) that collaborative work is less effective after investigation, in relation to the 'protection plan'; the implications of this finding will need to be considered in the protection of adults. Consideration should also be given to prioritise vulnerable adults whose proper health and development will be jeopardised without the provision of services for them by the local authority, much as children may be defined to be 'in need' within the Children Act.

## CASE STUDY

Helen Jones is 58 years old and has Parkinson's Disease. She lives with her husband Tom who has taken early retirement. Tom assists Helen with washing and dressing and other aspects of personal care. They have no immediate family and live in a small village, five miles from the nearest town. Helen has been attending a voluntary sector day centre in the town on two days a week for the last six months. Helen does not join in many of the activities at the day centre, and has told staff she would rather be at home. Her husband, however, has said that this is the only time that he has to himself or to pursue his own hobbies. One day when Helen attends the day centre, staff notice bruising on the side of her face and behind her ear. When this is commented on, Helen breaks down in tears, saying that her husband has hit her for being too slow in getting ready to go out. He frequently handles her roughly, and shouts at her. 'Please don't say anything though', says Helen, 'because he's told me that I will have to go into a home if I complain.'

If you were the manager of the day centre, how would you respond to this situation?

# 5

# Monitoring and Review

The evaluation of outcomes, monitoring and review are essential components of the 'production of welfare' approach to care management exemplified by early research into community care in Kent and elsewhere (Payne, 1995). The successful evaluation of outcomes of course depends upon the clarity of objectives at the care planning stage, where clear goals are specified and strategic plans are worked out in order to achieve those goals. The monitoring process will then check that services are on target to meet those objectives. A review, however, is an opportunity for change by allowing participants to stand back and reconsider what those goals should be, adjusting interim plans accordingly. Any method of social work practice which fits this model will need to give as much emphasis to monitoring and review as to initial assessment. If a mechanistic approach is taken to case monitoring and review, the complexities of relationships involved in supporting people in the community can become stereotypical. Short-term pragmatic issues will also tend to predominate over long-term aspirations. Searching for Service (SSI/DoH, 1996a) identified this as a particular problem for young people with a learning disability, where 'getting through the week' took precedence over the longer-term evaluation of educational and social needs. Monitoring and review are thus essential tools for good social work practice. They also assume that the effectiveness of social work intervention can be evaluated. Proper monitoring and review means that care packages should be reviewed as a whole and not, as they often have been, by way of separate reviews, for example, in residential care and day care. The contribution of day care, home support services and residential care is however evaluated in this chapter in terms of their efficiency and effectiveness in supporting vulnerable people in the community, and in the recognition of their pivotal role in contributing to care packages.

86

## Monitoring

The Managers' Guide (1991, para. 2.29) makes it clear that systems of monitoring (and review) need not involve formal meetings, but can be undertaken in writing or by telephone. However, the important principle (para. 2.30) is that, wherever possible, monitoring and reviewing should be undertaken by someone who does not have a direct stake in the services provided. This enables quality issues to be effectively addressed, and services to remain needs-led. The regular reassessment of changing perspectives and priorities in progressing towards agreed aims and the effectiveness of arrangements with adults, carers and groups is one of the evidence indicators within the practice requirement 'sustain and maintain working relationships'. It emphasises the continuing nature of the responsibility for service delivery.

Some users of service may move in and out of the system. This is particularly true for people with mental health problems (Huxley, 1993). Huxley regards care management as failing people with long-term but fluctuating needs and attributes this to the choice of an inappropriate administrative rather than a clinical model of care management. In the clinical model direct face-to-face work is undertaken by the case manager which is not only more effective therapeutically, but also enables continuous monitoring of relapse to take place. Huxley also commends Quality of Life Assessment (QOL) as developed by Oliver (1991) as a systematic tool for social workers to assess outcomes for patients living in the community. Results of the application of quality of life assessment to community services show that community treatment is more popular with service users and (in terms of public accountability) can improve mental health and social relationships, though it also highlights deficiencies in regard to meaningful occupation, consistency in the quality of residential care and high levels of poverty. The application of Quality of Life Assessment is also empowering of service users insofar as it puts their views on community care at the centre of service provision and planning (Oliver, 1991).

Raiff and Shore (1993) emphasise the long-term nature of care management systems in the United States and their particular appropriateness for people with long-term chronic conditions. They discuss involving family members as active partners in the monitoring of services and as proactive 'case management extenders' in pulling in other resources. With regard to the monitoring function, consumers and family members should be specifically asked if they think that services are making a difference, what they would like the next steps to be, and whether they are at this time feeling over-involved and burdened. The opportunity should also be taken to provide up-to-date information about new resources and issues. The valuable interventions are those that build on family strengths rather than correcting deficits, and those that support family decisions and consciously attribute successful outcomes to the family's, rather than the case manager's, efforts (Raiff and Shore, 1993).

### Review

Statutory reviews are familiar processes to social workers in child care, and intervals between reviews are fixed by regulations in the case of children looked after by the local authority. Reviews may be presented as important decision-making occasions, but Thoburn (1986) challenges the view that a review is predominantly a decision-making occasion, pointing out that it is often the 'small' decisions made in the intervals between reviews that alter the outcome of a case. The issue may be whether for example to spend money on supporting visits by the family, or whether to extend the child's network by involving other significant persons in the community. Reviews in community care are not statutory; there is nothing in the National Health Service and Community Care Act 1990 that requires reviews to be held. There has, however, been an administrative tradition of holding reviews for separate services such as day care and domiciliary care. As the Managers' Guide (1991) admits (para. 2.30), reviews have in the past been accorded low priority, so have either not taken place or have been subject to considerable delay. Preliminary findings from SSI inspections of community care services (1993) have referred to the 'review time bomb' as energies have been focused on assessment, rather than review. This can mean that services are being provided where there is no longer a need, or are not adapting to changed circumstances. The Policy Guidance (DoH, 1990a) reaffirms the importance of reviews in adapting services to changing needs of users and carers in a formal way.

   Termination of social work involvement or of a particular service is an issue not much dealt with in the literature; much more attention has traditionally been focused on beginnings rather than endings. Raiff and Shore (1993) acknowledge that 'planned termination of advanced case management services to targeted high-risk clients is often an ethically and politically difficult decision, implying a judgement that a client's gains have been maximised or that a prediction of risk warrants this decision' (p. 60). A number of different reasons for termination are identified by Raiff and Shore:

1. Spontaneous client-initiated requests for termination, or de facto 'drop out'. Either of these may signal incompatibility between the client and the worker or the programme and may require a good-faith demonstration of worker outreach to re-engage the client;
2. A request for termination as a healthy sign of client gains and growth in self-confidence;
3. There is some evidence that involuntary termination is occasion-ally used by the worker as a confrontational, last-resort tool to precipitate a crisis to re-engage 'uncooperative' clients.

More generally, the process of disengagement includes follow-up to ensure that a smooth transition is experienced and that achieved goals can be sustained, leaving the door open to possible return if a change of circumstances should occur. Making a more effective or expanded use of available networks is often a precursor of termination of involve-ment with formal services.

The ability to successfully disengage from relationships with children, young people, adults, carers and groups, is one of the evidence indicators within the practice requirement 'sustain and maintain working relationships' within the core competence 'intervene and provide services'. As such it links with an earlier evidence indicator under the same practice requirement 'identify and agree estimated time-scales for work and the conditions under which contact will end'. This shows the value respectively of being clear at the outset about the limits of involvement and the nature of the relationship, something which is especially important with students whose work on placement is necessarily time-limited. It also requires a criterion for success, or at least adequate progress, to be fixed at the outset; something which is fundamental to partnership and which enhances self esteem and confidence in the service user (Marsh and Fisher, 1992).

**What happens in practice?**

There is evidence that in practice the tasks of monitoring and review are sometimes confused, to the detriment particularly of the monitoring task. Mencap in their (1995) survey of service provision under community care noted the absence of clear local authority strategies for monitoring and attributed this partly to a paucity of government guidance on the issue. Only two out of thirty carers said that their care manager had told them about monitoring or how it is applied. Sometimes monitoring was substituted by review with little opportunity to discuss or alter service provision in the interim.

The purchaser/provider split may have attenuated the withdrawal of assessors from the monitoring task. An example of inadequate monitoring of a care plan, exacerbated by the purchaser's withdrawal from responsibility for this task, is seen in a report from the local government Ombudsman (complaint no. 94/A/0562) which led to a finding of maladministration against Newham London Borough Council. In this case a disabled woman with complex and rapidly changing needs was allocated predominantly a home care service for both cleaning and personal care. Once the original care plan was agreed, responsibility for monitoring was put on the provider team which, because it was a provider team, had difficulty accessing the assessment team when the care plan began to break down. It also appears that insufficient flexibility was built into the original plan to deal with contingencies such as the complainant suffering further ligament injury and needing additional care. The care manager was also not readily available to respond to queries from home care assistants about the tasks included in the care plan, and to be aware that the service received was sometimes erratic.

Close liaison between care managers and home carers who are closest to the day-to-day issues is easily lost if lines of communication are cut by the purchaser/provider split. It is also difficult to monitor a total package of care if provision is divided amongst a number of agencies. Evidence from Age Concern Scotland (Robertson, 1995) is that service users are keenly aware of the intimate and detailed knowledge that domiciliary workers have about their circumstances, and wish this information to be fed back directly into care management systems.

**Evaluation and effectiveness**

How do we know that the work we do and the services we provide are worthwhile? It may be possible to measure the effectiveness of a service in achieving a certain outcome, whether that is an older person

Gary Lewis is 19 years old and has just begun a computer course at his local College of Further Education. Gary has cystic fibrosis and is a wheelchair user. He currently lives with his parents who assist with personal care and physiotherapy. The need for such assistance fluctuates from week to week; sometimes limited help is needed; at other times, a lot of assistance is required. Gary is talking about leaving home to live with his friend Jack, whom he has met at college. Jack would not be able to provide the kind of assistance that Gary's parents now provide. Gary approaches the local authority for assistance.

Assuming that a package of care could be set up, what arrangements would need to be put into place for such a package of care to be:

(a)　monitored,
(b)　reviewed.

remaining in the community rather than moving into residential care, or the achievement of funding for a carers' support project, but such 'effectiveness' is not the whole of the story. For some clients, process – the human value of being there and appearing interested and supportive – is as important as a tangible output, particularly for clients with chronic needs whose circumstances are not easily changed (Sainsbury, 1975). Cheetham *et al.* (1992) also urges us to differentiate effectiveness from evaluation. Evaluation judges the intrinsic worth of an activity, rather than its outcome. This acknowledges that social work can be about caring, not necessarily about helping, in the same sense as a medical model is about treatment and cure. With this in mind, we can evaluate the contribution of different sorts of service.

## Evaluating day care

Day care services have always played an important role in maintaining people in the community, but the advent of community care, with its emphasis on individual care planning, contracting and inter-agency co-operation provides an opportunity for a reappraisal of why such services exist, for whom and with what effect.

There are a number of different models of day centre functioning (Seed, 1988), but even though objectives may be stated in terms of only one or two models, the competing needs of users and service systems almost invariably result in centres attempting to fulfil a number of different functions, ranging from work experience to further education, to social care. This is particularly true of centres for people with learning disabilities. Different models of provision are explored below.

## The social care model

The social care model is common in day care services for older people. Purpose-built centres, or in some cases annexes to residential facilities, provide a total environment within which care can be provided. This is often an alternative to intensive home care, and as such plays an important rationing role within 'a package of care' allowing domiciliary resources to be spread more thinly. Authorities which ration the number of hours of domiciliary care available commonly discount day care hours from this calculation. Usually such centres provide a hot meal, bathing facilities and social stimulation. Other services such as hairdressing or chiropody may be provided communally. Services are usually targeted upon the frailest or most vulnerable people, and may have an assessment element. Attendance can be time-limited, and users moved on to less intensive provision if deemed appropriate after assessment. Staff are often professionally qualified and activities may have a therapeutic as well as a social element; to this end formal groupwork may be undertaken.

## The continuing education model

The continuing education model has been common in services for people with a learning disability. Adult Training Centres have been the traditional type of resource provision – and often the only resource available. There has been an emphasis on skills training towards independent living, with facilities to practice cooking, shopping and dealing with money. Social and inter-personal skills may also be taught. Colleges of Further Education have also developed courses in literacy and numeracy as well as social skills for people with learning disabilities.

Innovations in day care provision for people with learning disabilities aim towards providing services directly in the community. This may take the form of outreach work, where the service provided is independent of buildings except as an office base. The work takes place in users' own homes. Staff are also used to facilitate access to ordinary community facilities such as leisure centres and shops. The emphasis is on integration with the community which again will facilitate independent living. Seed (1988) anticipates the development of more varied community-based provision from day centres with smaller groups of people spending a higher proportion of their time in integrated settings.

**Employment and work**

Adult training centres have also historically provided a segregated work environment for people with learning disabilities. Sheltered workshops have provided similar opportunities for people with physical disabilities. Work is culturally important and a source of self-esteem. 'Proper jobs' are hard to find, though workers' co-operatives and sheltered work groups may provide some opportunities. Real numbers of people seeking work may be disguised in this way.

**Leisure and recreation**

Clubs for older people have been based predominantly around leisure and recreational activities, and have been organised by users themselves. Luncheon clubs have also developed to meet the needs of people for a social meeting place as well as a hot meal. Drop-in centres have less of a care element, but may provide advice and assistance, for example about welfare benefits and other services, as well as offering a place to meet. They operate on an 'open-door' basis, but may have a core membership. Local authorities may provide funding through grant aid or contract.

**Influence of community care on day services**

Community care's commitment to wider user choice should mean the greater development of more individual programmes of care, rather than fitting people into existing resources. In order to achieve this, attention needs to be paid to the appropriateness of services; in particular, services for people from ethnic minorities are underdeveloped (SSI, 1998); and those with the most complex degree of disability are often offered the least amount of service (Mencap, 1995). To facilitate choice, care managers will also need to have access to spot contracts to buy in from a range of resources. Paradoxically. local authority funding has a tendency to push the independent sector into catering for those with higher levels of need, rather than those in the middle range. This in turn may lead to the preferred model being 'care' rather than self-development through social and leisure pursuits.

New sources of funding such as the Mental Illness Specific Grant have provided an impetus for community-based projects. The Social Work Services Inspectorate for Scotland in their (1995) report on day care services for people with mental illness 'Time Well Spent' found that in their survey 'Day services provide a range of services, drop-ins, structured groups, social and recreational facilities, skills training and employment support, advice and information and counselling' (p. 5). Ninety-nine per cent of users said that the service had made a positive difference to their lives, and eighty-eight per cent considered that it had improved their mental health. There was no quantitative evidence of the preventative effect of day care on hospital admissions, though qualitatively social workers were more likely than health professionals to say that attendance prevented hospital admission. There were however a number of shortcomings in the service some of which are relevant to the earlier discussion on the purpose of day care. The age range of service users was mostly 25–64, meaning that the needs of younger users were perhaps being overlooked; also, little consideration was paid to the needs of people from different ethnic groups. Thirty per cent of users would have liked more help in preparing for work, and links with leisure, recreation, education and employment services in the wider community were not well-developed. There was also an unmet need for weekend and evening opening, this being identified as a difficult time for people with mental health problems.

Evaluation of the formal integration of day care into care management and the care programme approach revealed deficiencies in planning and in the monitoring and review of services. Only one of the services could be said to have been constructed in a truly multi-disciplinary way and there was little evidence of clear agreements with psychiatric services about what the service should cover, arrangements for back-up and how to deal with emergencies. Clearly just referring someone to a service is not sufficient; to ensure that people with the greatest needs are included, a well-planned introduction and follow-up home visits are essential to secure attendance. In practice, individual follow-up at times of crisis was difficult to provide, and was partly attributable to a high degree of reliance on voluntary or sessional workers. The conclusion to be drawn is that though day care services are of value in themselves, they need to be properly integrated into a system of care management.

The Social Work Services Inspectorate found that few of those attending day centres had care managers or individually co-ordinated support on a consistent basis. This is particularly problematic for the functions of monitoring and review, where day services often fulfil the role of key worker (under the Care Programme Approach) by default; this usually occurs without consultation with social work and health care staff about who is most suited to undertake this role. Despite emphasis within care management on individualised response to need, it was found that day care services did not systematically draw up plans for individuals attending services:

> Our conclusion is that day services are effective in reaching people who need help; they provide services which benefit people with mental illness; and they provide good value for money in doing so. However services could be targeted more efficiently on people with serious mental illness. Although the number of services has increased greatly in the last four years it is still not sufficient to meet needs. (Social Work Services Inspectorate, 1995, p. 4)

### Evaluating home support services

Developing the role of home support services is absolutely fundamental to community care. Providing support for people to remain living in their own homes is the first service option presented in the Policy Guidance (1990). Home Support Services is the generic terms used by the SSI (1995a) to describe a range of tasks which may also be subsumed under the title of domiciliary care, or home care. These are:

- personal assistance with daily living activities
- domestic help with household tasks
- social and emotional support

The attributes of such services are that they should be sufficient, reliable, co-ordinated, flexible and affordable and based upon values which are shared between users and providers of services. These values are autonomy, respect, participation, knowledge, fulfilment, privacy and equality (SSI, 1995a).

The definition of home support services to include personal, domestic and emotional support is highly ambitious given the history of service development in domiciliary care. It was an earlier SSI report 'From Home Help to Home Care' (1987) which encouraged local authorities to move from providing a home help (cleaning) service towards providing a home care (personal care) service with the result that nowadays a domestic cleaning service is rarely available from the public sector to people who do not also have personal care needs. This is despite the fact that service users (RADAR, 1992; Age Concern, 1994) have consistently stated how much they value a domestic cleaning service. RADAR is also concerned that local authorities may not be fulfilling their statutory duty under Schedule 8 of the National Health Service Act 1977 to provide a home help (not home care) service 'adequate to the needs of the area'; s. 2 of the Chronically Sick and Disabled Persons Act 1970 similarly refers to the provision of 'practical assistance in the home' as a service that the local authority is under a duty to make arrangements to provide. The provision of 'social and emotional support' (service component 3) is rarely specifically provided for in care plans; given the rationing of home care tasks by time and function, there is little space for social and emotional needs to be addressed. The development of close, confiding relationships between home care staff and service users is also threatened by frequent staff changes and discontinuities in services. The SSI (1995) report recognises that this is an aspect of the service that has drawn critical comment from the local government Ombudsman in recent years. More fundamentally, consideration must be given to the disempowering nature of domiciliary care for people, particularly older women. The feelings of those who took pride in doing tasks for themselves, need to be sensitively addressed. There is evidence (Robertson, 1995) of a higher incidence of depression amongst users of domiciliary services than amongst the general population.

Private providers of domiciliary care, after a fairly slow start, in 1993 accounted for about 23 per cent of the market (Kestenbaum, 1993). Their growth has been promoted by the requirement that local authorities spend 85 per cent of the transfer element of their Special Transitional Grant money in the independent sector. Though the Burgner Committee (1996) recommended the registration and inspection of domiciliary care agencies, their position is currently unregulated. The UK Home Care Association has however developed its own Code of Practice for members, and some local authorities have voluntary registration schemes. The SSI (1995a) recommends that purchasers of domiciliary care monitor the availability of a quality workforce as well as user participation in service delivery, user protection from abuse or inadequate care, and quality assurance mechanisms within the agency. These are the services that the commissioners of services should look for (SSI, 1995):

- written statements of philosophy, objectives and standards, and action plans;
- involvement of users and workers in setting standards, objectives and plans, and in reviewing services;
- regular self monitoring of services based primarily on users' experiences and views;
- implementation and monitoring of equal opportunities, including religion, language and diet as well as ethnic origin;
- independent evaluation of services.

### Evaluating residential care

Though de-institutionalisation was a motivation in promoting care in the community, the peculiar status of residential care remains. Residential care may either be considered as 'an alternative to community care' (Alaszewski and Wun, 1994) or as part of it (Peace, Kellaher and Willcocks, 1997). It is not living at home, but it is part of care in the community. Residential care covers a wide spectrum from large residential homes of 35+ residents to small fully staffed group homes in ordinary residential locations. Though much of the literature on residential care is concerned with older people, only five per cent of the population over 65 lives in residential care. Residential care, widely defined, is still significant for people with learning disabilities; 35 per cent of people with learning disabilities *under* the age of 65 live in residential care (SSI, 1997a). In addition to these figures, there are more people passing through residential care on a short-term basis. Some of these will join mainstream residential care, whilst others will be accommodated in specialist resources.

The SSI has produced guidance on standards for short-term care breaks (1993a), which is addressed to social services managers and inspectors, users and carers. It is important, however, (Stalker, 1996) to be clear about the purpose of any service, and the means chosen to achieve it, before identifying appropriate indicators by which to judge its performance. Different criteria, for example, would be used to evaluate a short-term care break intended to be a holiday from that intended for medical assessment. The use of language again is significant – whether 'respite care', 'shared care' 'breaks and opportunities' or 'community links' – as each of these terms connotes a different balance between care and dependency and independence and opportunity.

Within residential care services, aspects of quality assurance and quality control have been given greater prominence than monitoring and review functions (see Chapter Six). This is due to the legal requirement of registration and inspection contained in the Residential Homes Act 1984. However, for the resident, issues of monitoring and review may have greater importance because they are the individualised expressions of quality, and a means of evaluating whether the resource provided actually meets the needs of the service user as an individual.

From its inception it was acknowledged that community care could not replace residential provision for the most vulnerable people, and the White Paper of 1989 said as much. This is despite the assertion of the Wagner Committee on Residential Care (1988) that people should not have to change the place in which they live in order to receive the care that they need. It remains true, however, (Jack, 1998) that the best institutions are those that have permeable boundaries and strong links with the communities within which they are located. The idea of residential care as part of a continuum of housing provision in the community is further explored in Chapter Eleven.

# 6

# Quality Assurance and Quality Control

Quality assurance and quality control are important means by which standards of service are set and maintained. Quality assurance is the term used to refer to those processes which aim to ensure that concern for quality is designed and built into services. Quality control refers to processes of verification or challenge and will include systematic monitoring, audit and inspection designed to establish whether standards are being achieved. Total quality management describes an approach to quality assurance which stresses the importance of creating a culture in which concern for quality is an integral part of service delivery (DoH, 1992).

This procedural approach to quality assurance of course does not answer the question of who defines what quality is in any particular service. Is it to be the service user, the commissioner of that service (the local authority), or the provider of this service? If the answer is 'a combination of all three', then whose voice is the most powerful, particularly where consumer choice is limited both through rationing processes and by the absence of providers? As issues of quality are explored, it may be helpful to keep in mind Pfeffer and Coote's (1991) perspectives on 'what is quality?' Is it

- the achievement of standards set by experts;
- a reflection of prestige or positional advantage;
- a managerial wish to achieve excellence – as measured by user satisfaction;
- empowerment of the service user?

This is a theme which will be returned to throughout this chapter.

**Ways of defining quality**

Quality assurance and quality control takes place within a paradigm which may be presented thus:

RIGHTS          POWERS

DUTIES          REMEDIES

Rights, duties and remedies are all inter-linked. Thus to say that someone has a right to a service, for example under the Chronically Sick and Disabled Persons Act 1970, is also to assert that there is a duty placed upon another person or organisation to provide that service. This is the duty of the local authority to provide services to meet the assessed needs of people with a disability under that Act. However, the assertion of a right in the abstract is of little value if there is no remedy for enforcing that right (if the local authority does not in fact provide the service needed). The development of accessible and effective remedies is therefore crucial not only to enforce rights in the individual cases, but also authoritatively to interpret and develop the law. This process was seen clearly in the *Gloucestershire* case (see p. 34) where the House of Lords authoritatively determined the extent of the local authority's duties under the Chronically Sick and Disabled Persons Act 1970.

The instances in which a clear duty is owed to a definable individual, are of course, the easiest to describe within this paradigm. There are, however, a whole host of decisions which are based not upon duties but upon discretion, where the local authority has a *power* to provide services, but no duty to do so. Assessments under s. 47 National Health Service and Community Care Act 1990 fall within this category. Quality assurance in these circumstances means adherence to the principles of good administration: openness, fairness, and account-ability. There is no individual right which can be directly enforced to receive a service, but there is a right to be assessed by a fair process for access to an available service, and to have a remedy available by which the process or the decision can be challenged. Although these are procedural rather than substantive rights, they are not inconsiderable, as will be discussed below.

## Trends within quality assurance and quality control

A number of trends are discernible within the development of quality assurance and quality control. These are (McDonald, 1997):

1. The development of Community Care Plans which describe priorities between and within services.
2. The use of national or local standards documents directed to quality but not quantity of service, e.g. the Patients' Charter, the Citizens' Charter, local Community Care Charters.
3. Debate around the continued desirability of registration and regulation of services e.g. residential care within a statutory framework.
4. The development of accreditation schemes which place reliance on service providers' own internal quality assurance systems.
5. Standard setting through contract compliance mechanisms at the collective and individual level.
6. The development of a range of remedies both administrative and judicial, including mandatory local authority complaints procedures.

For local authorities issues of quality assurance and quality control have been embedded in the institution in a number of ways. The Policy Guidance on the National Health Service and Community Care Act 1990 required local authorities to set up inspection units with responsibility for fulfilling the authority's statutory duties in relation to registration and inspection of services. These units were to be 'free standing', i.e. separate from line management, in order that they could also assume responsibility for inspecting the local authority's own services. The Director of Social Services is responsible for the performance of the unit, and the presentation of the annual report of the Inspection Unit to the Social Services Committee even if the unit is located (as it may be) elsewhere than in the Social Services Department (para. 58).

The term 'Quality', however, is mis-used if it is seen only as an operational term to describe a particular set of institutionalised review activities, not extending for example to the incorporation of users views into standard setting. As the DoH report 'Committed to Quality' (1992) itself found:

A clearer understanding of the terms Quality Control, Quality Assurance and Quality (or Total Quality) needs to be developed outside specialist units. That understanding needs to be broader than comprising the specific activities of the Inspectorate and the Quality Assurance Units, and needs to spring from the prime aim of Quality Assurance approaches, which is to improve outcomes for users. The creation of Inspectorate or review processes may assist in that process but their creation does not assure Quality; it simply ensures that systems exist to measure it. (DoH, 1992, para. 2.15)

Concern for quality may itself be pursued with four primary functions in mind:

- to demonstrate value for money
- to demonstrate achievement of policy objectives
- to improve the experience of the service user
- and to act as an integrating device in the management of Department change (DoH, 1992)

Measures of outcome may be different for each of these objectives; for example, a value for money service may do nothing to improve the subjective experience of the service user. Evaluation of a service is particularly problematic when that service is personal care (Hughes, 1995) given the constraints on users and carers expressing dissatisfaction with a service upon which they are dependent.

The Report goes onto describe a joint project between Humberside Social Services Department and East Yorkshire Health Authority to set standards for each of their client groups by co-opting a 'diagonal slice' (meaning people involved in each of those client groups at all levels of the organisation) including senior, middle and front line managers, professionals, practitioners and ancillary and support workers who combine with users to form a project team. The results are used to set unit targets for each Quality standard (Lynch and Pope, 1990). This is an example of quality being defined in terms not of managerial excellence but of the empowerment of all interested stakeholders, including service users.

**Measuring quality**

A number of instruments exist for measuring quality in service provision. Some local authorities, most notably Gloucestershire and

Norfolk, have adopted the British Standards Institute's BS 5750, a quality assurance system for manufacturing industries adapted for use in social care agencies by modifying the concepts of 'fitness for purpose' and 'safety in use' to include consumer perspectives. The British Quality Association, Social Care Agencies Sector Committee, have produced Guidance on the Interpretation of BS 5750 with reference to Social Care Agencies (1987). The same organisation has also produced Notes for the Application of BS 5750 to the Continuing Nursing Care Sector (1994). The latter provides guidance on how companies can establish, document and review quality planning and quality control and assess the training needs of staff. Other packages also exist for reviewing quality in residential care. One of the best known is 'Inside Quality Assurance', one of the projects developed by the Caring in Homes Initiative which followed the publication of the Wagner Report in 1988. The project is based on an accreditation system and monitors quality through Quality Group meetings of staff, residents and other interested persons. It is based explicitly on the core values of respect, dignity, rights, autonomy, choice, fulfilment and equality of opportunity.

The process of care planning also involves issues of quality. Monitoring and evaluating contracts is a crucial element in the contracting process (Hughes, 1995). Contributing to the monitoring and evaluation of purchased services, and negotiating adjustments to agreed services and support are also two of the evidence indicators for the core competence 'Intervene and Provide Services'. Research amongst consumers (Harding and Beresford, 1996; Robertson, 1995) has shown a concern for quality, particularly as regards domiciliary care where there is no legislative framework for registration and inspection, comparable to that which exists for residential care. This concern extended to the credentials of staff taken on by some private domiciliary agencies who could be temporary staff without any experience or training (Harding and Beresford, 1996). Devon County Council has initiated a system of accreditation for day and domiciliary service providers, which may serve as a model for other authorities (AMA, 1995). Among the quality standards required are:

- a 'fit person' test for managers
- evidence of consistency of helpers
- competence in care tasks

Each agency should have its own quality assurance policy, and involve users in identifying service requirements as well as measuring outcomes. The Joint Advisory Group of Domiciliary Care Associations has produced guidelines (1992) for a model registration scheme. Giving service users a 'voice' in setting standards should, however be balanced by an opportunity to 'exit' the system if the service provided is not acceptable to the individual user (Day *et al.*, 1996a). Whether or not this is a realistic prospect of course depends upon the availability of alternatives which may in turn be limited by the local authority's choice of approved providers in the contracting system (Kestenbaum, 1993). In the Social Service Inspectorate's (SSI/DoH, 1996) Overview of the National Inspection of Social Services Departments Arrangements for the Assessment and Delivery of Home Care Services, it was deemed to be too early to assess the impact of service specifications on the quality of services (para. 11.2) though where service specifications were seen they did incorporate quality assurance principles and equal opportunities issues. Purchasing arrangements to facilitate the provision of appropriate services to meet users' and carers' needs were at an early stage.

**Quality mechanisms in residential care**

Local authority residential care has historically been less closely regulated than the independent sector. Reliance has been placed largely upon the demands of professionalism and political accountability. Local authority residential homes are not required to register under the Registered Homes Act 1984, but quality will be monitored through the local authority's inspection unit. This will be looking for broad parity of standards. Independent Sector homes are by contrast highly regulated. Section 1(1) of the Registered Homes Act 1984 requires registration: 'in respect of any establishment which provides, or is intended to provide, whether for reward or not, residential accommodation with both board and personal care by reasons of old age, disablement, past or present dependence on alcohol or drugs, or past or present mental disorder'.

A wide range of establishments is thus included within the definition, with the unifying factor that both board and 'personal care' must be provided. The whole of the establishment is registrable, even if only four residents are in receipt of 'personal care' (s. 4). 'Personal care' includes counselling and other types of therapy, as well as physical care, Though residential homes are registered with the local authority, nursing homes are registered with the health authority (dual registration is also possible). A nursing home must have a registered medical practitioner or a qualified nurse as the person in charge. A nursing home is defined by s. 21 of the Registered Homes Act 1984 as: 'any premises used, or intended to be used, for the reception of, and the provision of nursing for, persons suffering from any sickness, injury or infirmity.'

Mental Nursing Homes are subject to a separate registration regime under sections 35 and 36 of the Act. In the public sector, Joint Provider Units between social services departments and health authorities may offer both residential and nursing care under the same roof and under the same management. Since health authorities are not allowed to charge for their services, while local authorities are, differentiating between patients and residents in the two halves is of very great importance. Certainly research by Bond (1989) found that in practice it was hard to distinguish between the different characteristics of residents in long-term hospital care, nursing home care, residential care and, indeed, in the community. There are suggestions that the current organisational divide could be changed into a continuity of care between residential and nursing homes, with unified registration practices reflecting this. At the present time medical and nursing services in residential homes are provided from the community, as for people in their own homes. The Annex to Circular No. LAC(92)24 makes it clear in para. 2 that local authorities' contracts for independent sector residential care should not include the provision of any services which it is the responsibilities of the National Health Service to provide. The Royal College of Nursing however, in a (1992) report 'A Scandal Waiting to Happen' has drawn attention to the inadequacy of health care in some residential homes, with unqualified staff taking on responsibilities which should be the responsibility of properly trained professionals. Market forces may put pressure on some residential homes to take residents who really need nursing care, or who deteriorate to the point at which nursing care is needed. Though continuity of care is desirable, the availability of proper nursing surveillance should be monitored in these situations.

In the interests of maintaining standards and promulgating good practice, local registration authorities have access to a considerable amount of guidance from central government. The Social Service Inspectorate document 'Homes are for Living In' (SSI, 1989) flags up the six basic values of privacy, dignity, independence, choice, rights and fulfilment as the yardstick by which to judge the practicalities of life in residential care such as the availability of shared rooms, choice of food, number of social activities and so on. The Code of Practice known as Home Life (CPA, 1984) has long been regarded as a model for good practice in residential care, and a yardstick by which to measure standards. The successor volume A Better Home Life (CPA, 1996) has attracted some criticism as a promoter of standards beyond basic registration requirements, that some homes would find difficult to attain. It applies, as its predecessor did not, also to nursing homes and to sheltered accommodation for older people. The SSI has also produced a number of what it calls 'standards documents' under the general title of 'Inspecting for Quality'; these distinguish between different types of desirable residential regimes, from young people with disabilities to elderly people with mental disorders. Increasingly, there is a diversity of standards to be attained beyond the registration baseline – age, sex, number of residents, category of persons accommodated. Local authorities may introduce specification standards in their contracts with the private sector which are lawful so long as they are not *ultra vires* the National Assistance Act 1948, and so long as they are reasonable. Market forces therefore will be a potent factor in honing and enhancing standards in each sector of care.

**Why regulate?**

Quality assurance in residential care thus derives from a number of different sources: from standards documents, from guidance, from statute and from regulations. It even involves the criminal law, since certain breaches of the Registered Homes Act 1984 and regulations are criminal offences. Inspections have gained an element of public visibility through the appointment of 'lay assessors' to complement the work of professional inspectors, and reports on individual homes are open to public scrutiny without being anonymised. Beyond this there exist Registered Homes Tribunals which hear appeals against the refusal or cancellation of registration, and there is an emergency procedure under s.11 Registered Homes Act 1984 whereby a local authority can apply for an order from a magistrates' court for the immediate cancellation of registration. Is all of this bureaucracy and legal control really necessary? This is what the government was asking when it published 'Moving Forward' (DoH, 1995b), a consultation document on the registration and inspection of social services which raised the prospect of deregulation. In 1996 the Burgner Committee reported and did endorse continuing regulation and even its extension to domiciliary care. It also endorsed the idea of national standards rather than local standards and more consistent training for inspectors.

The present system is, in many cases, overloaded. The Social Service Inspectorate itself found that nine of the 19 inspection units included in its (1995) survey had failed to meet the statutory requirement of twice yearly inspections (SSI, 1995c). The registration and inspection of residential care faces problems common to all regulatory systems: policing v. consultancy, rules v. discretion, stringency v. accommodation (Day *et al.*, 1996). Paradoxically, some aspects of the system may be intended to pose difficulties: 'registration is deliberately designed as an obstacle course ( a sort of initiation ceremony) that forces prospective home owners to demonstrate that they are 'fit persons', that their plans meet local guidelines and that they know what is expected of them' (Day *et al.*, 1996). Day et al's research, highlighted however, the inconsistencies within a complex task: 107 inspection units were during the period of the research responsible for the registration of 12000 homes for elderly and disabled people alone, apart from their responsibilities to children's services. There were also large differences in the size of the budgets held by inspection units not explained by the number of homes in the area. Considerable variation in standards and their interpretation were seen even within the same unit. It was these sorts of inconsistencies that irritated providers, who increasingly seem to be moving towards a common set of expectations with the regulatory bodies about good practice. Nevertheless, an analysis of 200 inspection reports showed that a disproportionate number of requirements for improvement were prompted by a small number of homes (Day *et al.*, 1996).

**Outcome measures**

The difference between process and outcome is an important issue in quality assurance, particularly from the perspective of service users. Formal regulatory processes such as registration and inspection have tended to focus on inputs and processes, rather than outcomes in the sense of achieving satisfaction for service users. So, for example, the regulation of residential care may focus on inputs such as staffing levels and bedroom sizes, and processes such as the accurate recording of medication and the holding of reviews, rather than the quality of life of residents. Those who draw up contracts for the provision of services may also confuse 'service standards' with the outcome specifications. Smith and Thomas in their early (1993) review of contracting within local authorities found that such contracts rarely contained an indication of specific outcome measures for users.

Since the same service can assist different people in different ways, it will be important to evaluate service outcomes for individuals, as well as to research the performance of a service as a whole. Thus quality assurance is a matter of concern to the individual care manager as well as the organisation. Nocon and Quereshi have explored the different tasks of care managers and administrators thus: 'individual practice requires flexibility and objective-setting related to the individual's unique combination of needs and circumstances, whereas aggregation for management information requires consistent structuring of a fixed set of information across different cases' (Nocon and Quereshi, 1996, p. 21).

Little research has, however, taken place into routine practice in community care. Studies of community care, as in the work of the PSSRU at the University of Kent, have been concerned with the evaluation of service innovations or deinstitutionalisation, rather than the continuing evaluation of individual practice. (Nocon and Quereshi, 1996). Personalising outcomes in this way is dependent in turn upon a needs-led rather than a resource-led approach to assessment at the beginning of the care management process.

Incorporating users' views into service planning again has two strands: the individual and the organisational. Gester (1991), focusing on the individual, discusses whether process and outcome are indeed separable, or inextricably linked. If process involves giving time to the service user, empathising, ensuring choice and accessibility in services, then it is likely to secure a good outcome. At an organisational level, a distinction exists between market and 'voice' models of empowerment (Bewley and Glendinning, 1994). Within the market model, users are expected to react to agencies' agendas, rather than propose the issues they themselves see as most important. Work by the Office for Public Management (OPM) looked at different approaches to involving users and carers in the planning and design of services by a number of social services managers in different localities in England and Wales (Goss and Miller, 1995). The project focused on two major steps in the process of user involvement: establishing communication and creating change. A continuum of approaches was found which ranged from non-involvement, to consumer education and marketing services, to listening and responding and, finally, to working in partnership.

The empowerment of service users is seen by Hirschmann (1970) as comprising two separate elements; 'exit' as well as 'voice'. 'Voice' means being involved in the making of decisions and potentially also in evaluating the outcome of those decisions in a way which leads to positive change. 'Exit' is based on free market principles whereby service users are free to go elsewhere if services do not meet their needs. Exit may also be linked to complaints procedures as part of quality control, if dissatisfaction with services is to be highlighted. The following discussions on remedies in community care focuses on this notion of quality control

### Remedies in community care

There is an increasing awareness, from a consumer perspective, that decisions of local authorities are challengeable in a number of ways see McDonald (1997). This includes a willingness to take legal action to support claims to legal rights. The existence of effective remedies is a necessary fourth element in the paradigm of rights, powers, duties and remedies. A number of ways exist by which decisions of the local authority can be challenged, depending upon whether what is sought is an apology, compensation or a changed decision (Payne, 1995).

### Complaints procedures

Section 50 of the National Health Service and Community Care Act 1990 inserts a new section 7B into the Local Authority Social Service Act 1970, requiring local authorities to set up representations and complaints procedures to operate in respect of matters arising after 1 April, 1991. This replaces the previous *ad hoc* system of dealing with complaints, and was intended to be a standardised system applying throughout all authorities. The evidence however is that there exist wide variations in interpretation and process throughout the country (SSI, 1993; Connolly, 1996).

Under this procedure, complaints must be made by and in respect of a 'qualifying individual'. A person is a qualifying individual if:

- a local authority has a power or duty to provide, or to secure the provision of, a social service for him or her;
- his or her need or possible need for such a service has (by whatever means) come to the attention of the local authority.

Local authorities may, at their discretion, deal with representations or complaints outside these categories. A wide variety of issues may be addressed: 'Complaints can result from an unresolved problem or from a measure of dissatisfaction or disquiet about the organisation, about the quality and appropriateness of services, or about their delivery or non-delivery' (DoH, 1990a para. 6.7, *Policy Guidance*). Complaints procedures should be kept separate from grievance procedures and disciplinary procedures which concern internal staffing matters. The Complaints Procedure Directions 1990 require local authorities to:

- designate an officer to assist in the co-ordination of representations and complaints procedures
- ensure familiarity with procedures by all members or officers involved
- monitor the operation of the procedures

The procedures themselves are in three stages:

1. an informal stage
2. a formal stage
3. a review panel stage

### The informal stage (usually involving a line manager)

If the matter cannot be resolved to the satisfaction of the complainant after informal discussion, he or she should be invited to submit a written representation and should be given assistance and guidance in the use of the formal procedure, or advice on where she or he can obtain such assistance. A major difficulty in practice is getting systems to recognise that an expression of dissatisfaction is in fact a complaint.

### The formal stage

A formal written complaint becomes a 'registered' complaint to which the authority should respond within 28 days. Alternatively, the local authority should explain why a response within that time is not possible and advise the complainant when he can expect a response, which in any case should be given within three months.

Complaints concerning voluntary and private sector provision contracted for through the local authority should, wherever possible, be handled at the informal stage by the service provider (DoH, 1990, para. 31). Complainants who are dissatisfied with the response they receive, or who do not wish to complain to the service provider, may choose to refer the matter to the local authority; complaints received by this route should be treated as 'registered complaints'.

*The review panel stage*

If the complainant informs the authority in writing within 28 days of notification of the outcome of the formal stage that he or she is still dissatisfied and wishes the matter to be referred to a panel for review, the local authority is required to convene a panel to meet within 28 days of the request. The review panel should be made up of three people, one of whom should be independent of the local authority. Complaints procedures under s. 26(3) of the Children Act 1989 differ in that they require an independent element at the second stage as well. Ten days notice should be given, during which written submissions may be made. There is a right to an oral hearing, and a right to be accompanied by or represented by some other person at the hearing, though legal representation is excluded. The panel's decision takes the form of a recommendation to the Director of Social Services and the Social Services Committee. Though the recommendation is not binding, its persuasive value is considerable. The Director and Social Services Committee could not overrule the review panel's recommendation without substantial reason, and without having given that recommendation the weight it requires as 'the obvious and intended forum of detailed examination of the facts'. The proper operation of the local authorities complaints procedures also comes within the jurisdiction of the Ombudsman, whose concern is with due process issues, and for whom the operation of complaints procedures has raised issues of fairness and undue delay.

The Social Service Inspectorate conducted an inspection of complaints procedures two years into their operation (SSI/DoH, 1993) looking at progress against standards of accessibility, visibility, clarity and efficiency. Progress had been slow; out of the standards set only a quarter had been fully met. However, it was found that both managers and staff had responded well to the idea that to complain was acceptable, and that 'the traditional social work value placed on being discreet and ensuring high standards of confidentiality' (para. 3.3) had been transferred with ease into the working of the complaints procedures at all levels. Information leaflets for users about complaints had been produced, though in some cases there was a limited amount of consultation with service users which was also reflected in annual reports required to be produced on the workings of the system. There was also inadequate collation and overall monitoring of informal complaints. Making complaints procedures accessible to all service users was problematic; in particular, arrangements for service users in residential homes to complain with privacy were seldom satisfactory. This difficulty in engaging with the most isolated and vulnerable clients, particularly where there are communication problems, is of continuing concern (Connolly, 1996). However, the standard that gave all social services departments most concern was resolving complaints within the recommended time scales, and allocating a proper amount of time to investigations. Consumer satisfaction with outcomes is low; in a recent SSI survey (SSI/DoH, 1996) 37 per cent were satisfied, but 52 per cent remained dissatisfied. The majority of complaints were against fieldwork staff (36 per cent), or were about residential care (30 per cent); domiciliary care attracted only 4 per cent of all complaints.

Enabling service users and their carers to make representations including complaints and assisting them in ensuring that such representations are treated with respect and dealt with promptly and courteously is one of the evidence indicators within the practice requirement 'contribute to the evaluation of the effectiveness, efficiency and economy of services'. Yet the first barrier that the user has to overcome is having the sense of grievance recognised as a complaint so that the procedures can be progressed. The SSI found a reluctance generally to recognise complaints for what they were. There was also a tendency to discontinue working on complaints through negotiation once the formal registration stage had been reached.

**Ombudsmen**

The idea of 'Ombudsmen' to investigate complaints of maladministration in public service comes from Scandinavia and was first introduced into England and Wales in 1967. The system now covers both central and local government as well as the National Health Service; it has also extended into the commercial field of finance. The system is a useful one where a complaint is about procedures or confusion and delay rather than the quality of a decision already made. Although complaints are individualised, very often patterns can be discerned, and the reports of Ombudsmen are a useful political tool to highlight difficulties in the implementation of policy. Those of the Local Government Ombudsmen in particular (who operate on a regional basis) are insightful and critical. Their reports have been referred to a number of times throughout this book to illustrate principles of good administration.

The Commissioner for Local Administration may investigate allegations of injustice caused by maladministration in the performance of its functions by a local authority. Maladministration is generally taken to mean those matters contained in the so-called Crossman catalogue (H.C. Deb., Col. 51, 18 October, 1966): 'Bias, neglect, inattention, delay, incompetence, ineptitude, arbitrariness and the like.' The function of the Ombudsman is thus to uphold principles of good administration, not to question the merits of a decision – for that the complaints procedure should be used. Complaints must be made within twelve months, and alternative rights and remedies must already have been exhausted, unless the Commissioner feels it is not reasonable to expect the complainant to use these rights. The complainant will usually apply in person, but where he or she is unable to do so, 'some body or individual suitable to represent him' may apply on his behalf (Local Government Act, 1974 s. 27(2)). An attempt is usually made to achieve a settlement without a formal investigation and only 5 per cent of complaints actually result in a final report. A copy of the final report will be sent to all the parties, and if the local authority does not act upon his recommendation, the Ombudsman may publish a further report leading to a statement in an agreed form which must be published in the local press. Local authorities may also be requested to pay compensation to those found to have suffered injustice as a consequence of maladministration.

The Ombudsman has been quite stringent in his criticism of local authorities for their failure to implement good practice. Complaints of delay in responding to requests for assessment or the delivery of services are frequently made, and on the whole priority criteria for assessment have not protected local authorities from criticism. In one of a series of complaints against Liverpool City Council alleging delays in assessment and the provision of occupational therapy services (report no. 94/C/3114) the Ombudsman saw fit to lay down maximum time limits of two months for urgent cases, and six months for non-urgent cases; even though these sound generous, they are in fact quite modest deadlines for some authorities who have both a shortage of qualified staff and of resources. A recent innovation has been for the Ombudsman in some cases to require local authorities to report back to him in three months' time on progress made in reforming systems. The Ombudsman may recommend that small amounts of compensation are awarded to those who suffer injustice as a result of local authority decisions.

The Parliamentary Commissioner for Administration investigates complaints against government departments and certain non-departmental public bodies. Members of Parliament are used as the filter to refer complaints on to the Parliamentary Commissioner. Investigations may involve the reading of government files and papers, and the consideration of oral evidence, and are held in private. Compensation may be paid on an *ex gratia* basis, but again the investigation is into maladministration and not into the merits of a decision. A majority of the complaints involve the Department of Social Security and the Inland Revenue.

Though the power of the Ombudsman is formally limited to publicising shortcomings in services in individual cases, the influence of the Ombudsman's reports can extend far beyond this, into the field of policy. This is particularly true of the Health Service Commissioner whose special investigation into the continuing care needs of a patient transferred to nursing home care from the National Health Service – the 'Leeds' case – led to a review of policy on continuing care and subsequent guidance from the Department of Health (see p. 190)

### Default powers

In the field of public law, if a local authority fails to carry out any of its statutory duties, the Secretary of State can declare the authority to be in default, issue directions to ensure that the duties specified are complied with, and if necessary, enforce those directions in the High Court. The process is a discretionary one, and there is no recorded instance of the power having been used, though the Secretary of State may enter into correspondence with local authorities against which complaints have been made. As the dispute is likely to be founded on a shortage of resources provided by central government to local government, the Secretary of State would hardly be likely to draw attention to this through use of the default power.

## Legal actions

Using the authority of the courts to enforce rights to service or procedural rights to fair assessment and service allocation, is likely to become an important avenue of complaint. Historically, recipients of community care services have not been prominent in taking legal action, and the law in this area has therefore not been developed as rapidly or as publicly as, say, child care law has developed even since the Children Act 1989. The National Health Service and Community Care Act 1990 itself provides only a minimalist framework, backed by policy and guidance. Beyond the duty to assess, nothing is explicit about how such an assessment should be carried out, or how resources should be allocated.

There are two routes by which to challenge the actions of local authorities before the courts: in private law and in public law. Private law actions are concerned with individual rights and have as their objective the clarification and enforcement of duties owed to individuals, not the public at large. Those who bring private law actions seek individual remedies such as injunctions and damages. Such actions are based on ordinary principles of contract and tort. Public law actions are often brought as test cases in order to clarify the law for the benefit of others as well. The remedies sought will emphasise the public rather than the private interest in having decisions properly made, and may be concerned more with procedural irregularities than with substantive issues; damages by way of compensation will be available only in a minority of cases.

## Private law rights

Despite the rhetoric of community care in claiming to incorporate users' rights into the provision of services, legal remedies for the enforcement of such rights are not much in evidence. Even with respect to contracts for the provision of residential, day care or domiciliary care, the arrangement may be between the local authority as purchaser and the independent sector as provider, with the user of the services simply a third party. In legal terms this is unsatisfactory, for unless the user is made a party to that contract he does not have the right to sue on it and thus to challenge the quality of care provided. The concept of a legal contract as a 'bargain' freely entered into by parties will in most cases not fit the reality of block service agreements whose terms are not variable in individual cases. Harden (1992) discussing National Health Service contracts makes the same point; the law does not provide a coherent framework for consumers' rights or for the separation of interests where public bodies provide or contract for services.

Some claims which can be brought in contract may also be brought in the tort of negligence, the basis of which is breach of a duty of care owed to another as a consequence of which that other person suffers damage which is foreseeable. An example might be of a residential care home which fails to provide an adequate number of trained staff. If as a consequence of lack of oversight a resident should fall and injure themselves, it is likely that they would have a cause of action in negligence against the owner of the home. That owner could, of course, be the local authority, in which case the local authority would be liable. But what if the home was providing a placement under a contractual arrangement with the local authority? The local authority will not be liable unless they were themselves negligent. They may have been negligent in not carrying out a proper inspection of the home under the Registered Homes Act 1984, or they may have continued to make placements there when alerted by complaints that staffing was inadequate.

A further cause of action may exist not in negligence but in an action for breach of statutory duty. For there to be liability to individuals, the test to be applied is whether or not the statute intended to give them this benefit. This is not often found to be the case; the usual interpretation is that statutory duties are owed only to the public at large. An example is the duty placed upon the Secretary of State for Health by s. 1 of the National Health Service Act 1977 to provide a comprehensive health service – a provision which has been unsuccessfully challenged by patients unhappy at the curtailing of National Health Service facilities. Such a duty is sometimes described as a target duty (Cragg, 1996) operating on the political rather than the legal plane. However, some specific duties may be owed to individuals so as to found an action for breach of statutory duty. Section 117 of the Mental Health Act 1977 (aftercare for patients under s.3) is one example. In *Fox* v. *Ealing Health Authority* (see McDonald and Taylor, 1995) a Mental Health Review Tribunal discharged a patient subject to conditions relating to his aftercare which were not accepted by the health authority. In upholding the patient's right to aftercare the court used the language of individual rights in relation to s. 117 aftercare which the health authority were under a statutory duty to provide. Another example of a duty owed in private law is the duty in s. 2 Chronically Sick and Disabled Persons Act 1970 to make arrangements to meet the assessed needs of persons with a disability. This private law right to sue the local authority if services are not forthcoming survives the decision of the House of Lords in the Gloucestershire case, provided the local authority's eligibility criteria have been met.

**Judicial review**

Applications for judicial review are the primary legal means of enforcing public law duties. Application is to the Divisional Court in London. The process is both complex and costly and may be undertaken only by persons with a sufficient interest in the matter in dispute. However, judicial review is being used increasingly on a 'test case' basis to clarify the statutory responsibilities of public bodies such as local authorities, health authorities, government departments and prison boards of visitors. The Child Poverty Action Group, RADAR and Help the Aged have brought actions in this way.

It is the legality of an action – whether that action is assessing resources for residential care, or limiting services by way of eligibility criteria – rather than the merits of a decision, which is challenged in this way. Judicial review is also used to challenge decisions taken without due process, with inadequate consultation, or in contradiction of already-publicised criteria. Decisions to close homes for elderly people have been successfully challenged for inadequate consultation with resident groups. Now that local authorities are required to be explicit about assessment procedures and service availability in community care plans (or where such procedures are explained elsewhere), judicial review might usefully be considered to hold such authorities to account for their actions.

**The importance of challenge**

The justification for such systems of quality control in public services lies in public accountability. It is empowering of service users for means of challenging local authority decisions to be made explicit to them. Legal actions have a particular potency because they give direct access to a major source of power in society: the courts. A major difficulty however is that substantive issues (how much of what kind of service) are more difficult to challenge than procedural lapses. This is in large measure an outcome of a welfare system that is based on needs rather than rights, where the definition of quality on the whole remains that of those who allocate the resources. Giving people a voice in the design of services is more potent than expecting them to 'exit' from services that they dislike, when the choice of service provider is limited and the services provided are essential to the maintenance of an adequate level of care.

*EXERCISE*

1. Collect information on your local authority's complaints procedure. How accessible is this information? What assistance may be given to people to use the system? What sort of redress is available? e.g. an apology, compensation, a changed decision.
2. Obtain a copy of an inspection report on a local residential care home. To what extent are the 'Homes are for Living In' values of privacy, dignity, independence, choice, rights and fulfilment, acknowledged in the report.

# 7

# Changing Roles

The debate about how social work fits into the framework of care management is complicated by the lack of consensus on what social work really is. One view is to see social work as essentially malleable. Based as it is on a framework of statutory duties, the role and tasks of social work will change as social policy and legislation change. If social workers are essentially state employees acting within a bureaucratic system, then the employer will legitimately define the parameters of the role. An alternative view of social work is that it exists not to ameliorate, but to challenge the inequalities that exist in the lives of people with disabilities and older people, and in the marginalisation of offenders. Being practised in so many different settings and with diverse groups of people, 'social work actually does cover a multitude of virtues which are remarkably difficult to characterise in a conceptually tidy manner' (Davies, 1997). This chapter examines the changing role of social work under community care by looking at different models of care management and the social work skills they require, and the response of users and carers to change. The satisfactions and difficulties that social workers have encountered in the transition to community care are also described.

Jordan (1997) argues that social work is necessary to compensate vulnerable individuals when communities break up under pressure from market forces. Accordingly: 'there is a contradiction at the heart of social work, because it is spawned by market-orientated economic individualism, yet its values are those of a caring, inclusive, reciprocal community that takes collective responsibility for its members' (p. 10). This contradiction is of course at the heart of community care policy itself with its emphasis on contract culture, rationing and regulation of scarce resources, whereas the real difficulty in peoples' lives may be the result of structural problems such as poverty and discrimination which market forces may help to sustain as well as create. An individualised model of social work practice thus needs to be set alongside models of social work which emphasise community action and collective responses to problem-solving.

### Care management: can social work survive?

Different models exist for the institution of care management which distinguish to a greater or lesser extent between role and task. In a role-based system the title of care manager is simply a job description of the title holder, and carries with it no necessary presumption of the professional qualification (if any) of the person within it. This was what Griffiths (1988) envisaged when he spoke of the role of care manager in procedural terms. Thus a care manager could be anyone who could follow through the principles of care management; they could be a social worker, an occupational therapist, or a community nurse. Care management as a task regards the process of care management as essentially one of method; a particular way of working which may be set alongside psychodynamic social work, for example, or cognitive behavioural therapy. The Managers' Guide (1991) (para. 3.33) states the dichotomy nicely:

> In deciding on the appropriate model or models of care management, the authorities/agencies will have to decide whether separate staff should be identified with specific care management responsibilities or whether staff can undertake care management as part of a wider range of responsibilities. The decision of agencies may be affected by the ease with which they are able to re-deploy and recruit staff of the appropriate calibre.

The choice is thus between intensive care management or a care management approach.

Care management may also be provided on an integrated or segregated basis (para. 3.34). An integrated model whereby all initial requests for assessment receive a care management response is likely to overburden professionally qualified people at the apex of the social services pyramid. People with substantial accrued skills such as domiciliary and home care managers may be deprived of assessment responsibilities and given a provider function. The SSI in its pre-liminary (SSI, 1993c) review of the operation of care management found such a top-heavy system to be widespread. One of their recommendations was for greater attention to be paid to the six separate levels of assessment themselves detailed in the Managers' Guide, whereby only the most complex cases requiring comprehensive assess-ment were assigned to professionally qualified staff. Care management as a specialist service has been developed by some authorities (now including Kent), with the vast majority of simple or single-service referrals going to administrative or non-professionally qualified staff.

The Managers' Guide identifies five models of care management:

1. the single care manager model (located either in separate teams or integrated in mainstream teams);
2. the social entrepreneurship model of a designated worker with devolved budgetary responsibility;
3. the shared case tasks model where tasks are shared by a combina-tion of professionally and vocationally qualified staff;
4. the administrative model for a co-ordination of inputs from other services;
5. the user model where the user of services acts as their own care manager.

Pilling (1992) gives examples of a further model – the multi-dis-ciplinary model – in which a multidisciplinary team is responsible for assessment and developing a care plan for an individual, usually through the development of a keyworker system. This model has similarities to the Care Programme Approach in mental health services (for which see p. 194). Raiff and Shore (1993) also describe a model similar to that favoured by Huxley (1990) for use in mental health services which they call the clinical model, and within which the provision of therapeutic help as well as services is within the domain of the care manager. Brandon and Towell (1989) describe a model of 'service brokerage' used in Canada in which the care manager acts as the agent of the service user in securing the best available package of care: as the care manager does not work for an agency he has no agenda to reduce costs or ration resources. The introduction of direct payments in lieu of community care services is a partial move towards the empowerment of service users, and the use of care managers as assessors and facilitators rather than as entrepreneurs of services. It would be misleading however to see such a system as truly user-led.

Adams (1998) sees care management as changing the nature of social work practice towards procedularism and away from theory-based and value-driven aspects of critically reflective practice. This is reflected in the competence based approach to student assessment which emphasises outcomes and performance rather than learning. The practice teacher will then have to mediate between the student's learning needs and the standards of service that the agency has to guarantee. Doel and Shardlow (1998) locate this firmly within the notion of accountability. They see the student's learning experience being underwritten in a number of ways within the agency. These underpinning factors may be subject to change in a system such as community care where there is increasing managerial control (Doel and Shardlow, 1998, p. 9).

- how much autonomy and responsibility do front-line workers have?
- do service users feel they are dealing with someone who can make decisions?
- how flat or deep are lines of accountability?
- how does the agency monitor the quality of service to users?
- what support systems are there for agency staff in terms of professional supervision, personal support or group support?
- who carries the can?
- who gets recognition?

**Working with other professions**

Close liaison with other relevant professions – in education, in housing and in health care – has always been an important feature of social work, whether with children and families or with adults. The advent of community care has made the need for that liaison more apparent, whilst fudging the boundaries between different professional groupings. The resulting dilemmas are neatly summarised by Øvretveit *et al.* (1997) as: 'how to assess needs and work together with different professional languages, how to shift from profession-services to more interprofessional working, and how to combine team leadership with profession and agency management services' (p. 6). Øvretveit sees the key issue as defining the 'team' and its purpose. Managers must first of all clarify whether a team exists for client co-ordination (referring on to each other and working in parallel), or for a collective service (with shared responsibility and authority). Teams vary on a continuum, from the highly integrated where the team's priorities are the strongest influence on the individual's work decisions to a network team which, though it may see the same 'type' of clients, is organised as a collection of disparate professional services each under its own management with its own policies, priorities and procedures. The former are multi-disciplinary teams the latter are interdisciplinary. Examples of each can be found in services for people with disabilities and mental health problems. *Interagency* working, by contrast, is not dependent upon teamwork, places less emphasis on professionals working together, and concentrates rather on strategic issues and planning.

Øvretveit sees inter-professional working as valuable for a number of reasons (the first four of which draw upon work by Hallet and Birchall, (1992), in child care but which are relevant to the objectives of community care). These are:

1. Avoidance of duplication and overlap.
2. Reductions of gaps and discontinuities in services.
3. Clarification of roles and responsibilities.
4. The delivery of comprehensive, holistic services.
5. The promotion of a service driven by objectives and outcomes rather than by professional interests.
6. The potential for replacement of staff with closely supervised ancillaries.

On the other hand, Øvretveit sees some disadvantages in interprofessionalism:

1. A reduction of choice in the absence of a diversity of assessment and service.
2. The possibility of collusion against the client which is difficult to challenge.
3. A reluctance to pursue risky or novel solutions.
4. Inward-looking attitudes.

This greater emphasis on 'what gets done' rather than 'who does what' (Øvretveit) in multidisciplinarity assumes a consensus model of working based on similar values and priorities. The major test of such co-operation is whether it can survive conflict. Dimond (1997) explores such conflicts in relation to legal rights and responsibilities. If a patient discharged from a psychiatric hospital, following involvement by a multidisciplinary team, commits a serious offence, who would be held responsible for his or her discharge? The answer would be: the psychiatrist in charge of his or her case. Given this, it is not surprising that such a person would seek pre-eminence in decision-making and would suggest resources that are within his or her control. In the case of nurses working in a similar role to social workers, the nurse is bound by the UKCC not to work 'beyond the limits of her competence'; thus professionally-imposed limitations have the effect of restricting the transfer of skills. This has implications, of course, which favour the survival of distinct professional groupings in community care.

## The status of social work within community care

Official statements on care management do little to clarify the status of social work within it. Neither the Griffiths report (1988) nor the White Paper (1989) nor the Policy Guidance addresses in any detail what the role of social work is intended to be. Bamford (1990 p. 159) was prepared to contemplate that this was because: 'the new role envisaged in designing, organising and purchasing services is so fundamentally different from that currently performed that a wholly different approach is required to which social work has a contribution to make.' Post-implementation surveys of social workers within a care management system have found major dissatisfactions with the bureaucratisation of the social work task. Both Macdonald and Myers (1995) and Petch *et al.* (1994) found widespread dissatisfaction with form-filling and the disempowering nature of the paperwork required to be completed. Lewis and Glennerster (1996) found that front-line workers were less enthusiastic than their managers about the community care changes and cited form-filling, hospital discharge procedures and the movement away from counselling as major sources of dissatisfaction. Managers themselves were showing a tendency (observed also by the SSI in 1993) (SSI, 1993c) to retreat from their professional role as 'super-visors' into a role as managers of budgets. Professional leadership in teams was thus being lost. The move from consensus management to general management not requiring professional qualifications for appointments which began in the NHS in the mid 1980s after the *first* Griffiths report is now being seen in SSDs (Simiç, 1996).

Lyons *et al.* (1995) in a survey conducted in 1993–4 of social workers' career patterns found that social workers' reactions to recent changes in their working patterns were closely related to their work settings. Probation officers, for example were highly critical of national standards, which were seen as limiting professional freedom and supporting the control/policing role. Social workers in child care, however, were approving of changes introduced by the Children Act 1989, which were seen as clarifying the role of the social worker and as addressing power imbalances with families. Social workers in adult care were hostile to the introduction of market principles and felt that flexible and locally based responses were inhibited by rigid and bureaucratic structures. Hospital social workers felt estranged from the process of consultation being carried on in social services departments and were also affected by difficulties occurring in the NHS. Workers in fieldwork teams felt that they had less opportunity for casework; they were deskilled by dealing only with assessments of a very proscribed kind and felt that their jobs were being reduced by the bringing in of other occupational groups. A feeling that social work was being fragmented was widespread, and led to an inability on the part of social workers to define and have control over their work. The overall experience of change as positive was however related to membership of an autonomous and reasonably well-resourced team with a specific remit, such as HIV/AIDS, working in a local authority where political values were consistent with the worker's own values, working in a rural area where community links and networks were more easily developed and maintained, and either recent, relevant training or a background in finance or development work. A willingness to see oneself as a change agent and to push forward new ideas was a positive view of community care which was also related to job satisfaction.

An alternative to seeing care management as a new role in social work is to see it as a new task (Petch, 1997) or an innovative method of working to be used alongside other methods of working. Superficially, this argument might be attractive because there are many features which care management has in common with traditional social casework in its emphasis on assessment, care planning, implementing, monitoring and reviewing as part of an individual care plan. To equate care management with social casework is, however, to divorce both from their historical context. As Simiç (1996) points out: 'it is not the method that distinguishes care management from casework, it is the social and economic context in which it is employed and the way its resources, intellectual, emotional and material are developed' (p. 13). Biggs (1991) sees care management as ultimately unworkable because it views interpersonal relationships as unproblematic; it is therefore fatally dismissive of a major method in social work practice – the psychodynamic. Anyone who has worked with carers under stress against a background of difficult family relationships going back over a number of years knows this to be true. It is the focus of Hughes' (1993) work on the assessment of elderly people in the community, and Parker's (1993) study of disability in marriage. To regard such problems of living as purely practical is to throw expensive resources at problems which they will not be able to resolve. Yet it is a common fault of social work practice, particularly in assessment, to over-simplify problems in this way (Ellis, 1993).

## Skills training in community care

The skills required of social workers in community care are a mixture of the old and the new. Smale and Tuson (1993) begin from the premise that there are particular skills that social workers need if their goal is not to be 'expert professionals' but facilitators of full participation in the way in which assessments are carried out. This includes skills in the process of assessment involving complex negotiations based on:

- expertise in facilitating people's attempts to articulate and identify their own needs and clarify what they want;
- sensitivity to language, cultural, racial and gender differences;
- the ability to help people through major transitions involving loss;
- the ability to negotiate and conciliate between people who have different perceptions, values, attitudes, expectations, wants and needs.

All of these things are of course major attributes of the social work task, and this has led Sheppard (1995) to see social workers as particularly well-suited to carrying out the tasks of care management. Challis (1992) challenges the view that community care is concerned simply with the efficiency of systems and looking back over the historical development of community care projects, notes that:

> The experimental inputs of the most successful projects were ideational as well as structural. They were substantially about commitments, values and skills. What the structures (including the resources) were intended to do was to enable and encourage people

to apply the commitments, values and skills of the new community care philosophy; that is, provide the incentives and rewards which harness individual motivations to achieve the equity and efficiency goals of public policy. (p. 118)

CCETSW (Best, 1994) offers guidance on training for purchasing and contracting skills, probably the most technical of care management skills, which at the same time incorporates ethical practice into an understanding of roles and tasks:

> Students who have successfully completed qualifying training in social work can be expected to understand the nature of health and local authority enabling/purchasing role, the characteristics and composition of the statutory, voluntary, private and not-for-profit sectors. Students should be expected to engage with the inequalities arising in purchasing through competent ethical practice. They should know how to make a contribution in the purchasing and contracting of social care services – with supervisor support in collaboration with other disciplines, service users, carers and relevant representatives. (p. 41)

Students should be able to evaluate whether services take into account ethnically sensitive and cultural considerations, whether they recognise users' and carers' rights of choice, and whether they provide opportunities for those aggrieved to seek representation through advocacy, complaint or legal redress.

### Social casework in community care

The medium through which services are to be delivered within community care is 'the package of care'. To what extent is this also an innovation?

Smale and Tuson (1993, p. 26) emphasise that in care management as elsewhere, 'social services and social work intervention are a response to the nature of a person's social relationships'; thus the relevant assessment is not that of individuals, but of social relationships. They point out that for most people the rudiments of a package of care already exist in the form of support provided by family, neighbours and involved professionals such as the GP. The basic task then is to resolve the 'who does what with whom' and 'who is responsible for what', all of which involve skills in negotiation, conflict management and weaving together formal and informal care. Smale and Tuson (p. 33) see such work as having four different components:

- work with individuals and their immediate families and network to tackle problems which directly affect them = direct work;
- work with wider community groups and other agencies to tackle problems which affect a range of people (including the individuals involved in direct work) = indirect work;
- work which involves the maintenance of certain social situations to avoid further distress or institutionalisation, by the provision of services = service delivery;
- work done to effect change in the ways people relate to each other, ways which precipitate or perpetuate social problems of family groups or at community levels = change agent activities.

Care management thus embraces both the social casework approach of traditional social work with individuals, and the development role of community social work. It also has both a maintenance component and a change agent component. Care management thus by the very breadth of opportunity that it presents is an exciting and radical new form of work. It requires social workers to think beyond the individual case and to confront a commonality of social problems.

**User satisfaction**

What sort of skills do service users want from social workers under community care? The answer is very similar to earlier surveys of satisfaction and dissatisfaction with social work (Sainsbury, 1975) in that service users want workers who combine practical help with an empathetic approach. Studies of consumer reactions to assessment in community care have been undertaken by Age Concern, England (1994); Age Concern, Scotland (Robertson, 1995); and Mencap (1995). All emphasise the importance of the personal but professional qualities of the social worker: reliability, empathy, good listening skills and efficiency; these qualities were more important than the professional qualification of the person concerned. The user groups surveyed were realistic (if cynical) about the amount of service that would be provided; one participant in the Age Concern, Scotland, research, took a view of service provision that became the title of the whole report 'Fed and Watered', protesting at how demeaning it was to be told that needs had been satisfied provided that the person receiving the service had been 'fed and watered'. However, there was also a strong message in this research that fundamental needs – the need for adequate warmth and an adequate income and the need for a telephone – had first of all to be met before care management at an individual level could make an impact on people's lives. There was a strong expressed need for information on services available, particularly in the Mencap research. The Mencap research also emphasised a desire for new and up dated services to be brought to the attention of individual service users. Responsive workers are required in any system, but particularly when information and access are complex.

### Care providers

Contrary to the hopes of policy-makers, there has initially been no large-scale expansion of independent sector provision in response to the introduction of a mixed economy of care (Common and Flynn, 1992). A survey by Kestenbaum (1993) on the development of private sector domiciliary providers found that there was a large variation in the size and type of provision, but for any one user the choice was very limited. There was also a very high turnover of small agencies. The Independent Living Fund, for whom the research was undertaken, had played a significant part in stimulating the private sector of care providers, though only a minority of service users (20 per cent) used private nursing or domiciliary care agencies. Commonly, the care agency will introduce their care staff to the service user. The contract however is usually between the service user and the individual carer, who is probably self-employed. Training and supervision may not be a part of that carer's relationship with the agency. The growth of such agencies has led to an increase in the number of people employed in social care, as opposed to social work. Employment is commonly available on a casual basis. Care staff in independent-sector residential homes may also be casual or bank employees. Concern over the proper regulation of staff at all levels has led to renewed pleas for a General

Social Services Council. Such a council would regulate the employment of staff at all levels by maintaining registers of workers with different qualifications and spheres of interest. Regulation by employment law alone is seen as inadequate given the diversity of employers and employment situations. The provision of direct payments by Social Services Departments will also increase the number of people employed as single employees in private households. A General Social Services Council could thus be of benefit to potential employers in establishing the credentials of people they employ as facilitators.

## Carers' issues

The vast majority of people providing social care are, of course, unpaid; they are families, friends or neighbours, and the majority will continue to care without any 'official' involvement whatsoever. Indeed, the system of community care is predicated upon there being such a group of people able and willing to provide assistance. Such people may often be grouped together as 'carers'. 'Carers' is a term which covers a range of social situations, however, and should be used with caution for a number of reasons:

- the amount and type of assistance that people provide varies widely and therefore results in qualitatively different situations. These different situations may become unhelpfully muddled by the use of the generic term 'carers';
- the word carer may carry unhelpful and inaccurate connotations of dependency in a relationship;
- 'caring for' is in this way given a status that 'caring about' does not receive, even though 'caring about' may, in the context of a relationship, be the more important role.

The extent of informal care in the community has been revealed by the analysis of statistics from the General Household Survey (Evandrou, 1997). From the GHS of 1990, One person in seven (16 per cent) was identified as having caring responsibilities, of which half were sole carers. The prime age for caring was 45–59, and the average amount of care provided was 20 hours per week; fewer than half of those people had any health or social services support, and this proportion had in fact declined since 1985. Fifty-two per cent of carers had not had a break since their caring responsibilities began, even though 20 per cent of carers had been caring for more than ten years. The overall impression given is that caring is isolating and unremitting and any formal support which is given is not asked for until caring is well established. Caring also has a negative effect on employment opportunities for both men and women, as well as on health, especially for women (Evandrou, 1997).

Social workers may relate to 'carers' in a number of different ways: as colleagues, as significant others in a relationship with the cared-for person, or as service users in their own right. The first approach is based on partnership principles, the second on ideas derived from psychotherapy, and the third on citizenship and legalism (Twigg, 1989). Public perceptions of caring may however differ from those of professionals; in Neill and Williams' (1992) study of hospital discharge, for example, a number of interviewees shrank from the application of the term 'carers' to them, seeing it as carrying connotations of obligation and responsibility. A distinction between *carers* (most often family members) who perform intimate physical tasks and whose input of time and energy is substantial, and *supporters* (often friends and neighbours), who do not become involved in physical care but who may do practical tasks such as shopping or housework, may therefore be more useful. Caring itself arises in a variety of different family situations. Caring for elderly parents is often seen in terms of duty, though there is no legal obligation to care for parents in old age. Such care therefore lacks the legal foundation that parental care for children has. Caring within marriage has been studied by Parker (1993). Such caring may evolve over a period of time as one partner becomes more frail; in other cases, the sudden onset of disability may provoke a crisis in the marriage. Caring for people with physical needs is also qualitatively different from caring for people with mental health problems, whose needs may fluctuate over time and may involve supervision and concern rather than direct help. Finch and Mason (1993) in a study of family attitudes towards responsibility for their members found that 'being deserving' rated highly in legitimising care by others. There is also a tendency for other family members to withdraw once one person is identified as a main carer.

Though spouse-carers are almost as likely to be men as women (Arber and Gilbert, 1993), Finch (1989) writing from a feminist perspective is critical of the extent to which community care is predicated upon the labour of women, particularly as women are also assumed to have the major responsibility for the care of children. Suggestions of a return to communal or institutional care are however resisted by Morris (1993a) who sees such a movement as divisive and discriminatory against disabled women. Less emphasis on 'care' and more on 'enabling' would seek to remove the negative connotations of exploitation and dependency. 'Caring about' as a replacement for the notion of 'caring for' humanises the situation being described and gives it dignity. The situation of children who care for adults in the same household is, for example, often interpreted narrowly as 'caring for', with concerns focused on the appropriateness, or otherwise, of the tasks that the child is undertaking, and on abrogation of the parental role. A more positive approach is to discuss each of the participants' feelings about the situation: there may be a good deal of 'caring about' going on, with the child wishing to contribute to the household, and the parent concerned for and involved in the emotional development of the child (SSI, 1996b).

The task for the social worker is to perceive how the system itself works: what sustains the carer/cared-for relationship, and what undermines it. Qureshi et al (1989) predicate that helping in its widest sense is characterised by exchange theory; in other words, people will calculate (consciously or not) whether what they gain from the relationship, in terms of satisfaction or reward, is worth the physical or emotional effort they put into it. As the balance will be different for each individual, and will change over time, exchanges need to be carefully monitored and, where necessary, supported. The Carers National Association has evolved a 10 Point Plan for Carers which seeks to quantify what most carers would want. These are:

1.  Recognition of their contribution and of their own needs as individuals in their own right.
2.  Services tailored to their individual circumstances, needs and views.
3.  Services which reflect an awareness of differing racial, cultural and religious backgrounds.
4.  Opportunities for a break, to relax and have time to themselves.
5.  Practical help.
6.  Someone to talk to about their own emotional needs.
7.  Information about available benefits and services.
8.  An income which covers the cost of caring.

9. Opportunities to explore alternatives to family care.
10. Services designed through consultation with carers, at all levels of policy and planning.

The Carers (Recognition and Services) Act 1995 gives carers who provide a substantial amount of care on a regular basis a right to assessment of their needs as carers. It is important that social workers bring this provision to the attention of carers, and that local authority eligibility criteria are designed with the needs of carers in mind.

Breakdown in the caring/supporting relationship is a more potent factor than level of disability in precipitating admission to residential care (Warburton, 1989). Research by Levin *et al.* (1989) has found that day care and respite care are services which are highly valued by carers of elderly people, and which enable them to carry on caring for longer. Nevertheless, social workers must be sensitive to a desire by carers to use such services to begin the process of disengagement from caring; not to be explicit about the purpose for which such services are being used means that social workers and carers may be working to different agendas.

## Community responses

The interlocking nature of individual and collective responses to the problem of need was identified in the Barclay report (1982). Social Services Departments were seen as having failed to come up with strategies for linking statutory and non-statutory sources of care provision into a coherent plan. Community care planning enables, indeed requires, such a strategy to take place. It is the responsibility not only of departments but also of individual social workers to develop skills in 'exploring communities of interest which may be important to a particular client' (para. 3.30). For care management to operate properly it is important not only that individual's needs are understood, but that individuals, groups and organisations within communities are prepared and able to provide the facilities needed (Coulshed and Orme, 1998). The theoretical base is close to that of radical social work with its emphasis on collective action and a perception of individual problems as political issues. This is not to deny, however, that networks may have a therapeutic role to play as change agents in finding solutions to the problems of individuals and families.

Seed (1990) sees individuals as having networks which comprise layers of close, or more distant social involvement. This may be represented diagrammatically:

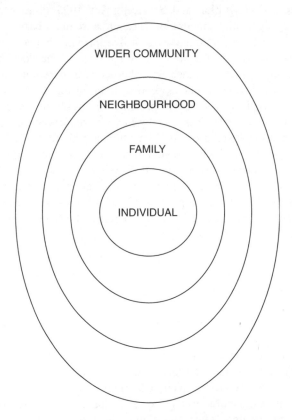

Figure 3    *Social networks*

The analysis of networking in social support systems has developed from systems theory, and offers a way of exploring how people's social networks operate in ways that help or hamper their ability to cope in the community. Network analysis has been successfully used to assist people with learning disabilities to move out of hospital care into the community; the role of the social worker being variously that of counsellor, mediator, planner or advocate (Atkinson, 1986). Its value to social workers is as a tool for understanding the social experiences of

clients and of composing a picture of the informal support systems that
may need to be mobilised or even created (Reigate, 1997). A network
might include close relatives, neighbours and friends, voluntary helpers, people with similar problems coming together in a self-help group,
and members of formal organisations like churches or trade unions.
Seed (1990) suggests that the keeping of a networking diary is a useful
tool for keeping the client as the focus of planning, and illustrating the
client's own ability to form networks in the community.

*EXERCISE* ▨▨▨▨▨▨▨▨▨▨▨▨▨▨▨▨▨▨▨▨▨▨▨▨▨▨▨▨▨▨▨▨▨

Construct a diagram to illustrate the social network of a person that you
know (or of your own social network). What are the significant individuals
and organisations within this network?

Smale and Tuson (1993) see social workers as being proactive in
making community resources available: 'Care managers will have to
work in partnership with local people to negotiate the need for, plan,
initiate, support, sustain and maintain local groups, voluntary organisations and schemes for meeting certain people's needs' (p. 40). The core
competence 'communicate and engage with organisations and people
within communities to promote opportunities for adults, their families
and groups, at risk or in need, to function, participate and develop in
society' explicitly recognises this community development aspect as a
competence. This is backed up by the evidence indicator: 'identify and
evaluate the roles, responsibilities, policies and potential contributions
of agencies, community resources, volunteers and other professionals.'

This echoes Goldberg and Warburton's (1979) conclusions from
their study of social work in the aftermath of the Seebohm reorganisation in the early 1970s. With regard to work with older people, they
concluded from an examination of case review records that local
authority social services departments could only hope to provide very
basic services for what was even then the growing number of very
elderly clients. There was a major demand for information and advice,
for example, on welfare benefits, which probably could be more
rationally supplied through citizens advice bureaux or neighbourhood
advice centres; there was need for specialist social work involvement in
dealing with issues relating to grief and loss, or major life changes such
as admission to residential care, and there was a need for heavy-end

domiciliary care and the provision of aids and adaptations. However, beyond this, occasional routine visiting by social workers was rarely an appropriate or effective means of support or anticipating approaching crises. 'Relief of isolation and loneliness, help with small chores, emotional and practical support to informal carers' would, they concluded, need to be provided by volunteers or 'good neighbours' under the sponsorship of either the statutory or voluntary sector. Similar convictions as to the appropriateness and a capacity for developing community support systems were behind the innovatory Kent Community Care Project (Davies and Challis, 1986) which provided the research evidence for the development of Community Care (see Chapter Two). In this project, local people with no previous caring experience were recruited to perform routine domiciliary tasks for frail elderly people and their main carers. Overall the project was seen to increase the likelihood of people remaining at home with an improved quality of life and at lower cost than conventional services. However, one difficulty within the project, and a reason for the later collapse of the community aspect of the scheme, was the low rate of pay given to helpers.

Finding, supporting and sustaining networks within a community can be a major part of the social work task. Also acknowledged is the fact that individuals, agencies, volunteers, community resources and other professionals within a network may have differing perspectives. Working with Difference (Home Office, 1995) is thus an important aspect of working within a community; structural factors such as gender, race and class may be more powerful in themselves than the inclusive idea of community. It is also necessary to acknowledge that people may have different motivations on a personal level for giving time, money and expertise to assist others, and that these need to be supported (Qureshi *et al.*, 1983). Some people may need time from the worker; some may need financial reward; some may simply need acknowledgement that they are doing a good job. Smale and Tuson's (1993) description of a package of care as 'a fluid set of human relationships' rather than 'a basket of goods and services' indicates the sort of social work skills in negotiation and counselling that may be needed here.

'Working Alongside Volunteers' (SSI, 1996a) seeks to emphasise the importance of clarity and commitment, co-ordination, equal opportunities and contract specifications in work with volunteers for Social Services Departments. However, this is very much a review of systems and does not explore client perspectives on volunteering, or the community development potential of the role. Though volunteering is often seen as an individual activity, it can also be organised collectively through self help organisations and community groups (Payne, 1995), and may include people who are service users in their own right. Again, social workers will have to contribute positively to exchanges in the relationship, not simply take the benefit of the volunteer's time.

Payne (1995) explores the difference between community develop-ment work and community work. Community development work is based upon pluralism – the idea that formal authorities, though they have an important role in providing services and taking a lead in planning, are not the only bodies concerned with public welfare. Voluntary organisations and neighbourhood groups will play a sig-nificant role in developing a truly local response to need. The basic tenets of community development are therefore highly congruent with those of community care, though as Payne points out (p. 169):

> The central conflict within community development is that between developing services and projects which respond to social services requirements, and promoting involvement in processes for commu-nity decision-making among people in particular areas or with shared interests, which may not reflect or may conflict with social services priorities. The evidence is that a degree of involvement in services and much better community responsiveness on the part of agencies can be developed. Genuine community influence or, to go further, control, may be much harder to achieve, even if it is desired. A distinction must also be drawn between the interests of the commu-nity as a whole and those of users and carers. There may be no interest in the particular needs of groups of users of community care services; priorities with other people may lie elsewhere.

Community development work is essentially proactive in developing community awareness as well as services or facilities, such as luncheon clubs or sitting services, so that carers can meet together. The role of the paid worker becomes one of a facilitator rather than a leader. Local groups, based around a common interest, can be helped to grow, enabled to use community facilities such as village halls or be given help in developing business-like tasks such as running a meeting or organising a budget. The most famous account of community *social* work in action is the 'patch' system in Normanton, Wakefield described by Hadley and McGrath (1984). Social workers working on a 'patch' within a closely defined geographical area would acquire 'on the ground' information about the local area, would develop an accessibility to local people and forge strong personal links with other professionals in the area such as GPs, community nurses, representatives of voluntary organisations and churches. Community social work was endorsed in the Barclay report (1982) but is currently out of fashion. Payne (1995) would judge the effectiveness of community social work in terms of its major objectives of involving local people in decision-making and making locally-sensitive services available.

Community work per se is outside the ambit of social work insofar as community workers have their own distinctive qualification separate from the Dip. SW, and do not work to statutory requirements. Community work mobilises the resources of the community itself to change. Mayo (1994) sees that there are two different perspectives on community work: the *technicist* and the *transformational*. The *technicist* promotes community initiatives within the framework of existing social relations, whereas the *transformational* seeks to develop strategies and build alliances for social change. Transformational community work is inherently political in that it challenges the location of power within officially sanctioned groups. Structural inequalities, poverty and racism are all confronted by community work. In so doing, it exposes the benign assumptions of community care policy that society is based on consensus and that formal and informal care can easily be interwoven.

The 'community' basis of community care is challenged from a different perspective by Bulmer (1987). Bulmer develops the idea of a community of 'limited liability' based upon temporary and highly focused alliances between people who have a common interest, for example in the provision of good quality education for their children at the local school, or the building of a bypass to alleviate traffic congestion locally. It cannot be assumed that this community of interest will extend to other matters, particularly as people's major ties remain kinship ties, which survive despite greater social mobility. The isolation and rejection of people with mental health problems or learning disabilities is seen as underlining the point that in many people's minds community care means care by the families (if any) of those in need of care, and not some wider conception of social responsibility. The consequence is that formal (statutory) sector involvement is necessary to support people who are without family ties. Yet, at the same time, informal care by families alone is not adequate, largely due to the absence of a proper family policy to compensate financially those family members who provide care. Community care policies which ignore these infrastructure issues are therefore built on shaky foundations.

*CASE STUDY*

Polly Richards is 35 years old and lives alone in her flat on a local authority housing estate. She has a diagnosis of schizophrenia and receives fortnightly visits from a community psychiatric nurse. Polly rarely leaves her flat, except to visit the local shops and café. The CPN has become concerned that local youths are visiting Polly's flat when they are supposed to be at school. Small amounts of money and some possessions have gone missing. Polly has said that she enjoyed their company at first, but now she feels harassed by them. She has asked them to stay away, but they have not done so.

The CPN asks your advice on what to do about this situation. What would you advise?

# 8

# Changing Values

Social work has been described (CCETSW, 1995) as a combination of knowledge, skills and values. But it is arguable (Banks, 1995) that no real distinction can be drawn between these three elements of practice. Knowledge is rendered sterile by an unskilled application, and is not in itself value-free. What we seek to know – more precisely, how we understand and make sense of what we know – is determined by our value position. The value-base of social work is here explored within a framework of community care. Particular attention is paid to social work dilemmas when values conflict, for example when a cared-for person's right to self-determination is in conflict with a carer's need for respite. Three particular areas are chosen for consideration in this chapter in terms of their value base: meeting the needs of black service users, the rights of people with disabilities, and difficulties posed by the onset of mental incapacity.

Values in social work are part of a professionally protected dogma; they are essentially collective, and may be in juxtaposition to the personal beliefs of the individual social worker. Thus the client's rights to self-determination – to make decisions for himself or herself, within the law – will require the social worker to facilitate the exploration of moral choices with which he or she would disapprove. So, a client contemplating a termination of pregnancy should be given the opportunity to explore such a choice even though abortion was deemed unacceptable by the worker as an individual. Social work values are not static; they evolve in line with changes in society and organisations to which social workers must respond. Though the classic social work values of respect for persons and client self-determination still subsist, they may nowadays emerge in a different formulation as working in partnership and empowerment. The proactive expression of social work's value base is seen in the development of anti-oppressive and anti-discriminatory practice.

Social work practice is in need of a moral base because its concern is with the care and development of vulnerable people. Social workers are called upon to make difficult decisions affecting the integrity of families and individuals' freedom to live the life they choose. Legislation under which social workers operate, such as the Mental Health Act 1983 and the National Assistance Act 1948, are the expressions of agreed social policy, but a mere reading of the legislation dos not decide actual cases. Social work decisions are 'decisions under uncertainty' which cannot be adjudicated simply by the application of technical or procedural rules. Banks (1995) uses the term 'dilemma' to describe the essentially moral choices that social workers have to make when considering which of two possible outcomes to pursue. Should the social worker, for example, section a person under the Mental Health Act for the protection of the public, or support his or her desire to remain in the community with (possibly inadequate) support? The social worker who has the choice between two equally unwelcome alternatives may be said to face a dilemma when it is not clear which choice he or she should make. Choices in such a situation should be guided by values, so that hopefully the least detrimental alternative can be achieved.

**What are values?**

A value may be described as 'the principles or moral standards of a person or social group'; this is the Oxford English Dictionary definition of values. Values ultimately help guide action: 'a value is something to do with what you ought to do in practice. This may not be the same as what you want to do or what it is in your interests to do, or in fact what you actually do' (Howe, 1996). There are also two kinds of values: primary, or intrinsic values, where things are seen as good in their own right; and instrumental values, things that are worth pursuing because of their end result. The difficulty is that none of these things is uncontroversial; people in different cultures and at different points in time will disagree over what primary values are and the authority from which they stem. In a religious society the word of God expressed in religious texts is the source of primary values. In a society where human reason is seen as the means through which progress can be achieved there is a reliance upon science and ethics to produce 'rules for living'. Social work, particularly when it emphasises legalism, measured change and control, fits well into this rational view of the world which is essentially that of modernism. The stance of post-modernism is to emphasise the relativity of values; there are no universal standards or laws by which we can understand either human behaviour or society. The ultimate consequence of rigid adherence to the idea of immutable truths is to be seen in totalitarianism. This is so whether those truths are seen as either self-evident, or objectively verifiable.

A search for 'social work values' may be an impossible quest given the diversity of situations with which social work has to deal, both in terms of user groups and the settings within which social work is practised. Social work has to deal with offending behaviour, mental illness, family breakdown, disability and frailty in old age; it is practised in community settings, hospitals, prisons and the courts. Social workers also operate in a world which is significantly influenced by gender, race, class and sexuality (Davies, 1997). It is not surprising then that any claim to a definitive value-base for the whole of social work may be illusory.

The divergence is therefore not only concerning what social workers do, it is also in the significance, meaning and value to be given to those actions (Shardlow, 1998).Thus in discussing anti-oppressive practice Clifford (1994) emphasises historical and cultural factors which lead to an approach based on social construction theories of oppression. Dominelli (1998) adopts a person-centred philosophy and an egalitarian value system, while Dalrymple and Burke (1995) emphasise reflex-ivity, requiring that social workers consider the ways in which their own social identity and values affect the information they gather, so that 'the act of challenging' relates to themselves as much as to others and to external systems.

**The historical development of social work values**

The development of value statements for social work was first of all grounded in the one-to-one casework tradition, with values appropriate to that relationship being propounded most famously by Biestek (1957). Biestek's 'Seven Principles' are summarised by Banks (1995) as:

1. Individualisation; the recognition of each person's unique qualities.
2. The recognition of each person's need to express their own feelings, both positive and negative.
3. Controlled emotional involvement.
4. Acceptance of people as they really are.
5. A non-judgemental attitude; separating out the person from the behaviour.
6. User self-determination.
7. Confidentiality.

This approach is derived from the philosophy of Emmanuel Kant who saw it to be a categorical imperative that people should never be treated as a means to an end, but always as an end in themselves, that is, intrinsically worthy and as people who have their own choices and desires. This is often condensed into the phrase 'respect for persons'. Biestek himself, however, recognised that such principles would be subject to legal requirements, to a 'higher duty' to self, to other individuals or to the community (Banks, 1995). Controversially this concept of 'personhood' applied only to people who were capable of rational thought and self-determined action; this in itself has led to difficulties in applying Biestek's principles to people lacking mental capacity (see below).

Principles which emphasise the integrity of the social worker – individual relationship are best suited to a professional model of social work, which sees the social worker as an autonomous professional and the other party as a 'client'. Such an analysis best fits a counselling relationship within a private or voluntary agency. It may be less appropriate where the social worker is an employee of a statutory agency working to a legal mandate. Given that the practice of social work is a socially-sanctioned role, other types of ethical principles concerned with utility (promoting the greatest balance of good over evil) and justice (distributing the good(s) as widely and/or fairly as possible) may claim to be a more relevant expression of social work values than simply individualism (Banks, 1995). The hospitalisation of people who are mentally ill (because of the risk that they pose to the public, rather than themselves) is justified by utilitarian principles because it is the greatest good of the greatest number. The client in competition for scarce resources becomes a service user; a person in receipt of care according to his assessed ability to pay. In this sense, utilitarian values are easily espoused by community care policy.

However, in community care there is little respect for the concept of distributive justice; services on the whole are not spread thinly amongst those who might derive some benefit from them. Instead the *amount* of benefit is measured and services are targeted only on those in the greatest need.

The New Right approach of turning the service user into a consumer has created a person with a narrow entitlement to a particular service of a defined quantity and of an assured quality. Legalism looms large through complaints procedures to ensure that services received meet contract compliance standards. The consumer's self-determination is bounded by legal parameters; his or her needs are not expressed in terms of self-actualisation. The emphasis is on process and instrumental values, such as the right to a fair hearing or access to records. In the negative manifestation of New Right philosophy, the user is treated as an object of concern – a risk to be assessed and later controlled. This has been most apparent in the mental health field with the introduction of supervised discharge and supervision orders.

A move away from both individualisation and utilitarianism towards a growing awareness of structural oppression, particularly with regard to women and black communities, took place in the late 1980s. A key theme (Banks, 1995) was 'praxis' the notion of committed action in which values are part of a radical challenge to structural inequalities. Under such an approach equal opportunities policies, for example, would be seen as racist for ignoring difference, and the task of the social worker is one of challenging injustice at a structural level. Anti-discriminatory practice of this sort is described by Kohli (1996) as being about 'helpfully holding on to uncertainty, whilst seeking to establish clarity of purpose in working with difference'. But it is not just about adopting a value position, it is about *doing*; in particular, making a commitment to the process of connection. In relation to competences, anti-discriminatory practice is about professionals using authority in a way that is helpful for someone less powerful than themselves: in order to achieve this, it is necessary to examine the impact of difference on oneself, to use knowledge and research to inform practice, to consider the use of language, both orally and in written reports, and critically to evaluate both agency policy and procedures.

The use of language is a fundamental indicator of the theoretical position held by the user and is a signpost to the type of practice that will follow. Thus Braye and Preston-Shoot (1995) are able to highlight traditional v. radical values in social care by juxtapositioning, for example, the traditional value of respect for persons with that of citizenship; paternalism and protection with participation; and partnership with empowerment or user-control. They perceive social workers as working either to a broadly reformist agenda where there are equal opportunities to reform the relationship between service providers and users within a social democratic framework, or a radical agenda where issues of power and oppression are uppermost and an individual's life chances are determined by his or her position in society.

Can different approaches to values from individualistic, utilitarian and radical perspectives be reconciled? Jordan (1995) argues that they cannot, because they are inherently in conflict with each other. Formal professionally-driven statements of values may juxtapose elements from each of these perspectives without acknowledging that the achievement of some is dependent upon the destruction of others. CCETSW's values requirement for the Dip.SW may be criticised in this way. It begins by listing traditional liberal values such as respect for individual freedom and choice, and ends with statements about the sources of structural oppression which social workers have a duty to challenge. Yet, as Jordan argues, these same liberal values are amongst the strongest intellectual defences of the privileges of wealth, whiteness and masculinity upon which structural oppression is based. Which values are to take precedence? There is no guidance on this, and, arguably there cannot be, if, as Howe (1996) argues, the task is really to acknowledge imperfections and the compromises, trading and negotiation that inevitably have to take place. This of course makes difficult, if not impossible, the attainment of CCETSW's view of values as objectively verifiable and hence assessable.

## CCETSW's values requirement

Why should bodies responsible for professional education put such emphasis on values? The possession of a distinctive code of values (written or unwritten, but usually written) has been seen as one of the attributes of a profession. CCETSW's revised Paper 30 (1995) contains within it a separately stated Values Requirement; unlike the earlier (1989) Paper 30, values are not wrapped around the competences, instead the emphasis is on their integration with practice.

In order to achieve the award of the Dip.SW, students must demonstrate in meeting the core competences that they (CCETSW, 1995):

- identify and question their values and prejudices, and implications for practice;
- respect and value uniqueness and diversity, and recognise and build on strengths;
- promote people's rights to choice, privacy, confidentiality and protection, while recognising and addressing the complexities of competing rights and demands;
- assist people to increase control of and improve the quality of their lives, while recognising that control of behaviour will be required at times in order to protect children and adults from harm;
- identify, analyse and take action to counter discrimination, racism, disadvantage, inequality and injustice, using strategies appropriate to role and context; and
- practice in a manner that does not stigmatise or disadvantage either individuals, groups or communities.

This statement is, of course, open to all the allegations of inconsistency raised by Howe (1996) and Jordan (1995) above. However, it is a useful position statement from which to examine not only 'the values of social work', but also the perceived role of social work in society, and the inherent demands made upon every person who aspires to become a social work practitioner.

The preamble to the values requirement contains within itself a definition of the social work task which is essentially reformist rather than radical: 'Social workers assist people to have control of and improve the quality of their lives, and are committed to reducing and preventing hardship and disadvantage for children, adults, families and groups.' A single-perspective approach is, however, recognised to be insufficient: 'in intervening in people's lives to achieve change, social workers must recognise their interrelationships of structural and individual factors in the social context in which services operate, and the need to address their impact on the lives of children and adults.' Social workers furthermore: 'must be self aware and critically reflective, and their practice must be founded on, informed by and capable of being judged against a clear value base.'

Jones and Joss (1995) in seeking to answer the question: what is professionalism? develop Schön's (1993) idea of the 'reflective practitioner' to explain the importance of CCETSW's first requirement that the competent student must identify and question their own values and prejudices and their implications for practice. Hence the importance of students bringing forward, analysing and dealing with their own life experiences. The reflective practitioner rejects the view that professional development depends on individual detachment and objectivity. Taking an essentially psychoanalytic stance, Jones and Joss see all potential professionals – whether in nursing, the law, teaching or social work – as whole persons who each bring their own background, values and culture to the specific context of professional practice.

The emphasis within professional training on competences and learning outcomes often disguises the fact that what actually happens in the learning process is not often studied or understood (Yelloly and Henkel, 1995). What develops in the relationship between the individual worker and the agency may itself be explicable in terms of the psychoanalytic concepts of conflict, ambivalence, anxiety and defence. Jones and Joss (1995) consider that the value-base of the individual worker may thus include informal rules and meanings which derive from sub-cultures within the organisation. Bion (1967) also uses psychoanalytic concepts to explain unconscious and unverbalised feelings of anger or depression aroused in the worker by the nature of the work that he is called upon to do.

At the same time there has also been a tendency to replace professional judgement with more stringent guidelines and policy statements, and to locate decision-making at managerial rather than individual practitioner level. Paradoxically, this abrogation of the opportunity for individual development may ultimately work to the detriment of the organisation. Where the individual social worker is sustained and enabled by their organisation to carry out a very difficult and challenging task, the experience thus gained fosters growth in the organisation. Thus capacity for creative individual thought will be weakened by demands that are 'off task', such as meaningless paperwork and sterile meetings, and will be lost altogether if energy is instead diverted to the construction of 'bad objects' at the level of management or policy making. The social worker who is asked to assess need without having the resources to meet that need is also likely to suffer (in a personal psychological sense, as well as in a professional sense) from cognitive dissonance as the gap between aspiration and reality becomes more difficult logically to sustain.


## Values within community care

Pietroni (1995) analyses the effect that community care changes have had on professionalism, and locates such changes within post-modernism. The loss of certainty, acceptance of a relativist philosophy, and the fragmentation of values, thoughts and belief are all accepted features of post-modernism. Most important, in terms of social work values, is what is termed 'the waning of affect' – people become 'commodities', 'bits', 'episodes' rather than significant individuals. Specifically in relation to community care, cultural change has been highlighted by the adoption of market mechanisms which in turn has led to (Pietroni, 1995, p. 45):

- The commodification of care through needs assessment, care packaging and care management.
- The emphasis on audit, information and databases especially to serve the welfare exchange market structured around the purchaser-provider split. Knowledge and information in this way themselves become marketable commodities.
- The near erasure of the term social work without official acknowledgement in the glossaries and directories accompanying the National Health Service and Community Care Act 1990.
- A world where the term 'quality' can in effect mean *quantity* of care provided. If care management is defined by resource-based eligibility criteria, care management as a process can also means managing the lack of care.
- The rhetoric of 'user-centred seamless service' and 'partnership' with a seductive undertow that evokes sentimentality in the place of a more rational appraisal of the viability of new policies given the existing resource framework.
- The constant change of senior managers and organisational structures leading to an absence of authoritative leadership.

The espousal of agency values as taken-for-granted expressions of the common good is also problematic insofar as it subordinates individual thought to organisational culture. The legitimacy of such definitions is accepted by CCETSW in the fifth of its Values Requirements in the mandate to identify, analyse and take action to counter discrimination, racism, disadvantage, inequality and injustice, which is qualified by the phrase 'using strategies appropriate to the role and context'. In the Probation Service this context would be the primacy of protecting the public. This primacy finds expression in the inclusion of an essential requirement that the risk to the public of re-offending be included in a Pre-Sentence Report; this, and other requirements, are 'National Standards' and the values they represent have dominated probation practice since the coming into force of the Criminal Justice Act 1991. Similarly, the fourth Values Requirement that competent social workers will assist people to increase control of and improve the quality of their lives, is subject to the recognition that control of behaviour will be required at times in order to protect children and adults from harm. Such protection, especially in the case of patients discharged from psychiatric care, is increasingly prescriptive. The introduction of supervised discharge and supervision registers has determined how such behaviour should be controlled. These procedures are initiated by health professionals under the Care Programme approach, and whilst it is true that concentration on 'task' rather than 'role' has cut across professional boundaries, clashes of professional values may occur between the 'medical model' of diagnosis and cure, and the 'social model' of understanding and support.

Are there, however, positive elements of community care which relate to values, an understanding of which supports good practice? The areas which best promote change in community care are seen by Shardlow (1998) as participation, empowerment, advocacy, and anti-discriminatory and anti-oppressive practice. These may be explored in turn:

- Participation may be said to be based on traditional Kantian principles of respect for persons; involving people in planning and in decision-making is inherently respectful and can be a source of personal growth.
- Empowerment is more than an instrumental value that enables people to make choices, insofar as it asserts the sovereignty of the decision-maker it is a primary value of citizenship.
- Advocacy is instrumental in a utilitarian sense by emphasising distributive justice and fair treatment for all and a (potentially at least) equal entitlement to bid for goods on offer.

- Anti-Discriminatory and Anti-Oppressive Practice positively promote differences as part of an agenda for change.

Thus the historical development of the value base of social work from the individual to the structural can be seen to come together within community care, as long as the practitioner remains aware of the different sources upon which such practice is based.

## Participation

Participation by service users in the design and delivery of services was heralded in the foreword to the Griffiths report as a basic cornerstone of community care policy: 'The whole thrust of my work has been to ensure a move from an administered paternalistic provision of service to a managed system of meeting consumer needs in a way which will provide a quality of service economically and effectively delivered and involving and motivating both the consumer and the staff' (Griffiths, 1988, foreword).

Croft and Beresford (1990) in their first enquiry into user involvement in Social Services Departments identified two vital components for effective user participation: a voice in the agency, and personal support to express it. Neither was sufficient without the other. Also of importance was the encouragement given to direct involvement by front-line staff from the agency; imposing participatory schemes top–down was likely to dilute their effect. Involving people in the planning of services was also found to take more time, skills and resources than expected. However, it also saved time and money resulting from ill-informed decisions.

Croft and Beresford also identified two competing philosophies underpinning user involvement: consumerism and self-advocacy. Consumerism was defined as the seeking of information from users by agencies that wish to improve their efficiency, economy and effectiveness. Agencies do this primarily in order to find solutions to their own problems, such as, is their product the one that the consumer wants? Self-advocacy, is by contrast user-driven, and here the aim is empowerment. Service users seek a direct say in agencies and services to gain greater control over their lives; their motivation is not the narrow one of wishing to be involved in the administration of services. An example of consumerism would be advisory committees set up under the Registered Homes Act 1984 to comment upon the registration process; an example of self-advocacy would be the setting up of Carers Forums specifically to raise awareness of the needs and rights of carers. Agencies should therefore clarify from the beginning what kind of involvement is being sought and what commitment can be given to act on what people say they want.

**Empowerment**

Shardlow (1998) observes the term 'empowerment' as being used in the literature in two different ways. He sees Stevenson and Parsloe's (1993) definition of empowerment in community care as being centred upon the articulation and meeting of social care needs. Braye and Preston-Shoot (1995) however emphasise both the developmental nature of empowerment – extending one's ability to take effective decisions – and its role in maximising people's quality of life by enabling disempowered people to have a greater voice in institutions, services and situations which affect them in the attainment of their own goals.

Hoyes *et al.* (1993) have produced a 'ladder of empowerment' to measure the extent to which users both individually and collectively have the power to take decisions or influence the decision making process. The 'top' of the ladder reflects he highest level of empowerment, and the bottom of the ladder is the lowest (Hoyes *et al.*, 1993).

*THE LADDER OF EMPOWERMENT*

| | |
|---|---|
| HIGH | Users have the authority to take all decisions |
| | Users have the authority to take selected decisions |
| | Users' views are sought before decisions are finalised |
| | Users may take the initiative to influence decisions |
| | Decisions are publicised and explained before implementation |
| LOW | Information is given about decisions made |

Jack (1995) however is sceptical of claims that empowerment can be achieved through participation in service planning: he poses the question (p. 6): ' Do participation and involvement 'empower' service users or is their involvement itself potentially disempowering through absorption, colonisation or the bureaucratic dissipation of legitimate protest?' Real empowerment involves control – over money and over resources – and is essentially a political activity. It is not something which is in the gift of professionals; it is something which arises from the demands of individuals or groups to have their needs met. The model of care management which best fits the idea of empowerment is that of service brokerage (Brandon and Towell, 1989). In this model, the care manager acts as agent of the service user and/or their family to commission services from a variety of sources which fit the agenda which he is given. The care manager has no resources of his or her own, but negotiates for individualised funding to obtain services that the user needs and wants. Thus it is the service user and not the professional who sets the agenda.

Jack contrasts empowerment and enablement; terms which are often confused in social work parlance. Empowerment involves establishing the legitimacy of user-determined goals as an attribute of citizenship. Enablement, however, is not a political concept, but a professional skill. In the context of community care, the professional may involve a user in the assessment process for a service; the worker may thus 'enable' the user to develop self-confidence, self-esteem and negotiation skills through this process. However, the power to purchase that service and to withdraw it is retained by the professional who has given over none of the power to control the process or its outcome (Jack, 1995, p. 11).

The new Diploma in Social Work does not in fact use the language of empowerment but uses that of enablement and opportunity. Core competence 2 is to 'promote opportunities for people to use their own strengths and expertise to enable them to meet responsibilities, secure rights and achieve change'. The emphasis is thus on 'New Right' values of individual responsibility for (non-radical) change. The practice requirements emphasise this ultimate personal responsibility. The practice requirement 'provide opportunities for learning and development to enable children and adults to function and participate' emphasises for example, the giving of *assistance* to children and adult service users and carers to *participate* in decision-making about arrangements for daily living and personal care. It does not locate the power to make such decisions within the province of service users and carers themselves.

Empowerment in its proper sense has not only a substantive but a strong procedural aspect insofar as it is about having access to decision-making processes. An interesting practice example of a well-meaning but oppressive system which was criticised in terms of its failure to empower service users is contained in a report from the local government Ombudsman (Report 95/B/0166 against Cornwall County Council). The complainant had been excluded from a day centre for people with mental health problems for alleged abusive behaviour. From the reading of the report it appears that the day centre was operating in an unstructured way akin to a therapeutic community. There was no clear guidance on how to manage or record difficult events and thus no channel of representation or complaint short of using the local authority complaints procedure. The absence of any provision for making independent enquiries effectively gave all power to the centre manager. In addition, no work was undertaken with the user to facilitate her eventual return. The laxness of the regime therefore meant that users effectively had no voice in the process of terminating attendance or its outcome. Empowerment therefore is dependent upon clear procedural provisions being made for decision-making which have the rights of users at their centre.

**Advocacy**

'Promoting the rights of children and adults at risk or in need in the community' is one of the practice requirements within the core competence 'promote and enable'. An evidence indicator for this is direct advocacy with, and on behalf of, children and adults. How feasible is such a form of advocacy within an administrative or entrepreneurial system of care management? Advocacy is 'speaking on behalf of' another, usually in a formal, and often in a quasi-legal, context. In contrast with empowerment, advocacy does not give power; it gives the right to make representations to those (others) who have the power. It implies partisanship; a sense of belonging to the person on whose behalf the advocacy is taking place. It is unlikely then that anyone who is an employee of the agency which makes the final decision on the granting of resources or the settlement of a dispute concerning property, money or even individual liberty, can properly be said to be acting as an advocate. The Practitioners' Guide (1991, para. 74) recognises this: 'the devolution of responsibility to allocate resources, changes the nature of the relationship between practitioner and user. Practitioners are less able to act as advocates on users' behalf. This highlights the need to develop opportunities for independent representation and advocacy in parallel with care management arrangements.'

This concern for advocacy is felt also by service users. There is a need to develop training for personal advocates who will support individuals through the community care assessment process. It is one of Age Concern's Infrastructure policies (Age Concern, 1994) that sections 1–3 of the Disabled Persons Act 1986 should be implemented so as to trigger the appointment of personal representatives to speak for people in assessment and review processes. Their appointment is even more critical when the person being assessed is mentally incapacitated. There is evidence (Harding and Beresford, 1996) that advocacy is seen by service users and carers as a very important service – a fact that is not reflected in what health and local authorities choose to fund: 'Advocacy is crucial to express their wants and needs, their preferences and anxieties, their complaints and objections' (p. 30).

Payne (1995) distinguishes different types of advocacy:

1. Citizen advocacy which operates on a one-to-one basis with one person representing the views of another, usually in a formal setting such as a case conference or review.
2. Self-advocacy in which training and support may be provided to enable people to represent themselves assertively.
3. Group advocacy which brings together a number of people with similar interests who operate as a group to represent their shared interests.

Models 1 and 2 are essentially individual and operate on a case-by-case basis. Advising and assisting a mentally ill person to present an appeal against compulsory detention for treatment at a mental health review board or tribunal is one example of direct advocacy which a social worker could perform in this sort of sense. Model 3 is directed not so much to individual change but to structural change. The power of the group is also greater than the sum of its parts. Group advocacy may in some circumstances become community action when sufficient people are involved. Group advocacy may be seen as the preferred method if the aim is for the group to become involved in service delivery decisions and to reframe how the group itself is perceived. This type of advocacy may thus be seen as *cause* advocacy rather than *case* advocacy (Rees, 1991).

## Anti-discriminatory and anti-oppressive practice

Braye and Preston-Shoot (1995) contrast anti-discriminatory practice and anti-oppressive practice. The former they see as a non-radical value which locates challenges to both personal and structural inequalities within equal opportunities policies based on voluntary change. Anti-oppressive practice, by contrast, places less confidence on the value of remedial action *per se* in changing a service user's experience of oppression when such oppression is endemic to the whole fabric of society. 'Thus, while personal and organisational action for equality is important, its focus must be wider than merely the relationship created through use of services if equality is to be addressed on a significant scale' (Braye and Preston-Shoot, 1995, p. 43).

Dominelli (1998) sees anti-oppressive practice as a normal part of citizenship entitlements. She locates it within the tradition of humanism by emphasising its importance in responding to people's needs through combating the effects of structural inequalities such as race, gender and class. Anti-oppressive practice values difference, whilst refusing to recognise a hierarchy of oppressions within race, gender, age or disability. Adams (1998) sees anti-oppressive practice as a collectivist professional approach to oppression and contrasts it with empowerment which is the achievement of powers from professionals by individual service users. Anti-oppressive practice is in this sense a manifestation of a radical alternative value base which is inherently political insofar as it (Thompson, 1993):

- recognises the socio-political context of service users' life experiences;
- aims to ensure that the ways in which services are provided do not contribute to oppression;
- aims to assist users in their struggles against oppression.

## Values in practice

Has community care in any case made ethically sensitive social work more difficult to achieve in practice? Jack (1995) argues that the introduction of market principles against the background of a breakdown in consensus about the size and function of the welfare state have necessarily had an effect upon the profession of social work. In particular, 'Any claims still made to moral integrity based on professional vocation and the primacy of the client's interests are seen to be increasingly suspect as the difference between the caring professions and other businesses become less and less apparent' (Jack, 1996, p. 3). The bureaucratisation of social care may also be disabling for the worker. In order to promote empowerment for service users, workers themselves need a flexible and open approach in which solutions to problems can be based on negotiation rather than the rigid application of rules and hierarchies. Stevenson and Parsloe (1993), however, ague that many workers do not experience their organisations as empowering. In psychoanalytic terms (Bion, 1967) the worker needs to feel contained and well supported in order to function effectively; if such containment does not happen, management may come to be seen negatively as a 'bad object' which frustrates and rejects.

## Working with black service users

The extent to which community care policies acknowledge and respect difference is crucial for the ability of individual practitioners to practice in an anti-discriminatory way. Devore and Schlesinger (1991) specify four prerequisites for ethnically-sensitive practice. These are:

- community profiling of needs and resources;
- cultural awareness;
- understanding of systemic discrimination;
- consideration of methods which enhance ethnic-sensitive practice.

Services for people from black and minority ethnic groups are a generally underdeveloped area of community care; recognition of structural issues may be further undermined by traditional divisions between client groups which ignore commonalties of interest, for example amongst black service users. The White Paper 'Community Care in the Next Decade and Beyond' (1989) acknowledges that 'good community care must recognise the circumstances of minority communities, be sensitive to their needs and be planned in consultation with them'. No further guidance, however, is given on how this is to be achieved. Cameron *et al.* (1996) consider that the system of community care may create further disadvantage for black and ethnic minority groups:

- because of the tendency to individualise problems;
- because services are organised according to white norms;
- heavy reliance is placed on the voluntary sector to make specialist provision; this can lead to marginalisation, particularly if such services are short term and inadequately funded;
- the values upon which assessments are based may be inappropriate. A particular example is the assumption that independence from the family is to be encouraged.

Ahmad and Atkin (1996) take this argument further by emphasising the pervasiveness of racist attitudes, which may lead on to health and social problems being defined in terms of cultural deficits, particularly in the mental health field. Certainly, Norman (1980) exposed the 'triple jeopardy' facing older women growing old in a second homeland; they were identifiable as the group least likely to receive appropriate psychiatric treatment and care. Access to services, being aware of what is available and how to use it is poor (Atkin and Rollings, 1993). Ahmad and Atkin see community care positively as an opportunity for new forms of provision to arise. However: 'A challenge for academics and practitioners alike, including in relation to community care, is to recognise the context of black people's lives, to which their cultural norms, values and resources and racialised oppression and marginalisation are equally pertinent' (Ahmad and Atkin, 1996, p. 6). Community care policies which give limited attention to structural factors will thus provide an inadequate basis for service provision.

*EXERCISE*

Find out if policy statements exist locally concerning services for people from black and ethnic groups. Find and describe examples of those services. Do they reflect the values of the communities they serve?
How are they publicised?
How are they funded?

## Disability rights

The rationing effect of community care planning may also detract from the proper recognition of some issues as fundamentally questions of basic human rights. Morris (1994), for example, sees the provision of physical care for people with disabilities as a fundamental human and civil rights issue. Oliver (1996, p. 24) cites the Fundamental Principles Document of the Union of Physically Impaired against Segregation which is to seek: 'necessary financial and other help required from the State to enable us to gain the maximum possible independence in daily living activities, to achieve mobility, undertake productive work and to live where and how we choose with full control over our own lives.' Such matters as direct payments, adaptations and appropriate housing thus become matters of right rather than negotiation. The issue is one of citizenship and respect for difference. Oliver sees segregated education, residential care and financial assessment as fundamentally infringing and even taking away these rights. In terms of community care planning Bewley and Glendinning (1994) found little evidence that, despite rhetoric to the contrary, disabled people were actually involved in the planning of services. Care management, if an administrative model based upon a combination of medical and personal tragedy approaches to disability, is also seen by Finkelstein (1993) as being centrally concerned with controlling disabled people. Oliver (1996) concludes that insofar as the concept of 'needs' rather than rights is at the centre of community care provision, it is almost certain to guarantee the failure of those policies as far as disabled people are concerned.

**Mental incapacity**

The application of values in practice poses real dilemmas for social workers particularly where legislation and professional practice are less well developed. An example of this is in the situation of people with dementia who are, or are becoming, mentally incapacitated, that is, unable to make decisions for themselves. Structural factors such as ageism and racism may be equally relevant to an assessment of the issues. The research evidence does not support the contention that it is possible for people at an advanced state of dementia, which typically includes behaviours such as wandering and incontinence, to remain in the community, even with considerable support (Askham and Thompson, 1990). Services for people from black and ethnic minority communities are also under-developed, particularly where there is not a large black population (SSI, 1998). Whilst care management projects in England (Challis and Davies, 1986; Davies and Challis, 1986; Challis *et al.*, 1995) showed positive outcomes for frail elderly people and their carers, a pilot care management project for frail elderly people in Scotland (EPIC) (Bland, 1996) showed very limited success in maintaining people with dementia in the community, and at some considerable cost to the well-being of their carers. The project also found that carers frequently did not receive a proper diagnosis of what was wrong with the elderly person (though they would have welcomed this), and GPs were on the whole not instrumental in helping carers to receive services. Interestingly, as the project progressed the care managers concerned began to see admission to long-term care more positively as an outcome and, to ease the transition, planning for this through periods of respite care. The strategic role of the care manager emphasises the continuing importance of inter-personal skills: 'The care managers themselves performed a very important personal role both for carers and the elderly people as confidante, as advocate, and as a channel of communication between all the services being provided and the service involved' (Bland, 1996, p. 68). The issue of how directly to involve people with dementia in the planning of their care has not yet been tackled at a strategic level (SSI, 1995b). Goldsmith, (1996) however, is positive that communication with people with dementia is not only possible but necessary for informed decision-making to take place. Knowledge of that person's previous way of life, preferences and personal strengths is essential to predict how well they might adapt to day care or even what type of residential care they would find amenable. Communication, moreover, need not be only verbal; it can be by gesture or conduct. Older people can show by their behaviour whether or not they are happy in an environment. As Winner (1992) suggests, this is more than the 'passive consent' that Marsh and Fisher (1992) refer to as the limits of partnership with people with dementia; it is a positive attempt to seek out wishes and feelings. The SSI (1998) also recognise that assessment should be a dialogue with the service user; in CCETSW's terms, proper communication can 'assist people to increase control of and improve the quality of their lives'.

Mrs Smith, an Afro-Caribbean woman of 76, lives alone in a three-bedroomed council house. Her husband died two years ago. Her daughters, who visit daily, are concerned that she has become increasingly forgetful, and neighbours have told them that she is in the street late at night, going to the Post Office 'to collect her pension'. Her daughters approach the Social Services Department saying that they want to talk about residential care for their mother. How should the allocated worker react?

The first step might well be to ask questions of the daughters to see how long this situation has been going on; whether there have been any changes over time, if there has been any previous involvement and what the outcome of that involvement might have been. The daughters confirm that Mrs Smith's difficulties have been apparent for the last five years, but have increased over the past six months. Both work full-time but are frequently telephoned by a distressed Mrs Smith who says that she has lost her house-keys and that her purse has been stolen. A home visit confirms that Mrs Smith is agitated and distressed about her memory loss. She also expresses a profound sense of loneliness since she is on her own most of the day. Mrs Smith accepts the suggestion of visits from a home carer and attendance at a day centre. The possibility of respite care is also discussed. This is a fairly conventional response to these types of situation. Where are the dilemmas?

The first challenge to the social worker lies in the need for a culturally sensitive assessment, which takes into account Mrs Smith's past history and present needs. It will also be relevant to how her behaviour is interpreted. The availability of services for older women who are Afro-Caribbean will need to be explored. If no such resources exists, should one be created? Does an advocacy scheme exist to speak for Mrs Smith if she is unable to speak for herself?

The second dilemma lies with Mrs Smith's capacity to consent to what is quite a complex 'package of care'. Capacity is a legal and not a medical concept and entails an ability to use and retain information so as to make decisions (or more often choices) about options available. Capacity covers a range of issues and the test of capacity for each is different (see McDonald and Taylor, 1994), the capacity to vote, to marry, to make a will, or (as here) to enter into a contract. The matter is complicated by the imposition of financial assessments. As Langan and Means (1996) discovered in their research, few local authorities have comprehensive and integrated systems to link financial assessments with devices such as Powers of Attorney or the use of the Court of Protection, which exist to delegate the financial power of people who are mentally incapacitated.

Levin *et al.* (1989) found that services such as domiciliary care, day care and respite care were highly valued by carers of people with dementia. Frequently, however, social workers and carers may be at odds with regard to the proper interpretation of a particular service. Carers could see the use of day care and respite care as a precursor of permanent care, whereas social workers might see its use as a device for keeping people in the community for longer. Such perceptions need to be clarified at the outset. In social work with persons who are mentally incapacitated, inevitably substitute decision-making will happen. This raises the question of according to what principles such decisions should be made. The Law Commission in reviewing the law on mental capacity (1995) have expressed support for a system which is based upon the person's 'best interests'. In deciding what is the person's best interests regard should be had:

- to that person's ascertainable past and present wishes and feelings;
- to the need to permit and encourage that person to participate as fully as possible in anything done for him or her or any decision affecting him or her;
- to the views of any person engaged in caring for him or her or interested in his or her welfare;
- to the principle of the least restrictive alternative.

Carers' views therefore are important (perhaps qualitatively so in relation to the amount of care that they provide), but are only one factor. Mrs Smith may resist the idea of admission to residential care, and this may be supported by an analysis of her past views on the subject. Yet she is not functioning well in the community. Giving a premium to the value of self-determination would indicate a decision in favour of her remaining at home with all of its attendant risks until *she* acknowledged that she could cope no more. Increased statutory services might support the family in any decision to withdraw. The emotional cost (to Mrs Smith) of entering residential care would have to be weighed against the physical security that it would provide. If there is no mandate from the client, then a legal mandate by way of compulsory intervention under the Mental Health Act 1983 is necessary (Fisher, 1990). The use of guardianship, in the context of an agreed care plan, is endorsed by the Mental Health Act Commission as a legitimate use of compulsory intervention. Using legal powers in this way is something that social workers often shrink from, yet as McPherson (1988) points out, for many elderly people with dementia, admission to hospital under the Mental Health Act 1983 is usually a temporary episode, but hedged around with legal safeguards, whereas entry to residential care is often achieved by stealth, and is usually for life. It is important therefore for social workers clearly to identify the point where they move from upholding self-determination as the greater good, to an acknowledgement that mental capacity has been lost and that substitute decision-making is necessary.

The social worker in the case of Mrs Smith would therefore need to approach the issues on a number of levels:

- their own value system and feelings about ageing and incapacity;
- their skill in ascertaining Mrs Smith's wishes and feelings;
- the feelings and rights of her daughters as carers;
- structural issues relevant to older women in black communities, and their agency's response to those needs;
- concepts of fairness in the allocation of resources, if Mrs Smith is one of a number of people with similar needs;
- issues of voluntary and compulsory intervention.

The complexity of interlocking values in community care should not therefore be underestimated. The whole gamut from individual to collectivist approaches is relevant to an analysis of Mrs Smith's situation. To see solutions in terms solely of resource allocation is to ignore the professional dilemmas with which the social worker is faced.

# 9

# Financial Matters

Social workers have traditionally shown little interest in thinking about financial matters except, perhaps, about welfare benefits. The cost of care has been a concern of planners and senior managers, but not of individual practitioners. Community care has changed all this. The introduction of a market for care services has meant that services, even the social worker's own time, have to be costed and assessed for value-for-money. Choice between different options in a care package may be influenced by cost as well as by other qualitative differences between services. This is especially so if demand for a given service such as domiciliary care exceeds supply. Social workers who are care managers in charge of a budget will themselves have to cost packages of care, and prioritise their caseloads within the limits of their total budget. Identifying implications of the cost of purchasing services for an individual on the total budget available for the caseload is put forward by CCETSW (1995) as a relevant example from practice in meeting the practice requirement 'contribute to planning, monitoring and control of resources' within the core competence 'intervene and provide services'. This is a formal acknowledgement of how the social work task has changed to incorporate responsibility for financial issues. This chapter will examine the policy context of charging for services and will analyse the impact of that policy upon the social worker/service user relationship. The social worker's role in enabling service users to manage their personal finances is also explored through an examination of welfare benefits, direct payments and legal devices such as powers of attorney and receivership in the Court of Protection.

Charging for services is something that has developed apace. Charging for residential care has always been a requirement of local authorities imposed by the National Assistance Act 1948 and has always been means-tested for both income and capital. Charging for other services has been discretionary, and, apart from meals and transport, not widespread (Chetwynd et al., 1996). Charging has now, however, become the norm, with the user of services cast in the role of consumer. This has implications in a number of ways: it may affect assessment practices by introducing affordability issues into a needs-led process, it raises questions of value-for-money in relation to the efficiency and effectiveness of services, and it raises administrative issues around charging procedures, payment of independent providers, and recovery of debts. All this may have to take place within a therapeutic relationship or one which is involuntary. The impact of service charges upon income means that it is increasingly important for users to maximise their income through receipt of benefits. Focused and accurate welfare rights advice and support through review and appeal procedures are therefore of crucial importance. Dealing with financial issues has thus in a number of ways become an essential component of the social worker's knowledge and skills. It is important that social workers' involvement in financial matters is supported by their managers beyond the managerial agenda of working within agency budgets. There is some evidence (Dowling, 1998) that managers are unsympathetic towards workers having piecemeal involvement in financial matters when operating a duty system which is seen as distracting them from their caseload responsibilities. This means that people seeking limited financial assistance or advice on welfare benefits may be dealt with in a cursory fashion. Social workers also need to be aware of the waning of affect caused by poverty being such a common part of the everyday work of a social services office or voluntary agency. The danger is then that the impact of poverty can be overlooked, ignored or treated superficially.

### Charging for services

The more widespread introduction of charges for services has certainly developed in the 1990s. Local authority charging policies must operate within the law and within guidance. Section 17 of the Health and Social Service and Social Security Adjudication Act 1983 states that charges must be 'reasonable'. What this means is amplified in the 1994 Advice Note on Charging from the Department of Health; charges must be based only on the income and capital of the user of services and not, for example, on that of another member of the household, including a partner or spouse. Charges should not exceed what is reasonable for a person in receipt of services to pay, and although those on benefit are not automatically exempt from charges, there should also be a reviewing system to deal with individual challenges to charges imposed. Local authorities should also monitor the effect of changes in charging policy on service take up and use.

A survey by Baldwin and Lunt (1996) into charging policies in six different local authorities found many wide variations in policy and practice. Many different schemes are possible based on flat-rate charges, banding, simple and complex means-testing, and single service or care package assessments. A survey by the Disability Alliance (Chetwynd *et al.*, 1996) looked at experiences of, and satisfaction with, charging policies amongst disabled people. This is against the policy background (AMA, 1994; NCC, 1995) that 85 per cent of authorities were charging for home care. The report considers a number of practical deficiencies within charging systems but also raises general and far-reaching issues of concern to do with the psychological impact upon disabled people of paying for care. The practical issues raised by the report include:

- poor dissemination of information about charging policies
- resentment at paying for unreliable and inflexible services
- insufficient knowledge about how and when services should be reviewed

The report casts doubt upon the ability of service users to act as real consumers in a mixed economy of care – matching services to costs and making choices. There was still a high degree of dependency on services provided by the local authority to supplement informal care by relatives and friends, nor was the independent sector much used except for domestic cleaning. Lack of information about how charges were calculated and how they related to the services to be received made it difficult for people to make informed choices about the care they could afford or to check if the correct charge had been levied. There was little evidence that people knew that charges were discretionary or that local authorities had the power to waive charges or were required to continue statutory services, even though charges were not paid.

In the provision of personal care, market mechanisms may not work. There is no spare or unnecessary care that people can just drop in response to increased charges. The perception that services are overstretched means that users are unwilling to release any part of their current service. Lack of understanding can also be a deterrent to requests for further care and can make it difficult for people to know what will happen if their financial circumstances change. To this end, there was support for a move away from blanket charges to a more finely-tuned banding system; no local authorities in that particular survey, however, took into account general household expenditure, including expenditure on other care needs, as part of a comprehensive assessment of social *and* financial circumstances.

The longer-term impact of charging for services that were once free is that people are beginning to wonder if they can still take it for granted that they will always have the care they need. This sense of vulnerability is greatest for those who have other sizeable costs related to their disability and for those with dependent children. Looking at where the money comes from to be able to afford care raises the whole question of the purpose of disability benefits. Chetwynd sees disability benefits such as Disability Living Allowance and Attendance Allowance as compensation for a diminished quality of life; to impose charges based on this income is to impose a penalty for disability.

Few authorities were monitoring the impact of their charging policies despite the finding in Baldwin and Lunt's (1996) survey about the inappropriateness of some charging systems for people living in community settings. Reduced use of services, increased financial hardship, poorer quality of life and bad effects on user-professional relationships were all unintended outcomes. Baldwin and Lunt found that social workers and care managers typically had responsibility for gathering financial information, a task for which they often felt ill at ease, untrained and lacking in up-to-date information. It is not a responsibility, however, that can easily be avoided. The position is unlikely to change given the financial constraints upon local authorities, an assumption that charges will be made in fixing the Revenue Support Grant, and aspirations to provide the highest standards of service possible within available resources.

How should social workers respond to these dilemmas within charging systems? First of all, it is important to be open and honest at the assessment stage that charges will be levied. Chetwynd *et al.* (1996) found that assessments were perceived by users to have worked best when there was a high degree of interaction between the service user and assessor. For the assessor to possess accurate and up-to-date information on their authority's charging policy is, of course, vital.

Users should also be informed of their rights to challenge assessments seen to be unreasonable. The importance of regular review and making users aware how, and in what circumstances they may apply for more help, is emphasised in the research. As a necessary component of care management, review should not be overloaded; it is not simply an administrative exercise rather it is an assurance that users with fluctuating needs will not be overlooked.

**Direct payments**

The emphasis in legislation has been on local authority provision of services, and a prohibition (reiterated in the Policy Guidance, 1990) on cash payments instead of services. This has limited choice and not enabled service users to act as their own care managers in a way seen as empowering by Smale and Tuson (1993).

The Community Care (Direct Payments) Act 1996 came into force in April 1997. The Act gives Social Services Departments the power to make direct cash payments to individuals in lieu of the community care services they have assessed those individuals as needing. There are regulations and s.7 guidance produced by the Department of Health on the Act. Only disabled people under the age of 65 but over the age of 18 who are willing and able – with help if necessary – to manage direct payments, will be eligible to receive them; this includes people with physical disabilities, learning disabilities, people who are mentally ill or those with HIV and AIDS. The eligible group will be reviewed once the Act has been in force for one year. Certain groups of people are ineligible, as the law intends that they should receive an agreed package of services in the community, which could not be guaranteed if they were to receive direct payments in lieu of those services.

These are:

• people detained under mental health legislation who are on leave of absence from hospital;
• patients subject to guardianship under mental health legislation or subject to supervised discharge;
• offenders serving a probation or combination order with a condition of treatment;
• conditionally discharged detained patients subject to Home Office restrictions.

Regulations also prevent services being bought from close relatives or partners living in the same household. Guidance in contrast, advises that local authorities may not normally allow direct payments to be used to secure services from a close relative who lives elsewhere, or someone else (e.g. a lodger) living in the same household, though local authorities do have a discretion here. Direct payments will not replace care provided by the NHS, or cover housing costs.

The direct payments scheme is itself subject to existing policy and practice guidance on community care generally. However, it is up to individual authorities to decide how flexible their own schemes should be, how often payments should be made, and for what services. All direct payments should, however, form part of a care plan, and should follow on from a comprehensive assessment. The main limitations in the guidance are:

1.   That a local authority should not make direct payments unless they are at least as cost effective as the services it would otherwise arrange. However greater 'effectiveness' may ensue from enabling the person to manage his or her own finances.
2.   The person for whom the direct payment is made must retain overall control over the money and the final responsibility for how much is spent. This should be monitored and reviewed. Repayment for mis-management of funds may be required.
3.   Any financial contributions due from the user will be taken into account in setting the amount of direct payment.
4.   The local authority may step in as back up in emergencies.
5.   The local authority's duty to arrange residential accommodation when needed is not affected.
6.   The scheme itself is subject to the local authority's complaints procedure.

In principle the scheme seems to offer an alternative opportunity for users to prioritise their own spending on care services and to choose their own providers. Local authorities should not set a condition that only certain providers should be used. Monitoring of quality is thus, initially at least, the user's own responsibility and choice. Carers, however, may well be disadvantaged by the legislation if they are close relatives.

Recruiting and employing personal assistants can be a complex task. An innovative project in Norwich (Dawson, 1995) was set up in advance of these legislative changes to channel local authority funding to people with disabilities. The project acted as a broker of services to 60 people in its first year, providing advice on National Insurance and tax structures as well as a support service. One of the findings was that shortfalls in other services such as adaptations, physiotherapy and nursing, may lead to additional costs being incurred by employers, who have to purchase additional time from personal assistants. These personal assistants may then be acting up to the limits of their competence, undertaking complex tasks which could potentially involve legal liability for their negligent performance. One positive effect of the project, however, was to reduce the workload of social services staff, who valued the growing expertise of the co-ordinator in facilitating self-assessment of need. As an exercise in user empowerment therefore the project was a success.

Before 1993, additional cash payments for severely disabled people were available from the Independent Living Fund, supported by monies from central government. After 1993, this money was replaced by the Independent Living (Continuation) Fund for existing claimants, and the Independent Living (1993) Fund for new claimants. Preference is given to younger disabled people seeking to live independently. The Independent Living Fund continues alongside the new regime for direct payments. The Independent Living Fund provides direct payments following assessment of need by the local authority. The minimum financial support given is for care in excess of a £200 floor provided by the social services department. Any need for care above the value of £500 per week reverts to the social services department. The Independent Living Fund thus operates between the £200 and £500 levels. Money is paid directly to the disabled person. Only persons under the age of 65 are eligible. For younger people with disabilities therefore a complex package of care can be put together using direct payments in tandem with Independent Living Fund money.

*EXERCISE*

Find out whether your local authority has a scheme for direct payments. Does it cover people with learning disabilities and mental health problems, as well as those with physical disabilities?

How does the local authority decide whether a person is 'able' and 'willing' to receive direct payments instead of services?
Is any evaluation being undertaken of the effectiveness of such a scheme?

**Welfare benefits**

Although social workers are not equipped by their training or role to give extensive advice on welfare benefits, nevertheless being aware of the range and type of benefits available is a necessary part of effective working in community care. 'Providing information and advice to individuals, families, carers and groups' which is a practice requirement within the competence 'promote and enable', includes as evidence indicators both the direct provision of advice, and the giving of information to users on where other sources of advice can be sought. Maximising income enables people to buy in resources not otherwise available, and to exercise choice. Some welfare rights services concentrate on take-up campaigns rather than advice in individual cases. Older people in particular may be unaware of their entitlement to benefits or reluctant to take them up. Successful claims for disability payments in particular can substantially increase income and standards of living.

Benefits may be either contributory or non-contributory, i.e. dependent upon a minimum number of National Insurance contributions having been paid or available regardless of contribution record. Non-contributory benefits can be means-tested or non-means-tested. Income replacement benefits such as income support are means tested and are payable only below a certain threshold of need. Other benefits, such as disability living allowance, are compensatory benefits and are based on eligibility criteria which are independent of income. Payment of benefit may be affected by stays in residential care or in hospital (or in prison) for which different rules apply.

The Child Poverty Action Group produces a range of publications on the different types of benefit available; these are updated annually. The best known are the National Welfare Benefits Handbook (for means-tested benefits) and the Rights Guide to Non-Means-Tested Benefits. Some benefits are highly specialised, such as war pensions and widows' benefits, and will not be dealt with here. What follows is an outline of the major income replacement and disability benefits available. These are:

- Jobseeker's Allowance;
- Income Support
- Retirement Pensions
- Incapacity Benefit

- Severe Disablement Allowance
- Disability Living Allowance
- Attendance Allowance
- Disability Working Allowance
- Invalid Care Allowance

Entitlement to housing benefit and council tax benefit are also covered.

## *Jobseeker's Allowance*

Jobseeker's Allowance was introduced in October 1996 to replace Unemployment Benefit, for those who had paid National Insurance contributions, and Income Support (for those who had not). It applies to all those who are required to 'sign on' as available for work as a condition of receiving benefit. There are thus two types of Jobseeker's Allowance: contribution-based (which lasts for six months and is paid independently of other income) and income-based (which is means-tested). Claimants are required to sign a jobseeker's agreement and are to agree their 'pattern of availability', which is normally being available for work up to 40 hours each week. The eligibility criteria for Jobseeker's Allowance are stringent, and after six months claimants can be required to take work which is different from, and less well paid, than the work that they are used to doing. There are, however, exceptions which may apply to people in the context of community care. Those with caring responsibilities may limit their hours of availability to fewer than the normal minimum of 24 hours per week. People who have a disability, physical or mental, but who are not eligible for incapacity benefit (see below) may limit the type of work they are able to do without having to show that they have still a reasonable prospect of securing employment.

## *Income Support*

Income Support is available as an income maintenance benefit to those who are not required to sign on; for example, those with dependent children, and men aged 60–65. It can also be a top-up to other benefits such as retirement pensions and severe disablement allowance. Payment of income support is based on a formula whereby the 'applicable amount' (i.e. the amount deemed necessary to live on) minus any income from other sources, is the amount of income support to be paid.

The applicable amount comprises a personal allowance plus any premiums to which the claimant is entitled. There are lone parent premiums, a family premium, two disability premiums, a carers premium and three types of pensioner premiums, rising in value according to age.


## The Social Fund

The Social Fund covers needs arising from exceptional circumstances that cannot be met from normal income. There are both discretionary and non-discretionary payments. Discretionary payments are paid out of a fixed annual budget allocated to each Benefits Agency district. Though there is national guidance on priority groups (the elderly, disabled, families under stress) and district priorities (details of which should be publicly available) each case should be treated on its merits. For unsuccessful claimants there is a two-stage review process, an internal local office review, and a social fund inspector review. There are three types of discretionary payments:

- crisis loans
- budgeting loans
- community care grants

Anyone can apply for a crisis loan, not just those getting income support: crisis loans are available for emergencies, being 'the only way that serious damage or serious risk to health or safety can be prevented'. Living expenses at the beginning of benefits claims may be paid by way of a crisis loan. Budgeting loans are available only to those continuously on Income Support for six months or more; the minimum loan is £30. Furniture, bedding, clothing and home repairs are a priority. Such loans are not available for domestic assistance in the home. Deposits to secure accommodation are not covered, but rent in advance to secure board and lodging or hostel accommodation is covered.

   Community care grants are intended to cover:

- re-establishment in the community following a period in institutional or residential care (usually of 3 months or more, but this is not an absolute rule);

- support to remain in the community;
- travel in the UK to cover a domestic crisis;
- visit a sick person; or
- move to more suitable accommodation.

There is no maximum amount, and the normal minimum figure is £30. Savings of under £500 (£1000 if aged over 60) are disregarded. It is advisable to cost items sought, e.g. from a catalogue. The usual items covered are furniture and bedding, clothing, removal expenses, fuel connection charges, laundry needs, and travel needs (when a lump sum for up to 26 weeks can be awarded). Community care grants may be claimed not only to allow a disabled person, for example, to move into more suitable accommodation, but also to enable a carer to move to live with a person for whom they will provide care.

Non-discretionary payments are maternity payments, payments for funeral expenses and cold weather payments. The maternity payment is a one-off payment of £100. Funeral expenses (up to a maximum of £600) are payable only to the person responsible for arranging the funeral, a test which has become narrower in recent years. Cold weather payments, payable for periods of very cold weather, do not need to be claimed but will be paid automatically to people on income support who are pensioners or disabled or who have a child under five.

### Retirement Pensions

Entitlement to a retirement pension depends upon the following factors:

- having reached 'pensionable age' (currently 65 for a man, and 60 for a woman)
- making a claim for a pension to be paid
- satisfying contribution conditions

The pension paid may consist of a basic pension, plus an additional pension (payable under the SERPS scheme unless contracted out) and a graduated pension (based on contributions between April 1961 and April 1975). There is a small age addition for those over 80. The Department of Social Security will give individuals a 'pension forecast' on request. All retirement pensions are taxable and taken fully into account for income support purposes.

### Incapacity Benefit

Incapacity benefit has replaced sickness benefit and invalidity benefit for people who are unable to work due to sickness or disability and who have paid sufficient national insurance contributions. There are two tests:

- the 'own occupation' test which applies for the first six months of incapacity, and
- the 'all work' test which applies thereafter, or from the beginning of a claim if there was no usual occupation.

Incapacity for work is assessed according to a functional test of disability across a range of competences which cover both physical and mental impairments. Some people are deemed to have passed the test of incapacity by virtue of the nature of their condition; others will have to satisfy a benefits agency doctor that they are incapable of work if their condition is not chronic. The position of people with mental health problems is particularly problematic as only recognised forms of mental disorder will constitute 'incapacity'.

The Incapacity Benefit Monitoring Group co-ordinated by RADAR (Bulletin no. 263, September 1996) has looked at the implementation of the new benefit and has reported difficulties in filling in claim forms allowing only yes/no answers, and problems with medicals which ignore pain, fatigue variability and length of time taken to complete an activity. Appeals, however, have had a relatively high success rate. Incapacity benefit is paid at short and long-term rates (long-term after twelve months incapacity), but unlike its predecessor invalidity benefit, is not payable to people of pensionable age.

### Severe Disablement Allowance

Severe Disablement Allowance is a means-tested benefit available to people who are severely disabled but who do not meet the contribution requirements for incapacity benefit. To qualify, the disability has to be at least 80 per cent, though there are more liberal criteria applied to people whose disability arose before the age of 20. Previously discriminatory rules against married women have now been changed to enable them to qualify for Severe Disablement Allowance.

### Disability Working Allowance

People with a disability who are able to work but who are limited to low-paid jobs may qualify for disability working allowance as a top-up benefit. This benefit, introduced in 1992, got off to a slow start, with few claimants and a high rejection rate for claims. Potential claimants may not be aware of its existence. Links with employment provisions of the Disability Discrimination Act 1995 will be important to secure access to employment. It is proposed (April 1999) to replace Disability Working Allowance with a Disability Tax Credit scheme for those in employment. Disabled people moving into employment may find themselves facing a drop in income with the loss of disability premiums linked to income support and the sharp taper which exists within housing benefit (see below).

### Disability Living Allowance and Attendance Allowance

Benefits which are compensatory for disability are payable on the basis of need regardless of income or capital. Disability Living Allowance consists of a care component and a mobility component; Attendance Allowance is payable to those over the age of 65 and has only a care component. There is no need to show that the benefit is used to purchase care, or that care is actually given. Entitlement is based on the effects of disability on a person's life rather than the presence of a particular disabling condition. There are three rates for the care component of Disability Living Allowance – lower, middle and higher – but only two rates of attendance allowance – higher and lower – corresponding to the higher and middle rates of Disability Living Allowance.

The *lower rate* of the care component of Disability Living Allowance is payable to people aged under 65 who need 'limited attention', e.g. getting up and going to bed, or people over the age of 16 but under 65 who are unable to prepare a cooked main meal for themselves. This lower category was first introduced in 1992; many people with learning disabilities will be eligible for the lower rate.

The *middle rate* of Disability Living Allowance is available to those who need frequent attention (e.g. to help with toileting) or continual supervision throughout the day or night. This can include people who are distressed and unable to sleep at night as a symptom of their mental disorder.

The *higher rate* is payable to those who are in need of attention or supervision day and night (most people in residential care will qualify for this).

Children may be awarded Disability Living Allowance if their care needs are substantially greater than the needs of other children of the same age. The *mobility* component of Disability Living Allowance is payable over the age of five, and if awarded before the age of 65, it will continue beyond that age. Though the higher and lower rate tests for the mobility component appear to be two halves of a unified benefit, in effect the criteria they employ are so different that they are best considered separately. The higher rate is available to those who are unable, or virtually unable, to walk or who are both deaf and blind and need someone with them when outdoors. The lower rate is payable to those who can walk but who need someone with them when outdoors, or who are severely mentally impaired with severe behavioural problems. People with cardiovascular complaints who find it difficult to walk any distance out of doors may qualify.

To receive Disability Living Allowance, help must have been needed for three months (six months for Attendance Allowance). There is a special procedure for people who are terminally ill, that is, not expected to live longer than six months; application may be made by someone other than the recipient who need not then be informed of the prognosis for their condition.

Sainsbury *et al.* (1995) have evaluated Disability Living Allowance and Attendance Allowance. Although application forms are complex and based on self-assessment, half the decisions made were based on evidence from the form alone without further medical assessment. Accurate completion of the form is therefore essential; however, Sainsbury *et al.* reported a high level of satisfaction with assistance given by Benefits Agency staff in filling in forms. Nevertheless a substantial minority of people experienced a lot of difficulty in describing how their lives were affected by disability, and claimants with mental illness were particularly affected. There is considerable scope for review and appeal (to a Disability Appeal Tribunal). In Sainsbury's sample, 36 per cent of lower rate recipients and 50 per cent of unsuccessful claimants had their case reviewed within nine months. For social workers, therefore, knowing how the system works and how to guide people through it is vital.

One surprising finding was that rejected claimants were not on the whole recently disabled, and were as likely to report extra disability-related costs as successful claimants. Even people with obvious, long-standing needs are therefore being overlooked. One reason for this may be an inhibition about fully describing the extent of one's disability on the form. One-quarter of the survey sample admitted that they gave a 'rosy' picture of themselves. People with mental health problems, in particular, might find it difficult to express their disability in terms of how it prevents them from performing simple tasks or leaving their home. Needing support and encouragement to take medication should not be overlooked as a basis for a claim. People, however, do need time to absorb the fact of how illness has affected their lives. There is obviously an important role for the social worker here in enabling people to assess honestly the extent of their disability, and to fit it within the benefits criteria which are described.

### Invalid Care Allowance

This allowance is paid to the carer not to the person who is cared for. It is an income replacement benefit which is payable only to those who provide 'regular and substantial care' to one individual for 35 hours per week or more. Invalid care allowance is not means-tested, but is taxable and is subject to the rules on overlapping benefits and so cannot be paid out at the same time as, for example, widows benefit or retirement pension. An underlying entitlement to invalid care allowance will, however, attract the carers' premium included in the calculation of income support, housing benefit and council tax benefit. A major disadvantage in claiming invalid care allowance is that the person being cared for thereby loses their entitlement to the severe disability premium for income support (which is substantial).

### Housing Benefit

Housing benefit may be available to people on low income who have capital of less than £16 000 to cover the payment of rent, including board and lodging and hostel payments. It will not be paid on rents deemed to be 'unreasonably high' (as determined by the valuation officer) and will only be paid on the 'eligible rent', which will exclude payment for such items as heating and laundry costs, and may exclude payments for supportive or counselling services unless these are substantial. Housing benefit is not available for those living with close relatives unless payment is on a strictly commercial basis, or the accommodation is self-contained (such as a granny flat).

### Council Tax Benefit

Council tax is payable on the basis of one bill per dwelling, regardless of the number of people living there – though a single person household will automatically receive a 25 per cent discount. Second adult rebate (maximum 25 per cent) is available if a second person with a low income is living with the householder. Thus a relative on a low income who moves into the household to share costs or to receive care will not disentitle the householder from claiming a deduction on council tax, regardless of their own income or capital. A 'status discount' also applies to people who are severely mentally impaired - they pay no council tax - and to live-in carers of people in receipt of the higher or middle rate of the care component of Disability Living Allowance, or of Attendance Allowance. Disabled people who need additional space for wheelchair use, or a second bathroom, may apply under the disability reduction scheme to have the valuation of their property reduced by one band.

### Going into hospital or residential care

Particular rules apply to benefits received by people who are in hospital. After six weeks in hospital, non-contributory benefits will be reduced, and after twelve months in hospital only a basic personal allowance will be paid. Dependants of people who are in hospital for more than twelve months may apply to the Benefits Agency to be assessed in their own right as single claimants. Entitlement to Disability Living Allowance or Attendance Allowance is lost after a stay of 28 days in hospital or residential care; periods of care separated by less than 28 days are counted together for reasons of eligibility. Periods of respite care should be carefully planned with this in mind. There are indefinite exemptions from council tax for people in hospital or in residential care; this exemption also applies to carers who leave their own home to live elsewhere to give personal care. Housing benefit may be paid to cover absences of up to 52 weeks in hospital, but is limited to 13 weeks for people in residential accommodation for a trial period, and for convicted prisoners.

## Paying for residential and nursing home care

Local authorities are required to charge for the care that they provide in residential or nursing homes by s. 22 National Assistance Act 1948; they have no discretion not to do so. The Department of Health regularly publishes guidance and updates on the factors to be taken into account on assessment. Under the Charging for Residential Accommodation Guide (CRAG) rules, residents will be assessed on their income and capital (up to a maximum of £16 000). There is no legal requirement for a spouse to disclose his or her income and assets; all that the local authority can do is to seek an agreement with this person as a 'liable relative'; other relatives have no obligation to contribute to the cost of care. However, a relative may voluntarily enter into a third party agreement to 'top up' the cost of care beyond the local authority's usual maximum. Conversely, the person entering care may have a private pension which has been used to support their spouse as well as themselves in the community; on entry to residential care this pension used to form part of the assessment; in 1996 however, the rules changed and one half of the pension can now continue to be used for the support of the spouse who remains at home. Different rules apply to those residents who have 'preserved rights' under the system of Department of Social Security payments available before 31 March 1993, by virtue of their placement in private or voluntary or nursing homes on or before that date (when the new arrangements came into force). These people will continue to be funded by the Department of Social Security.

Having to sell one's home to meet residential or nursing home fees is a frequent source of contention; 40 000 people annually are in this position. The value of the property is not counted when a spouse or partner, or a relative over the age of 60, or someone who is disabled remains living there. In other cases the local authority has a discretion to ignore the value of the property. If the owner does not wish to sell, then a legal charge can be placed upon the property as part of the resident's estate. The charge then becomes payable to the local authority upon death.

Different rules apply to temporary residents. Local authorities may at their discretion impose a reduced or flat-rate charge for short-term care for periods up to eight weeks. The value of property is not taken into account in short-term care assessments or for temporary residents whose stay is unlikely to exceed 52 weeks. Income support and housing benefits may be paid for home commitments for up to 52 weeks on admission into residential accommodation.

Deprivation of capital in order to reduce the accommodation charge is dealt with under CRAG rules and the Health and Social Services and Social Security Adjudication Act 1983. The burden of proof is on the local authority to prove that the deprivation of capital was undertaken in order to avoid an accommodation charge. Although there is no time limit on the tracing back of capital the CRAG Guide (1996) para. 6.064 makes it clear that: 'The timing of the disposal should be taken into account when considering the purpose of the disposal. It would be unreasonable to decide that a resident had disposed of an asset in order to reduce his charge for accommodation when the disposal took place at a time when he was fit and healthy and could not have foreseen the need for a move to residential accommodation.'

What action can a local authority take if it decides that deprivation has occurred, so that the resident is to be treated as having notional capital? The local authority may either:

1.  recover the assessed charge from the resident (even invoking the insolvency legislation to do so); or
2.  in appropriate cases, it may use the provisions of the Health and Social Services and Social Security Adjudication Act 1983 to transfer liability for the payment of that part of the charge to the person to whom the capital was transferred.

An example of the latter would be where a relative had been given money or property in anticipation of the donor's transfer to residential care. However, in order to invoke the provisions of the Health and Social Services and Social Security Adjudication Act 1983 s. 27, the transfer must have taken place no more than six months before admission to residential care. Older people who are considering transferring assets to friends or family members should be referred for specialist legal advice. Statistically the chance of entering residential care (a maximum 1 in 4) is less than the chance of a relative's marriage breaking down, or them becoming unemployed and unable to pay a continuing mortgage. Law Society rules (see McDonald and Taylor, 1995) require solicitors to clarify in these circumstances who the client is, so that if a conflict of interest arises the relatives may need to be separately represented.

**Paying for long-term care**

Discontent at the cost of long-term care, and a system which penalised people for saving and acquiring assets over their lifetime (Age Concern, 1994) has led to a review of long-term care policy. The Health Committee on Paying for Long Term Care (1996) considered a number of insurance-based schemes, but acknowledged that people would need a financial incentive to enter into such schemes; being able to retain assets up to twice the value of money invested in an insurance scheme was put forward as such an incentive. Recent research sponsored by the Joseph Rowntree Foundation (Diba, 1996) considered such a scheme to be morally justifiable (even if it were practicable) only for residential care; paying for placements in nursing home care was seen to be an National Health Service responsibility, though of course, at present in the vast majority of cases the local authority pays. The issue is as much a moral and political one as a legal one, and the question is ripe for wider public debate. A Royal Commission on Long Term Care has been appointed to consider both social and financial issues.

**Financial management**

Assessing financial contributions raises professional dilemmas for the social worker. Bradley and Manthorpe (1995) describe this work as 'beyond welfare rights' insofar as it requires practice which not only maximises income, but is also aware of the need to monitor expenditure and offer protection to people who may be vulnerable. Existing protective mechanisms such as the use of the Court of Protection are often unfamiliar to social workers, and local authorities may have no adequate procedures for dealing with day-to-day financial concerns. Research by Langan and Means (1994) found responsibility divided between professional social workers and staff and officers in the finance departments of local authorities. The latter were often critical of social workers for overlooking financial matters. However, the CCETSW supported workshops organised by Bradley and Manthorpe, confirmed that social workers (in this instance, those with older people) were sometimes uneasy and ill-informed about legal devices for handling other people's money and welcomed opportunities to discuss dilemmas such as the restriction of choice that financial assessment may bring, feelings about the deprivation of capital, and reactions to the possibility of financial abuse by relatives.

Legal devices that those working with the financial affairs of other people need to know about are:

- agency and appointeeship
- ordinary and enduring powers of attorney
- receivership

A brief account of the workings of each of these is considered below, but for further details see Letts (1998) and McDonald and Taylor (1995).

### Agency and appointeeship

An agency comes into being when one person (the principal) delegates to another (the agent) responsibility for a given transaction. Commonly this takes place when another person is authorised, by the signing of an order book, to collect a social security benefit for another. However, if that other person is, or becomes, incapable of handling their own financial affairs, then it is possible for another person to become their appointee; the order book is then given out in the name of the appointee and the collection of the money and any dealings with the Benefits Agency become their responsibility. They are still bound, of course, to use the money for the benefit of the person for whom they act as appointee. Local authorities may act as appointees for the people they place in residential care and though owners of residential homes are discouraged from becoming appointees, in practice this often happens because there is no one else to do the job. Monitoring of this should take place through the bi-annual inspections of residential care homes by the local authority.

### Ordinary and enduring powers of attorney

A power of attorney is a formal document made by deed which appoints another person (or persons) to act on behalf of the donor in financial matters. This may be a general power, or it may be limited to particular transactions. The donor does not lose his or her own right to act, but in effect shares it. The difference between an ordinary and enduring power of attorney is that the former is no longer valid if the donor should become mentally incapacitated. However, an enduring power of attorney does remain valid when the donor becomes mentally incapacitated. Enduring powers of attorney have to be registered with the Court of Protection when incapacity is reached; thereafter they cannot be revoked. Enduring powers of attorney are immensely useful for a trusted friend or relative to manage the financial affairs of someone whose mental capacity is likely to deteriorate. These are overwhelmingly private arrangements; local authorities on the whole (Langan and Means, 1994) do not act as attorneys for their clients.

## *Receivership*

Mental capacity is needed to grant a power of attorney; if this has already been lost, then an application to the Court of Protection for the appointment of a receiver is the only legal avenue. Local authorities may initiate receivership and may be appointed receiver. Annual accounts must be submitted to the Court of Protection. The procedure is costly, and those with capital of less than £5000 are unlikely to come within the jurisdiction of the Court. Langan and Means (1994) found that few local authorities had considered the advocacy role of the receiver in securing access to community care services. Indeed one of the difficulties of the present system is that it separates out the responsibility for financial decisions from responsibility for personal well-being, not only in the area of receipt of services, but also in the decision of where an individual might live and the range of people with whom he or she may come into contact. Thus, for example, a receiver has no authority to negotiate a placement in residential care though she or he will be expected to finance that placement if one is made.

## The social worker's role

The Law Commission (1995) have reviewed the provision for mentally incapacitated people, i.e. those unable to make decisions for themselves. Because of the way in which the law has developed, personal and financial decisions are separated. So, for example, a person may delegate responsibility for paying for medical care, but not make the decision about whether he or she should enter care – or where such care may be. The Law Commission has proposed the adoption of Personal Attorneys to cover personal and medical as well as financial decision-making, to be known as a 'Continuing Power of Attorney'. They also propose a 'New Jurisdiction', an expanded version of the Court of Protection which could make such decisions for people who have not appointed their own attorney. Clarification and development of the law would be supportive of social services staff who were unsure how to assess or provide for people who were incapacitated. Staff in Langan and Means (1994) study of people with dementia felt particularly vulnerable themselves to allegations of fraud; this was against a background of only one out of 27 local authorities surveyed having guidance on financial assessment for elderly people with dementia. Relatives also may be making financial decisions without any legal authority to do so. 'Fieldwork staff interviews suggested practice varied considerably in terms of a willingness to clarify with carers the legal basis of their involvement in the financial affairs of their elderly relative with dementia' (p. 29).

This lack of clarity concerning legal rights and responsibilities was what led Bradley and Manthorpe (1995) to convene workshops for local authority social workers to explore their knowledge of the law, their definition of the limits of their role in financial matters, and dilemmas that they encountered. The workshop was based partly on a case where resources were not disclosed, and where money was withdrawn from the older person's bank account prior to their entering residential care. Appreciation of the workshop by the participants indicated their need for greater clarity in dealing with financial matters; an issue on which little formal training is often given on social work qualification courses.

Training in financial matters is not given sufficient prominence in the context of the number of opportunities to challenge decisions which currently exist. Social workers have come in for criticism from the local government Ombudsman for failing to provide proper information about welfare benefits, which was seen as maladministration. In one case (Report No. 94/C/1027 on a complaint against Humberside County Council) delay, amounting to maladministration in securing 24 hour care for a severely disabled man discharged from hospital, had been caused by the social worker's failure to apply for the highest rate of the care component of disability living allowance as a prerequisite for an application to the Independent Living Fund. Similarly, in Report No. 93/A/3738 involving East Sussex County Council, a social worker's statement that a person registered as blind was not entitled to additional benefits was inaccurate, and therefore maladministration. In fact the claimant was entitled to Severe Disablement Allowance because of her disability. Interestingly, the Ombudsman in this case interpreted the duty placed upon local authorities by s.9 of the Disabled Persons Act 1986, to provide information about 'any relevant services' as including the giving of advice about services provided by the Benefits Agency. This places welfare rights advice amongst the statutory duties of local authorities.

Social work involvement in legal and financial matters, and the growing need for knowledge and expertise in this field, opens up the possibility of whole new areas of inter-professional working – with accountants and with lawyers in particular. Each of these professions has an obligation to clarify in a complex family situation 'who the client is', and to act in the best short and long-term interests of that client. Given the desire of many people to 'put their house in order', the making of a proper will or of an enduring power of attorney are matters which may need to be discussed, and could well be the subject of a referral on for independent legal advice. At a minimum, social workers will need to have an awareness of basic welfare rights knowledge and of local authority financial policies, acknowledging that this is part of the statutory framework in which they work. Research has shown that service users need reliable information about services, and that they value openness and honesty in this respect.

# 10
# Social Needs and Health Care Needs

Holistic assessment of people's need for services demands that not only social care needs, but also health care needs are addressed. A package of care will commonly contain both elements; co-ordination of services is then of primary importance. The reason why such co-ordination is in practice so difficult to achieve often relates back to historical divergences between services, compounded by different budgetary arrangements and, in some cases, by a difference in perspectives between services, or between individuals within them.

This chapter will look at problems in the definition of social care and health care needs, at the historical development of the NHS outside local government; and at three areas which illustrate points of contact between systems:

- hospital discharge
- continuing care
- mental health services

### The role of health care services

The role of health care services in promoting well-being is not uncontroversial. Currently the emphasis is on preventative health care. 'The Health of the Nation' (DoH, 1990b) identified five key areas for action in a strategy for health up to the year 2000:

- coronary heart disease and stroke
- cancers
- mental illness
- HIV/AIDS and sexual health
- reducing accidents

186

The relationship between poor health and poverty is well known; health care services may not be uniformly available to all sections of the population. There are geographical variations in the availability of services according to local priorities, and the priority normally given to acute care cases may mean cut-backs in services for people with chronic conditions, particularly older people and those with long-term mental illness.

## Definitions of health care and social care

There is no firmly fixed boundary between what is health care and what is social care. Government guidance is notable by its absence in this area; this means that individual health authorities and social services departments have to work together to produce local guidance on where the boundaries lie between different services. A notional policy shift did, however, occur in 1993 with the implementation of the National Health Service and Community Care Act 1990, which enabled local authorities for the first time to make placements not only in residential care homes but also in nursing homes. The legal responsibility of the NHS, however, remained unaltered by this legislation; its brief is still 'to provide a comprehensive health care service designed to secure improvement in the physical and mental health of the nation' (National Health Service Act 1977, s. 1).

Now that the home help service has become largely a home care service, providing personal care to people in their own homes rather than domestic cleaning, the point at which the responsibilities of the home care assistant ends and that of, say, a community nurse, begins, will need definition. Though dressing of wounds and the giving of intravenous injections is clearly a nursing activity, there are often areas of overlap where local agreements may have decided that an individual home care assistant may, for example, give injections to an individual patient who is diabetic. Overlapping responsibilities and anomalies may arise; Age Concern (1994), for example, drew attention to risible definitions of what constitutes a social bath (responsibility of social services) and what constitutes a medical bath (responsibility of the health authority).

Definitions need to cover both care in the community and a consideration of the boundaries between residential care, nursing home care and continuing care in hospital. Research by the Association of

Metropolitan Authorities (1995) illustrates the wide variety of approaches to the question in practice. They asked all member authorities to respond to a number of case studies where setting the boundary between health care and social care was at issue. The response revealed a wide variation in responses to common issues critical to resource allocation.

One example was of an elderly man with an inoperable brain tumour who needed constant attention for pain and constant nursing care, but no acute medical intervention. Fourteen per cent of the respondent social services authorities considered that he needed continuing care funded by the National Health Service, but 86 per cent of authorities would have funded his nursing home care despite the fact that they were not funded by central government – according to the AMA's (1994) interpretation – for arranging and paying for palliative care. A further example, from the other end of the scale, concerned a patient who had just had a cataract operation and was being discharged home. In order to avoid undue strain, patients who have had cataract operations are advised not to bend or carry heavy loads. For people living alone or without support this means that they will need help with shopping and cleaning. In response to a scenario of this sort, 10 per cent of authorities decided that such low-level need would not come within their eligibility criteria (this was 1995; financial constraints probably mean that the number would be larger now). The majority of authorities, however, did allocate home care, but usually two hours or less per week. The AMA see the issue as highlighting the care needs of people who are treated in either short stay surgical units or for day surgery who might previously have spent a period of time recuperating in hospital. Therefore they conclude (p. 142): 'Health authority purchasers need to have early discussions with local authorities about the care which people recuperating in their own homes may require.' These two examples are illustrations of the effect that policy decisions in one part of a welfare system will have on obligations within another.

## Changes in the NHS

Managerialism and competition within the 'internal market' of the NHS has had several consequences for patients at the level both of primary and secondary care. At the level of primary care, the New GPs' Contract of 1990 introduced the principle of 'open lists', meaning that patients may move freely now from one GP practice to another; conversely, GPs may remove patients whom they deem to be unsuitable from their lists. This newly created competition between GP practices, combined with opportunities for fundholders to manage their own costs, can lead to what Holliday (1995) calls 'skimming' and 'skimping'. 'Skimming' is the process of shedding patients who make greater than average demands upon practice budgets or GPs' time; people who are chronically sick are more likely to come into these categories. 'Skimping' is the rationing of resources by cautious prescribing of medications or selective referral-on to secondary services. Initiatives such as the Patients Charter also give a premium to acute care and rapid response services. Some services where there are strong social components in health care needs require expensive and long-term involvement. Appleby and Ham (1995) in their review of challenges and policy options for Healthcare 2000 cite the case of one Health Authority that is working to reduce referrals for 'high cost' treatments for alcohol and drug addiction and behaviour disorders, all of which have increasing numbers of patients.

The Health of the Nation targets also fail to take into account the structural relationship between poverty and ill-health. Though they emphasise preventative health care, the approach is largely based on personal responsibility for health. The radical agenda advocated by the Black Report (Townsend and Davidson, 1992) 'Inequalities in Health' continues to be ignored. Looking at the disparities in health status (both mental and physical health) between different income groups, the Black report recommended a broad programme of public action covering not only health but also unemployment and housing. Appleby and Ham (1995), whilst not concentrating on causation, nevertheless see action as being required to close the gap between what is provided by health and what is seen as the province of social services. They propose that consideration should be given to the development of a 'clinical pathway' purchased for a particular cohort of patients and incorporating the purchasing of necessary social services and voluntary sector services at appropriate points along the continuum of care. This would be an attempt to individualise joint purchasing arrangements which are normally confined to capital projects or 'dowry' payments made to support discharged long-stay hospital patients.

Only a small minority of the population (less than 10 per cent) ever come into contact with a social worker, and that contact is usually an episode limited in time. NHS services however particularly community services, touch everyone's lives. Important relationships and a fund of knowledge are built up over time. If proper liaison does not exist between services to ensure (subject to the requirements of confidentiality) that information is shared and plans are jointly made, a fund of worthwhile information will be lost. This is particularly true of patients who move between hospital, community and residential care (McDonald and Taylor, 1994). The consequences of recent structural changes for liaison between social services departments and the NHS is that a multiplicity of providers may exist with whom separate arrangements have to be made either in cases involving individuals or where jointly financed projects are envisaged. Philosophies and priorities within the NHS have also changed over the last decade. Some points of difficulty are addressed below.


## Continuing care

Prior to April 1996, there was no compulsion upon Health Authorities to state explicitly their policies on continuing care. Guidance issued in 1995 – HSG (95)5 – however, required all Health Authorities, after consultation with social services departments and GP fundholders, to formulate policies for the continuing care of all adults and children in their area other than those suffering from mental illness. Continuing care is defined as care provided by the NHS beyond the acute phase of illness and rehabilitation, in whatever setting is most appropriate: hospital, nursing home, or the patient's own home. Crucially, this service will be free at the point of delivery. The most controversial facet of a continuing care policy is deciding who will remain in a NHS – funded bed and who will be referred on for assessment for nursing home or residential care. The guidance is clear that this should be a decision taken only after consultation with all relevant parties (including the multi-disciplinary team), and according to publicly available criteria, based on HSG (95)5. The criteria in HSG (95)5 are that the patient should be in need of continuous or frequent medical intervention, or specialist nursing care. Clearly, the majority of those in need of nursing care alone will not be included. Social circumstances, such as stress on carers or financial status, are not specifically to be taken into account. A review procedure has been made available for patients, or their carers, challenging the applicability of the criteria in an individual case.

The role of the social worker is not to explain or justify the application of the criteria, but they may usefully contribute to the assessment, particularly where rejection as unsuitable by one or more residential or nursing homes is given as a criterion for continuing care, or where discharge to the community would be unsafe, given knowledge of the patient's previous functioning at home.

*EXERCISE*

Find a copy of the Continuing Care Policy which operates in your area.

Describe a case in which the policy has been applied to an individual, and discuss the outcome of the decision in that case.

HSG (95)5 also covers the provision of palliative care insofar as it advises against discharge from hospital for those who have only a short time to live. This may be restrictively interpreted by the Health Authority. Providing palliative care services in the community will be equally important, however, if people are to be given a proper choice of where to die. Equally, continuing care policies should be read for their applicability to return to hospital for someone whose condition deteriorates in residential or nursing home care.

**Hospital discharge**

In 1979–89 the number of available beds per 1000 population fell from 7.4 to 5.7. Average length of stay in acute specialities fell from 9.4 to 6.4 days (DoH/SSI, 1992). By the time community care was introduced, therefore, more people were leaving hospital more quickly than 20 years previously.

Discharge from hospital is a critical time for social work intervention, when emotional as well as physical needs must be addressed; an assessment which focuses only on functional capacity will ignore the effect of a hospital admission on the patient's self-confidence. Hospital authorities tend to emphasise the 'safe' discharge within which the emphasis is on an assessment of medical risks. The aim should instead be to secure a 'good discharge' that is, one that is planned, acceptable to the patient, and enduring. Neill and Williams (1992) found in their research that only one in three of the hospital discharges of elderly patients they followed through met their criteria for a good discharge. Many were flawed by a lack of attention to detail, such as adequate transport arrangements or notification to friends and neighbours of the discharge plan. Deficiencies in discharge arrangements were still marked six months later at follow-up where a high correlation was found with depression. Assessments of people's ability to cope supported only by low levels of domiciliary care was also found to be over-optimistic. Proper monitoring and review of arrangements was critical.

Quality assurance arrangements entered into by hospital trusts and social services departments normally provide for minimum response times to a request from ward staff or consultant for a community care assessment. Despite fears of bed-blocking, research by Giller and Tutt (1995) found that slow response from hospital social workers was not a significant factor; more significant was unexpected deterioration in the patient's physical condition requiring longer stay.

Good practice on hospital discharge is contained in the Hospital Discharge Workbook (DoH, 1994c) which emphasises the importance of planning and assessment from pre-admission through assessment, treatment, discharge and follow-up. The interlocking nature of systems is emphasised: the workbook focuses primarily on discharge from hospital. However, it is also apparent that a discharge from hospital is an admission – or transfer – to community care, and an admission to hospital is a transfer *from* the community. It is crucial, therefore, to recognise that actions and decisions made at any point in a care episode can have consequences for other parts of the health and social care system.

> The costs of getting it wrong include a poor service to patients, and unnecessarily slow recovery; GPs not knowing what has happened to their patients; social services staff receiving inappropriate referrals; disputes breaking out; unplanned re-admissions; a general waste of resources, and the risk of bad publicity on bed blocking. (Hospital Discharge Workbook, 1994, p. 1)

Such is the premium placed on effective inter-disciplinary working that evidence of jointly agreed discharge arrangements between health and social services departments was made a pre-condition from the outset for the payment of the Special Transitional Grant. The Patients Charter furthermore includes the discharge of patients from hospital as one of its national charter standards (Standard 9). It states that:

> The Charter Standard is. that before you are discharged from hospital a decision should be made about any continuing health or social care needs you may have. Your hospital will agree arrangements for meeting these needs with agencies such as community nursing services and local authority social services departments before you are discharged. You, and with your agreement, your carers will be consulted and informed at all stages.

The admission, treatment and discharge process is broken down into stages which examine what an individual patient, and their carer, should be entitled to expect. They are:

- to be made aware that an assessment of their needs is being undertaken;
- to be adequately consulted when plans are made;
- to have an agreed discharge plan and their own copy of it.

Effective procedures are particularly important in the light of research which shows (SSI, 1992) that around three quarters of hospital admissions to medical and geriatric specialities are unplanned. Many of the issues which arise in hospital discharge will also be relevant to patients presenting at A and E departments who are not subsequently admitted but who are referred on to community services. Procedures, including eligibility criteria, need to be understood by front-line staff. There also need to be agreed procedures for community care assessments of individuals who live in different local authority areas. Specialist hospital discharge schemes have been developed in some areas; these have been seen to offer a timely and well integrated service (Neill and Williams, 1992) but need to be planned as an overall policy, lest they increase inequity of provision and become overburdened by an inability to move people on to adequate longer term provision.

**Mental health**

Services for people who are mentally ill exemplify the two sides of community care: preventative work with people in the community to maintain them in the community, and the movement to discharge people from the large mental hospitals into the community.

## The care programme approach

The Mental Health Act 1983 contained a presumption against compulsory admission to hospital, and, in s. 117 a right to aftercare facilities upon discharge for certain patients compulsorily detained for treatment. Health Authorities were, however, and remain, the lead authorities in the provision of services for the mentally ill. This in itself has led to anomalies within the system of community care. Concerned by reports of inadequate care being provided for patients discharged from hospitals the government in 1991 issued guidance to all Health Authorities on what is called 'The Care Programme Approach' to the care of people referred to the specialist psychiatric services. This system pre-dated the system of care management introduced in the wake of the National Health Service and Community Care Act 1990. The two systems continue to run in parallel; one is health authority-led, the other local authority-led, but both often concentrate on the very same people. The care programme approach focuses on the appointment of a key worker (who may come from any discipline) to co-ordinate the care of the patient in the community.

A fuller explanation of the care programme approach and its relationship to care management was provided by the Department of

---

### DIFFERENCES BETWEEN CARE MANAGEMENT AND THE CARE PROGRAMME APPROACH

| CARE MANAGEMENT | CARE PROGRAMME APPROACH |
| --- | --- |
| General application | Applies to people referred to specialist psychiatric services |
| Focuses on social care needs | Focuses on health care needs |
| Relevant worker is care manager employed or commissioned by Social Services Department | Relevant worker is the 'Key Worker', who may nevertheless come from outside the NHS |
| Services may be means-tested (except for s. 117) | Services free at the point of delivery |

---

Health in its 1995 Report 'Building Bridges' (DoH, 1995a); it stresses that the two systems are based on the same principles and are capable of being integrated through a consistently applied initial screening process and jointly agreed criteria for allocating keyworkers to ensure the most effective deployment of professional skills on a cross-agency basis. Public concern over inadequate follow-up of previously detained patients and uncoordinated involvement by different professionals found its expression in the Christopher Clunis Inquiry (1994). As a consequence, supervision registers were introduced to monitor those patients seen as a risk to others, or to themselves in the community. There are considerable discrepancies in the operation of such registers (Bird and Davies, 1996) and the social work role is unclear.

These developments are bound to have an effect on multi-disciplinary working As Bird and Davies (1996, p. 2) have highlighted:

> Although the introduction of supervision registers was in some degree a tactical response to media coverage of a small number of high profile personal tragedies, it is likely that, in the longer term, it will be seen to have been a policy development of strategic significance. For one thing, the administration of the registers highlights the evolving complexity of the working relationship between psychiatric, nursing and social work staff; secondly, because of its focus on the needs of violent or self-destructive people, it encapsulates in potentially explosive form some of the problems and opportunities that go with the Care Programme Approach; and thirdly, as in some other areas of contemporary social work practice (probation and child protection, for example), it juxtaposes caring and policing functions of a kind that present both theoretical and practical challenges.

Bird and Davies' research found that social workers were almost as likely as community psychiatric nurses to be appointed as keyworkers for people placed on the register (10 cases compared to 12 in the county surveyed). For those patients in the community weekly or fortnightly visiting was the norm; all those on the register *ipso facto* required continuing medical supervision. The effect of registering high risk mentally ill people in a formal manner was to create a specialised caseload based on new patterns of administrative responsibility and a new role for the social worker. In effect the supervision register is a tool for risk management. The guidelines (HSG 94/5 and HSG 94/27) make it clear that the register is not for patients with low-level need, nor for those who have only short-term contact with psychiatric services. The register is to be used for those with 'severe and enduring mental illness' (HSG 94/5, para. 2) who are of significant risk of either serious violence to others; significant risk of severe self-neglect, or significant risk of suicide. Despite the history behind the policy, Bird and Davies' research found that the category of risk of violence to others was never used on its own as a reason for registration.

A more recent development has been the introduction of a power of supervised discharge (but not treatment) in the community by the Supervision of Patients in the Community Act 1995 (in force April 1996). There the role of the social worker is clearly subordinated to that of the Responsible Medical Officer, as it is the RMO and not the social worker who makes application for a supervised discharge order; a reversal of the roles undertaken when the patient is sectioned. Nevertheless, a social circumstances report is an essential part of the initial process, and should be available upon appeal to a mental health review tribunal.

Both supervision registers and supervised discharge are likely to prioritise the case loads of both social workers and community psychiatric nurses in favour of long-term high risk clients. They also emphasise the control rather than the care aspect of community services. This would reverse the trend observed by Barton (1996) for less chronically ill patients, e.g. those suffering from neurotic disorders, to become the larger group of service users in community mental health teams, perhaps because they exert more pressure for service and are reluctant to accept case closure. The following case study provides an example of the need for careful risk assessment and monitoring within the Care Programme Approach.

*CASE STUDY* ▬▬▬▬▬▬▬▬▬▬▬▬▬▬▬▬▬▬▬

Philip Charles is 26 years old and Afro-Caribbean. He has been diagnosed as paranoid schizophrenic and has had a number of hospital admissions in the past. Most recently he has been admitted under s. 3 Mental Health Act 1983 for treatment, after threatening his mother with a knife. Philip lives with his mother, who is willing to have him home, but feels she needs help in looking after him. Philip's condition deteriorates when he fails to take his medication.

What legal provisions would apply in anticipation of Philip's discharge from hospital?

What sort of support might assist him and his family?

### The nature of hospital social work and the role of the social worker in a health care setting

The role of the social worker in a hospital setting post-community care has been examined by Davies and Connolly (1995a). They found that personal factors such as approachability, good time-keeping and responsiveness were valued more highly by medical and clinical staff than social work skills. However, those who valued the social worker as a professional with a distinct body of knowledge and skills different from their own were more realistically satisfied with outcomes than were those who saw the social worker as a technician – able, or unable, to respond to a request for a particular service. Emphasis on holistic needs-led assessment rather than on referral for specific services such as day care or residential care is therefore more likely to enhance multidisciplinary working. Hospital social workers may feel marginalised compared to fieldwork colleagues and may have a less strong management structure. Their role in bringing services to people who might not otherwise come to the attention of Social Services Departments is, however, seen as critical by McLeod (1996). Social Services Inspectorate research on the discharge of hospital patients (SSI, 1992) also found that both patients and carers were overwhelmingly grateful for the support provided by hospital social workers.

Five practice elements may be identified as central to hospital social work: inter-disciplinary collaboration; assessment; communication between the hospital and the community; networking and negotiation; and using financial acumen. The discharge planning process has attained pre-eminence; in Davies and Connolly's (1995b) research social workers who had worked in hospitals for some time were clear that their practice had changed as a direct result of the passing and implementation of the National Health Service and Community Care Act 1990. There were two areas of dissonance: counselling and clients rights. Counselling in hospital was seen not primarily as a social work task, but one which was also undertaken by nursing staff. Indeed, the processing framework of the 1990 Act (as it was perceived to be) undervalued the need for counselling. In terms of client rights, there was conflict between medical notions of safety and seeing that the wishes of the patient were followed, though social workers attached to specialist units tended to have their role of representing patients' interests more commonly recognised as legitimate.

Ahulu (1995), writing from a nursing perspective, sees early discharge of patients appropriately as fitting the philosophy of primary nursing. 'Early', however, needs further definition: is this early in terms of the patient's stay, or his or her medical condition, or in terms of availability of other accommodation? Ahulu counsels against centring concern over issues of dependency and control only in the community, he sees these as equally relevant to hospital care. It is therefore false to assume that vulnerable people living in hospitals or institutions present no problems, and that difficulties arise only when such people are discharged into the community. Vulnerable people in hospital and institutions deserve the same level of concern and attention as advocated for those living in the community.

**The value of hospital social work**

The Social Services Inspectorate in its (1992) study of Social Services for Hospital Patients noted that hospital social workers comprised 20 per cent of fieldwork staff; however, it found little evidence to suggest that the potential of such staff was fully recognised. It was also apparent that they were a relatively under-managed group of staff with little evidence of senior management representation of their interests and skills. There were also failures of process, an absence of clear priorities and criteria to ensure equitable access for all patients, limited opportunities for home assessment and inability to follow up discharged patients. Though users and carers with hardly any exceptions found that their contact with the hospital social worker was positive, they had received little background information on the range of service available or how to access them; they were not made explicitly aware of the assessment process, and involvement in multidisciplinary meetings was limited. The impression was therefore given that patients were people to whom things were done. Research in the United States (Fillit *et al.*, 1992) found that early and frequent social worker interventions were associated with significantly shorter hospital stays, for non-medical reasons. How to maintain autonomy despite continued health-care requirements is discussed by McWilliams *et al.* (1994); central to this is a patient-centred approach based on the individual's goals, aspirations and sense of purpose within a larger life context. Hence the importance within the social work task of a holistic but person-centred assessment.

McLeod (1995) sees hospital social work as of strategic importance in contributing to a more equitable experience of health in Britain (p. 21) 'It is not simply being carried out in a 'health setting' which makes hospital social work health related. It is hospital social work's capacity – as social work – to foster health, which makes it so valuable.' A social work presence in health care gives access to social services to those previously unknown to the system; it necessarily targets those in greatest need, has a beneficial effect on re-admission rates and enhances well-being by securing greater material and social resources.

## Working together in health and social care

Working together in health and social care is full of paradoxes. Co-operation is necessary to produce coherent care plans, but institutional barriers to co-operation remain. 'Who will pay for what' is a question not easily resolved. Medical services on the whole emphasise 'cure' rather than care and are unlikely to prioritise chronic needs. There are, however, proven benefits in physical proximity, the location of social work teams in hospitals, and out-based social workers in GP surgeries (DoH, 1994b). Research suggests that psychiatrists and GPs have been disappointed by the community care reforms and have not seen the hoped-for expansion of choice in the provision of services (BMA 1994). Amongst GPs, disillusionment was particularly marked in the provision of mental health services.

GPs in the 1994 BMA survey of community care generally identified lack of appropriate information as a deficit in community care. Social workers therefore should not assume that GPs are aware of what services the local authority has available, and the eligibility criteria employed. The involvement of GPs in care planning was also confused; GPs were often unsure about whether they were being asked solely to provide medical information or whether they were seen as people who could express an opinion on the viability of a care plan and were expected to have an active role in its implementation. Clarification of role therefore appears to merit further consideration. GPs were also not commonly provided with copies of the care plan; satisfaction increased the more this was done. Seeing other professionals as active partners in community care is crucial for multidisciplinary working. Respecting limitations imposed by the statutory framework within which work is accomplished is, however, also an important part of working in community care; not expecting more of the other services than they are legally able or obliged to offer is crucial.

Unless, and until, jointly commissioned and paid-for services can be developed, clashes of perspective are bound to occur. Widening the choice of information carried out during routine health checks, or aiming for a 'health and well-being check' to bring in social needs would more appropriately address the causes and the consequences of ill-health (DoH, 1994b). The same report on the Role of the GP and Primary Healthcare Team in Implementing 'Caring for People' also recommended the development either on a practice or on a locality basis of collaborative commissioning arrangements between GP fund-holders and care managers. Appleby and Ham's (1995) proposal for 'clinical pathways' would extend this joint approach to secondary care and would enable longer-term strategic planning to take place. New developments in primary care within the NHS are likely to be seen in the very near future. The 1998 White Paper on the NHS, *The New NHS: Modern and Dependable* (DoH, 1998a), proposes the setting up of Primary Care Groups as commissioners of services on a locality basis. One of the aims is the better integration of primary and community health services with social services in terms of the planning and delivery of services. In the interim, collaborative working is important for a seamless service to be achieved.

# 11
# Social Needs and Housing Needs

Housing and its association with community care services is increasingly being recognised as vital to maintaining people within the community. This is true for mainstream housing as well as for the specialist housing sector. It is not only public sector housing that has an essential contribution to make; given that the majority of people in the UK are now owner-occupiers, properly utilising and maintaining private sector housing is important as well. Homelessness, whether hidden or overt, may be a trigger for the provision of community care services, or a consequence of their absence. There is a further link between deficiencies in housing services and admissions to residential care. In the continuum of need, therefore, housing has a vital role to play.

## Types of housing

Means and Smith (1994) begin from the premise that 'Community care policy in the UK is based on the belief that nearly everyone prefers to live in ordinary housing rather than in institutions, because institutions lack the capacity to be a home' (p. 166). 'Home' in this sense means more than bricks and mortar; insofar as it defines the sense of self, particularly if there is continuity over time, it meets fundamental attachment needs. This is the reason why relocation for older people especially can be so traumatic in circumstances when there is little choice over whether, and to where, the move should be made (Willcocks, Peace and Kellaher, 1987). People's housing needs, in this sense, will be very particular to them as individuals, and need to be recognised as such in any joint assessment of need. Freedom of choice, however, is often limited by policy decisions, as, for example, in the operation of housing benefit rules (Griffiths, 1997), or by administrative processes, such as the allocation of funding for adaptations to property.

Housing policy in the years since 1979 has supported

- an increase in owner occupation;
- the diminution of the local authority's own housing stock;
- the expansion of housing association provision;
- the development of supported housing; and
- differentials in the receipt of public assistance through the housing benefit scheme.

These policy trends were well established in their own right, before the introduction of the system of community care. Integration of the two systems, however, received very little attention. Arguably, this lack of integration has been a major defect of community care policy.

### *Owner occupation*

Levels of home ownership are projected to reach 66 per cent by 2001 and, for the first time, will include substantial numbers of older people (Means, 1997). Redundancy and early retirement will mean that one-third of owner-occupiers aged 65–74 in 2011 will still have a mortgage to pay (Hancock, 1998). Middle-class impoverishment related to housing is likely therefore to become an important issue for social policy in the future. The cost of housing is not, however, an issue which can be divorced from wider economic issues.

The implication of the trend towards owner-occupation is that substantial amounts of capital are tied up in bricks and mortar. A tension is then created between the potential of that capital as inheritance to be passed down the generations, and its availability as a resource for meeting the care needs of the present generation – particularly when admission to residential care is being contemplated. How this dilemma is related to current charging policies is discussed in chapter Nine. Social workers may then have to deal with very real feelings of disappointment and loss when assets have to be cashed in order to meet continuing care needs.

Owner-occupation brings with it responsibility for maintenance and repair. Disrepair is a major issue for low income owner-occupiers (Mackintosh, Means and Leather, 1990). The majority of those living in housing which is lacking in basic amenities or in need of considerable repair are older people. Most people would prefer to stay in their own property, if it can be renovated, rather than moving elsewhere. There are a number of possible solutions to the difficulty of low income and high housing costs. Some banks and building societies provide 'maturity' interest-only loans, where only the interest is payable, the capital being repaid when the property is disposed of or on death. Such loans are only available to borrowers over the age of 60. Also generally limited to older people are home income plans, also known as mortgage annuity schemes, which involve the taking-up of a loan against a proportion of the property's value. The loan is used to purchase an annuity which brings in an additional source of income. Tax is, however, payable on this income, and entitlement to income support or council tax benefit may be affected. Legal costs also have to be borne in mind, and interest on the loan has to be paid until the property is disposed of. In order to realise a more substantial capital sum, it is possible to enter into a home reversion scheme, whereby the property or a proportion of it, is sold to a reversions company; sometimes a nominal rent remains to be paid. However, under such schemes ongoing responsibility for maintenance and buildings insurance remains.

Assistance with adaptations and improvements may be available through the system of grant aid, though this is subject to means testing. Renovation grants are available for larger repair and improvement works such as structurally unstable properties, unsuitable sanitary facilities and dampness severe enough to damage health. Grants may also be available to convert a property to provide separate living accommodation, to provide adequate insulation, or to make 'satisfactory internal arrangements', for example to deal with a staircase felt to be too steep. Renovations grants are, however, means-tested, which may discourage potential applicants (Mackintosh and Leather, 1992) and are no longer mandatory; assistance for landlords is also confined to renewal areas. Help with minor works is now called 'home repair assistance' and is also discretionary. There are also 'staying put' schemes designed specifically for people over the age of 60 who need minor works assistance in order to 'stay put' in their own property or to move in with relatives, in which case the grant will cover additional standard amenities, e.g. showers, toilets or handbasins, as well as additional cooking or heating facilities. Insulation grants for draught-proofing and loft insulation are also available through the Energy Action Grants Agency, and since April 1994 grants have been available to all persons over 60 without a means test.

It is a common complaint that resources are often not adequate to meet the level of demand placed upon them. The introduction of the Disabled Facilities Grant in 1990, designed to enable properties to be made more suitable for the needs of disabled residents, has not attracted increased spending by social services departments themselves. Spending in 1994 was only 3 per cent above 1989 levels (Heywood and Smart, 1996), yet requests for adaptations have been increasing at the rate of 15 per cent a year since 1990, as public awareness of community care has grown. The brunt of the increased cost of adaptations has been borne, without subsidy, by housing departments, out of their housing revenue account – often from repair budgets. The increasing cost of demand for housing adaptations was not something foreseen or planned. Early hospital discharge, and the introduction of EU regulations regarding lifting, have increased demand. Any unfulfilled potential for funding from health sources has not been exploited (Heywood and Smart, 1996). Social services departments and Housing Departments jointly have a responsibility for housing adaptations, such as the installation of stair lifts and showers under the Chronically Sick and Disabled Persons Act 1970. Preliminary assessment is usually carried out by occupational therapists employed by the local authority. The current legislation is the Housing Grants, Construction and Regeneration Act 1996. Under this Act the housing authority must approve grant applications which will facilitate access, make the dwelling safe or improve the heating system for the benefit of a disabled person. The housing authority is required to consult with the social services authority in deciding whether the relevant works are necessary and appropriate and then decides whether it is reasonable and practicable to carry them out. Thus disabled facilities grants are the only mandatory grants to remain under the 1996 Act. It is a condition of receiving a grant that the home owner or tenant will remain in occupation, health permitting, for a period of five years. The statutory financial limit for grants approved on the recommendation of the social services department is £20 000. The housing authority may add discretionary grants for adaptations above the £20 000 limit. Means-testing takes into account not only the income of the applicant but also that of other persons occupying the house. A waiting time of a maximum of twelve months (extended from six) from the date of application has also been given statutory approval.

### Local authority housing

A seminal feature of housing policy in the last decade has been the introduction by Part V of the Housing Act 1985 of the 'right to buy' legislation. Although such a right extends also to tenants of housing associations and housing action trusts, it is the local authority housing stock which has been irretrievably depleted by the 'right to buy'. There are, however, certain exemptions to the right to buy legislation for specialist housing, which preserves this as a resource for the public sector.

On an individual level, one consequence of exercising the 'right to buy' is that housing benefit is no longer available. At a collective level, it means that public subsidy is no longer available through bricks and mortar, but by means-tested financial assessment for those who remain council tenants.

### Housing associations

Alongside policy developments in council house sales have come cutbacks in the housing investment programmes of local authorities (Malpas and Means, 1993) The lacuna has been expected to be filled by housing associations as the main providers of new rented housing. Housing associations are quasi-autonomous organisations operating under the general control of the Housing Corporation. The 1988 Housing Act introduced a new funding regime for housing associations which provided only part of their capital finance from public funds, but required them to raise the majority of their funding on the open market. One effect of this has been to push up rents (Means and Smith, 1994). Another effect has been to remove much responsibility for housing development out of direct democratic control, and to create an internal market within the public and not-for-profit sectors. Generally a proportion of housing association lets are reserved for local authority nominees from the housing list. Older people are currently over-represented in the public and private rented sector; according to the 1991 census, 46 per cent of council house tenants and 44 per cent housing tenants were aged over 65 (Means, 1997). Issues of security, disrepair and community support in these types of housing will therefore disproportionately affect older people.

### Specialist housing and supported housing

The growth of specialist and supported housing schemes, and their seeming appropriateness within a system of community care, should

not obscure the vital role still to be played by mainstream housing. To
do so is to the detriment of both housing and social care agencies; the
former, because tenants who are in need of supportive services may
have those needs overlooked because they are 'mainstream' and not
'special', and the latter because they may ignore the normalisation
potential of mainstream housing and a package of services, as opposed
to specialist provision. Special needs housing has nevertheless been a
major growth area, which in the 1980s accounted for one third of all
housing completions (Stewart and Stewart, 1993).

The earliest and most common type of specialist housing to emerge
was sheltered housing for older people which now covers a wide range
of tenure arrangements (to buy, rent or own), and varying degrees of
support therein. Support may range from on or off-site warden
provision to 'very sheltered housing' schemes (sometimes known as
Part 2½) where personal and domestic care as well as housing is
provided. There is evidence ( Watson and Cooper, 1992) that residents
of existing sheltered housing schemes are becoming more frail and are
tending to remain there. On the other hand Tinker (1989) found that
some specialist housing schemes were hard to let, and one quarter of
the sample in that research would have preferred to remain in their
original home with more domiciliary support. The danger is that some
poorly designed sheltered housing for older people with unpopular
bedsit accommodation around shared facilities may become the slum
housing of the future (Means, 1997).

Funding the care element of sheltered housing is problematic also.
Watson and Cooper (1992) describe how funding through the Hostel
Deficit Grant influenced the types of schemes subsequently developed.
Such funding was only available where there was a minimum of six
residents. Its successor scheme, the Special Needs Management
Allowance, was available for self-contained housing but was cash
limited with a ceiling of 3000 places per year. Neither scheme was
intended fully to cover the revenue costs of the full time care
component required by many scheme. Watson and Cooper (1992)
identified two main mechanisms for dealing with this deficit; either
registration as a residential home (undertaken reluctantly, as one would
expect, in some cases), or the use of staff provided under contract by
health and social services authorities.

A recent report by Values into Action (Collins, 1996) was critical of
schemes which combined as a package housing and social care. In the
case of people with learning disabilities, such schemes were seen as

less likely to respect their rights as citizens to make individual choices than where the two functions were clearly separated. Written agreements between user and provider were used not to guarantee rights as tenants, but explicitly to support the unit's operating policy, and focus concerns on the user. The National Federation of Housing Associations has, however, proposed that it might take over a commissioning role for clients with social care needs (NFHA, 1995). This is in response to their findings that many people are being inappropriately housed because they have not had their care needs assessed. In a survey of members, 44 per cent had no experience of clients whom they saw as 'vulnerable' ever having come with care packages. Who does the assessing, and who provides the service needed are essential questions to resolve.

**Inter-agency collaboration**

Inter-agency collaboration is once again seen to be the key to successful community care, both at a strategic and at an individual level. This includes addressing health as well as social care needs within a housing context. The willingness to work together is, however, threatened both by the lack of resources within each agency, and by the competitive ethos created by the introduction of markets; links between housing and health in particular are not well developed (Arblaster *et al.*, 1996). Research has shown little evidence that users and carers are being involved in strategic planning around housing and support needs; what involvement there is feels tokenistic and prone to be dismissed as unrepresentative by agencies. This is at a time when people with care support needs form an increasing proportion of those living in the rented housing sector. Co-operation is important not only for those people being considered for specialist housing but also for those living in ordinary housing. As many as 60 per cent of new tenants housed by general needs housing associations are considered by those associations to be vulnerable (NFHA, 1995) In addition, long term tenants may become vulnerable due to illness or age. Housing management staff and those in voluntary agencies have expressed concern about their capacity to cope with the growing number of vulnerable people living in unsuitable areas and estates with no other support (Arblaster *et al.*, 1996). From the users' perspective, some people found it very difficult to attract the interest of a professional to help them through the process of achieving a move (Hudson *et al.*, 1996); social workers were seen as making referrals to specific services rather than offering broader information on housing and support options. There was little evidence that formal care management was offering a more co-ordinated response. Real barriers can be created by social services departments' eligibility criteria being pitched at such a high level. Arblaster *et al.* found that there were serious shortfalls in care support for people with medium and low levels of need who were not given priority in community care provision.

The housing allocation process itself, with limited choice and short response times, assumes that people are poised to move and can make a rapid response to a given offer. Yet there are not necessarily systems in place to help people deal with the practical and emotional difficulties of moving house. Lack of skills in money management and running a household were identified by Hudson *et al.* as a major barrier to people moving into new accommodation. Users are often fitted into a limited range of options, rather than being given significant choice. This raises particular issues of anti-discriminatory practice when what is on offer is plainly unsuitable.

Examples of a lack of fine-tuning in housing policy are provided by an analysis of housing policy in respect of Asian residents with mental health problems and older people with deteriorating mental health. Research into the housing and mental health care needs of Asian people (Radia, 1996) found that housing for Asian people with mental health problems was in many cases inappropriate and often added to their difficulties in daily living. Myths and stereotypes of Asian people, particularly the ability and willingness of families to provide care, continued to dominate the thinking of both policy-makers and professionals. There was a shortage of specialist residential projects and an absence of good financial advice. Support services were inadequate and sometimes of poor quality. Age Concern in Scotland (Adams and Wilson, 1996) also found that few community care plans considered the special needs of older people with mental health problems, or how they might be provided with more suitable housing. This is despite statistical evidence that 25 per cent of over-55s on local authority waiting lists cited mental disorder as a reason for seeking priority in re-housing. For this group, good housing brought physical as well as mental benefits; conversely the impact of poor housing on a psychologically frail person could be disproportionate. Given the importance of social support and the overriding need to avoid loneliness and hostility from neighbours, shared living – with careful attention paid to the mix of residents – was found to have real advantages. Caution was, however, expressed about orthodox sheltered housing – it is by no means certain that successful integration with neighbours will occur. Within an overall housing policy the specific needs of different interest groups within community care services will need to be considered.

The relationship between poor health, disability and housing allocation is complex. Advice from the Scottish Federation of Housing Associations, for example, is that weightings given to medical factors must be 'appropriate', but need not be overriding. Despite the amount of hope and energy expended in obtaining evidence for medical priority, other factors, such as, the absence of security of tenure and lack of basic amenities are likely to be of overriding importance. The trend in medical priority allocations (SCFA, 1995) is towards self assessment, with endorsement by GPs at the appeal stage. The model of self-assessment form produced by the SFHA is designed to give housing staff a real impression as to whether re-housing would result in a significant reduction in the applicant's health/mobility difficulties, to clarify whether the applicant would actually prefer to stay put if he or she had the choice and to get an idea of what improvements may be needed to enable this to happen if practicable. Certainly, visible physical or mobility problems attract priority far more readily than psychological/mental health considerations. Indeed, many housing associations have chosen not to give points for anxiety or depression not requiring current treatment, given the generalised nature of these conditions. Asthma is another condition which, contrary to popular belief, is not high priority unless there is overwhelming evidence that particular characteristics of the property severely exacerbate the condition. HIV and AIDS are often treated as 'special lets' outside the main points system, given both the need for confidentiality and the deteriorating nature of the conditions. Social workers for their part find housing problems among the most difficult to handle 'possibly because the solutions are so obvious yet so hard to achieve' (Stewart and Stewart, 1993). The consequences of not dealing effectively with a housing problem may of course mean greater deterioration in the health, financial and relationship difficulties of those concerned. The National Health Service and Community Care Act 1990 requires social services departments to consider housing needs, thus highlighting the issue as one component of a comprehensive assessment of need; housing need in itself cannot be divorced from whatever else is going on in people's lives.

**Homelessness**

A substantial proportion of the community care caseload passes through both housing and social services departments at some stage or other. The legislative framework within which housing departments work determines that their culture is a 'gatekeeping' one rather than one based on need (Cowan, 1995). Part VII of the Housing Act 1996, which deals with homelessness, is a good example of this. In order fully to qualify for assistance under the Act, an individual applicant must satisfy the following criteria:

- that he is homeless;
- that he is in priority need;
- that he is not homeless intentionally;
- that he has a local connection with the housing authority to which he applies.

The definition of 'homelessness' is wider that that of 'rooflessness'; persons living in crisis accommodation, refuges or in night shelters are homeless, as are people who have accommodation that it would be unreasonable for them to occupy, for example because they are threatened with domestic violence. A person who is threatened with homelessness will qualify if he or she is likely to become homeless within 28 days. An example of totally unsuitable accommodation would be that which is overcrowded or unsuitable for a physically disabled occupant. An adult living with family in circumstances where he or she is not the householder may also seek to present himself or herself as homeless, if, perhaps as a result of a dispute, he or she is asked to leave. Much actual homelessness may in fact be hidden by multiple occupations or families moving in with friends.

Local authorities are obliged to provide advice and assistance to all persons who are homeless. However, it is only people who are in 'priority need' who are owed a duty by the local authority to secure that accommodation becomes available for their occupation. Those in priority need are defined as

- pregnant women (at any stage of their pregnancy);
- persons with dependent children;
- those who are homeless as a result of an emergency such as fire, flood or other disaster;

- persons who are vulnerable as a result of old age, mental illness or handicap, physical disability or other special reason. Persons with whom such a person resides or might reasonably be expected to reside will also qualify under this heading. In considering vulnerability due to mental or physical illness or disability authorities should have regard to medical advice and where appropriate seek social services advice.

Entitlement to accommodation may, however, be lost because of a further finding that the applicant is homeless intentionally, e.g. by doing something which leads to his or her lawful eviction, such as causing a nuisance, or not paying the rent. The behaviour concerned must however, be deliberate; 'real financial difficulties' leading to default, or circumstances where the authority has reason to believe that the applicant is incapable of managing his/her affairs, for example on account of old age, or mental illness or disability 'should not count as deliberate behaviour'. Those who are homeless intentionally still have a right to temporary accommodation for such period as the local authority consider will give the person a reasonable opportunity of securing accommodation (normally 28 days). Note that it is for the authority to establish intentionality, not for the applicant to disprove it.

The final hurdle to be overcome is that of 'local connection', not to be confused with that of ordinary residence under the National Assistance Act 1948 (see p. 215). Under the homelessness legislation, a local authority may refer on a person who has no local connection with their own area, but does have a local connection with the area of another authority. Local connection can be established by prior residence, employment, family association, or other special circumstances. A person who is at risk of domestic violence in that other authority should not be referred on. If a person who is unintentionally homeless and in priority need has no local connection with the area of any housing authority in Great Britain, then the duty to secure accommodation for that person rests with the authority to which application is made.

The basic legal framework for working with homeless people has changed little since the Housing (Homeless Persons) Act of 1977 moved responsibility for homelessness from social services departments to housing departments. The Housing Act 1996, however, introduces two major policy changes. One is that the housing authority will owe no duty at all to a homeless person if there is an adequate supply of suitable accommodation in the area in the private sector and that person fails to avail themselves of the advice and assistance provided by the local authority. Secondly, there is no duty to offer permanent accommodation; suitable accommodation for a limited period of two years is all that is required. Local authority-provided housing is thus seen increasingly as a residual safety net.

The social work role in housing is acknowledged within the Dip. SW competences. An example from the guidance of the practice requirement 'enable people to use their own strengths and expertise to meet responsibilities, secure rights and achieve change', is the giving of assistance to homeless people who present their needs and establish their eligibility for accommodation. The legislation is complex and those applying under it will need support and, in some cases, legal advice, as the basic concepts of homelessness, priority need, intentionality and local connection are all open to differential interpretation. However, it is fair to say the courts have not interpreted the legislation with a sensitivity to community care issues. Cowan (1995) cites the case of 'B' a person who was both mentally ill and vulnerable. The point at issue was whether or not there was an obligation on the part of the housing authority to ask for the intervention of the social services department. It was held that there was no such obligation; indeed, the onus was on B to request such involvement, despite the exhortations of Circular 92/10 for the two authorities positively to work together. *Begum*, cited in McDonald and Taylor (1995) was a case in which a learning-disabled woman put herself forward as the applicant when her family, with whom she lived, were deemed to be intentionally homeless. The House of Lords, dealing with the case by way of judicial review, held that she was ineligible in that role; the appropriate duty to a mentally incapacitated person being that under s. 21 National Assistance Act 1948 to provide residential accommodation. Not only was this a denial of an opportunity to receive care in the community, it was also more fundamentally a denial of citizenship, since a person not mentally incapacitated would not have had their claim blocked in this way.

Homelessness as a *consequence* of previous institutionalisation is a situation faced by people who have previously been admitted to psychiatric hospital or been given a sentence of imprisonment. The Homeless Mentally Ill Initiative (LAC (96)11) was designed initially to meet the housing and care needs of homeless mentally ill people in central London. The target group is 'rough sleepers' with mental health problems. The original scheme was used to fund five community psychiatric outreach teams, the capital costs of 10 high care rehabilitation hostels, and, through top-sliced Mental Illness Specific Grant, the care costs of hostel residents. The 'second wave' is looking to provide high care permanent accommodation and services for younger mentally ill people with secondary problems such as drug or alcohol misuse. The scheme is being extended to other big cities, and is inviting bids jointly from local authorities and housing associations.

## EXERCISE

Refer to a particular case to illustrate how housing is integrated with care management and the care programme approach.

Find out what types of accommodation are allocated by your local housing authority to people who are accepted as homeless.

The housing needs of ex-prisoners (Carlisle, 1996) need to be addressed both within the criminal justice system and within housing policy. Prisoners who do not find satisfactory accommodation on release are more likely to re-offend within the first twelve months than those with accommodation deemed to be 'good'. The problem is numerically large: approximately 90000 prisoners are released into the community each year. Less than half the prisoners in Carlisle's study were able to return to their previous home. Three factors were instrumental in determining whether ex-prisoners succeeded in retaining their homes:

- quality of family relationships
- availability of housing benefit
- financial status

The largest group to lose their housing in the community were owner-occupiers who had no financial support otherwise available to them; all prisoners in rented accommodation were poised to suffer from a reduction in the period during which housing benefit would be paid from 52 weeks to a maximum of 13 weeks. The group most likely to be disadvantaged, however, were single mothers.

Organisational factors were also found to militate against a well-planned transition back into the community. Though probation officers within prisons were actively involved in discussing housing matters, nowhere were there written procedures or guidance relating to housing.

Local authorities and housing associations would not accept onto their lists people who were in prison, although very few ex-prisoners were happy to accept hostel accommodation even when available. There have, however, been some positive recent developments. NACRO (1996) has produced guidance for prisoners and those working with them on housing issues, which include some standard letters relating to applications and finance. The voluntary sector has also entered into partnership agreements with the probation service through the Home Office Probation Grant Scheme (devolved to local probation areas from April 1996); part-funded shared and single person housing may thus become more available in future.

**Residential care**

An increasing range of accommodation now exists for people with care needs (Means and Smith, 1994) such that the boundaries between 'home' and 'institutional' care are by no means clear cut (Higgins, 1989). The traditional dualism between residential care and care in the community has been questioned by Jack (1998) who sees good quality residential care as necessarily having links into, and being supported by, the community within which it is located. Very sheltered housing, core and cluster schemes and shared living schemes have all developed to meet a spectrum of need. Yet the basic question remains: why should people have to change their permanent residence simply in order to obtain the services which they need? (Wagner, 1988). In other words, why cannot services be brought to the people, rather than people to the service? Housing schemes which allow people to move within the same site from very sheltered housing to residential care, and then on to nursing home care, are one solution. Better co-ordination between health and social care to put together a package of care at home is another. Inflexibility and deficiencies in mainstream housing are often at the root of the problem, particularly given the large body of research that shows that for many people entering residential care is more a matter of circumstances than choice:

> Many people enter residential care and other forms of supported housing, not from positive choice, but through the major inadequacies of availability, affordability, repair and access within main-

stream housing provision. Community care planning needs to consider these kinds of issues and not just indicate the main gaps in the availability of supported housing. (Means and Smith, 1994, p. 183)

Fundamentally different ways of funding packages of care in the community are needed through a combination of capital funding, housing benefit for maintenance and charges for services. The historical division of services which means that 24-hour care is only available in a residential setting persists in limiting choice for individuals. This is compounded by inflexibility in funding (Griffiths, 1997).

Concern about the over-provision and high cost of residential care was, of course, a prime incentive behind the community care changes in the early nineties. Subsequent policy however has been riddled with inconsistencies to do with funding and with registration requirements. For example, the rising cost of domiciliary services may mean that the hours available are insufficient to support people in the community; the only service offered to meet their needs may then be permanent residential care. However, this may be expensive for local authorities to fund and therefore diversion into schemes funded by housing benefit may be more attractive. However, the legal status of such schemes (and consequently their funding status) was radically affected by the coming into force of the Registered Homes (Amendment) Act 1991 in April 1993. This Act included 'small homes' with fewer than four residents within the homes registration scheme for the first time. This means that such schemes no longer attract housing benefit but are regarded for funding purposes as residential care. Many 'housing with care schemes' will be caught by the registration requirements as will many adult care schemes on the fostering model.

The current position is that residential provision effectively represents a mixed economy of care with contributions from the public, private, voluntary and not-for-profit sectors. Part III of the National Assistance Act 1948 still governs local authority provision of care, with s. 21 of that Act imposing a duty upon authorities to make accommodation available 'for persons who by reasons of age, infirmity, or any other circumstances are in need of care and attention which is not otherwise available to them'. The duty of any particular authority is limited, except in cases of 'urgent need' to those who are 'ordinarily resident' within the area of the local authority, though Circular No. LAC93 (7) makes it clear that where an individual does not appear to have any settled residence, it is the responsibility of the authority where that person actually is to provide the residential care to meet their needs. Disputes between authorities concerning patients discharged from long-stay hospitals, prisons or other forms of care (and unfortunately such disputes are not infrequent) are to be determined by the Secretary of State. People who, under private arrangements, have spent long periods away from their home area, will normally become ordinarily resident in their new area; however, if the placement was made originally by the local authority their ordinary residence will not change.

The National Health Service and Community Care Act 1990 has enabled local authorities to seek placements in other sectors and, for the first time, to make placements in nursing homes. There is no continuing obligation upon local authorities directly to provide residential care services and some authorities have either sold off their remaining homes or have transferred managerial responsibility to not-for-profit organisations operating as trusts. Financial implications for residents of moving into different types of residential care are discussed in Chapter Nine, but residents will also be concerned about the quality of the care that they receive and how this can be assured.

Choice in residential care, whether that is choice of whether or not to enter the residential sector in the first place or choice of location is probably still more apparent than real. Changes in the funding arrangements for residential care, with top-up funding being removed from the Department of Social Security budget to individual local authorities were designed to ensure that no-one entered residential care supported by public funding without the appropriateness of that move being assessed. It is doubtful, however, whether large numbers of people were being misplaced in this way (Phillips, 1990). Statistics themselves disguise the fact that for most people in residential care the decision to enter that type of care was neither a matter of free choice, nor were they necessarily consulted about the decision. Relatives, friends and GPs are prime movers in the process. There is an extensive literature summarised by Warburton (1989) on the reasons why some people enter residential care whilst others remain at home. Warburton's conclusion, based on a sad catalogue of limited user choice and limited user involvement in decision-making, is that a key challenge for community care is for professional and organisational goals and interests not to supersede the interests of service users, and to coincide more often that they apparently do.

The challenge for the social worker (and for the local authority) is how best to build upon the strengths and to work to overcome the negative factors which may precipitate people into residential care. Some of the factors are organisational, some of them are due to poor practice, and some are psycho-social in origin. A number of themes emerge (Warburton, 1989):

- fears about living alone, precipitated by crisis or bereavement;
- increasing impairment and disability;
- a shortage of community services;
- carers' stress and lack of support for carers;
- poor or ineffective assessment and care management;
- inadequate preparation for leaving hospital;
- lack of service innovation and inflexibility;
- professional and organisational concerns and interests, examples being over-concern about risk, insufficient time to allocate to assessment, the precipitate closure of continuing care beds.

Careful handling of the admission to residential care is vital; the process of giving up one's own home, leaving neighbourhood and friends and adapting to communal living may correctly be perceived as a crisis (Sinclair *et al.*, 1990). Being given real options, and a real choice, at this stage is a good indicator of a successful outcome (Willcocks, Peace and Kellaher, 1997). Choice may be limited, by availability or cost or by the contracting arrangements of local authorities.

If choice appears unreasonably to be limited reference should be made to the National Assistance Act 1948 (Choice of Accommodation) Directions 1992 (issued with Circular No. LAC (92)27); local authorities are *bound* to follow these directions. If a person (or their carer if that person is unable to express a preference) expresses a preference for particular accommodation (known as 'preferred accommodation') within the UK the authority must arrange for care in that accommodation provided that:

- the accommodation is suitable in relation to the individual's assessed need;
- to do so would not cost the authority more than it would usually pay for accommodation of that type, unless the individual or a third party is willing to meet the difference in cost;

- the accommodation is available;
- the person in charge of the accommodation is willing to provide it subject to the authority's usual terms and conditions for such accommodation.

The local authority that imposes a rigid ceiling on the cost of residential care that it is willing to fund will not be interpreting this direction properly. Individual assessment of need should lead to individual service response. Psychological needs are as important as physical needs in the assessment; the Guidance itself which accompanies the Directions specifically refers to the need to be near family (albeit in a different part of the country) as an important need to respect; the fact that care charges may be higher in that other region is an irrelevant consideration in this respect. The scope of the Directions was tested in the case of Mark Hazell, a young man with Downs Syndrome living in Avon who challenged through the complaints procedure, and later by judicial review, his authority's refusal to fund a placement for him at the Home Farm Trust. This was an expensive resource, but one to which the local authority had made referrals in the past. Mark was able to show that it was a feature of his Downs Syndrome that a desire for certainty over his placement had become a psychological need. All the evidence then was that this was not only preferred accommodation, it was the *only* placement that could meet his psychological as well as his physical needs. An account of the case is given by Catriona Marchant in *Community Care*, 15 July 1993, p. 18.

Good practice would involve the provision of appropriate information about the range of accommodation on offer, with an opportunity to visit individual homes to compare their facilities and their philosophies of care. When residential care for elderly people is under discussion, social workers should be aware of the 'F' factor (DoH, 1995a) – F for fear – the fears that elderly people have about remaining in their own home whether that is fear of falling, fear of illness or fear of crime. This fear is a reality for those oppressed by it and must be addressed: other means may exist to deal with that fear – occupational therapy assessment for example, or the installation of an alarm system – but it must be addressed because it is a major factor in moving into residential care. Crisis admissions, which by-pass or condense normal admission processes should be carefully monitored, as should admissions precipitated by being in hospital; in one study (Neill *et al.*, 1988) one-half of admissions to local authority homes were perceived as crisis admissions and six in ten applicants and seven in ten carers overall said that being in hospital had influenced the decision to apply. The role of monitoring and review in such situations will be crucial.

*EXERCISE*

Describe good practice in admission to residential care. What barriers exist to good practice and how can they be overcome?

Undoubtedly there remains a role for residential care within the spectrum of community care services. Any hope that, following the implementation of the 1990 Act, numbers in residential care would significantly fall has proved to be illusory. What has happened is that the escalation of provision apparent in the 1980s has been halted. Since 1991 there has been a small decrease in residential provision of between 1 and 2 per cent per annum (Peace, Kellaher and Willcocks, 1997), though overall numbers in institutional care have remained stable, largely due to the growth in the nursing home sector. Residential care provision may be a symptom of the structured dependency of older people or it may simply be too tied up with bricks and mortar to be dismantled (Peace, Kellaher and Willcocks, 1997). The delivery of services remains very practical with the emphasis on physical well-being and a safe environment, which is why it is appropriate for residential care to continue to be considered as an alternative form of housing.

# 12

# Working in Adult Services

Although the system of community care described in this book spans all adult client groups and is also applicable to childrens' services, the development of social work in the 1990s has seen a movement towards specialisation and away from genericism as the knowledge base and skills relevant to each client group have become more specific.

In their examination of how community care is working out in practice, Lewis and Glennerster (1996) conclude that unified social services departments on the Seebohm model are becoming less sustainable for two important reasons. First is the explicit rationing of services on the basis of cost efficiency which leads departments away from an open-door policy of service. Second is an organisational and philosophical split between childrens' services and adult services, which echoes the division between childrens' departments and welfare departments which existed from 1948 to 1970. A third reason is also proposed, and that is the split between purchasers and providers of service: between care managers and those who work in domiciliary, residential and day care.

An assumption of unity may already be more apparent than real even within adult services. The term 'adult services' is a very wide one, covering a range of different client groups with varying needs, interests and priorities. It is unlikely that any one model of service could be found that applies to all. The major groupings are here identified to be:

- older people
- physical disability
- learning disability
- substance misuse
- HIV and AIDS
- mental health

Although all of these groups will have been marginalised in the ways described in chapter 1 through cultural stereotyping and service neglect, policy development post-community care has been somewhat different for each of them. In terms of theory and method, social work with these different groups will show distinctive differences. This chapter therefore traces the historical development of social work with these different client groups, and analyses what community care has meant for each of them. Examples of innovation and good practice are given as appropriate.


## Services for older people

A CCETSW study in 1990 began with the premise that work with older people has often been seen as a less prestigious area of social work, often allocated to unqualified staff, and with a low profile on Dip.SW courses (CCETSW, 1990). This is despite the fact that the number of referrals for this group exceeds half of the total referred to social services departments. Research into effective working with older people has, however, shown the value of intensive involvement by qualified staff, (Goldberg and Warburton, 1979). Work with older people in the community was the focus of the Thanet community care project in Kent (Davies and Challis, 1986) which became the blueprint for the development of care management as a general scheme. The production of welfare approach adopted there indicated that focused work by budget-holding managers could be effective in at least delaying admission to residential care for frail older people, whilst at the same time raising the morale of their carers. Results from this user group were extrapolated into a general system for all adult client groups. Thus work with older people was at the forefront of community care development. How has community care worked out in general for older people? Age Concern in 1994 identified some early difficulties in shortage of information, patchy services, stringent eligibility criteria and insidious charging policies. Black service users have also been shown to present a particular challenge to social care agencies, as they are liable to suffer significant disadvantage in gaining access to community care services (SSI, 1998).

Older people have also been particularly affected by changes in NHS provision. They are major consumers of health care. Seventy-five per cent of those aged over 65 will visit their GP at least once a year (Victor, 1991) and 36 per cent of over 75s will have an in-patient stay in hospital (Tinker *et al.*, 1994). The provision of informal care by relatives and other informal networks is most marked in the case of older people, with 48 per cent of those people identified as carers in the 1990 General Household Survey caring for parent or parent-in-law. Thus it is in the care of older people that the assertion that community care is care by the community can be judged. Henwood (1992) identifies a number of policy issues of relevance to community care for older people in the 1990s:

- establishing support for carers as a central priority;
- testing out in practice the belief that community services can provide a viable alternative to residential care;
- the need for substantial investment in care management training and resourcing;
- negotiating the interface between health and social care both at organisational and practice levels.

*EXERCISE*

Examine your local authority's Community Care Plan. What priorities does it identify for older people? Does it contain explicit targets to redress the inequalities expressed by ethnic minority older people?

Early responses to organisational issues in care management have been provided by the PSSRU (Bulletin, 1996). The focus of the Evaluating Community Care for Elderly People project is investigating the patterns of need which now discriminate between groups of people allocated community care services. Preliminary findings show that there is a higher concentration of resources on those with greater disabilities and on those with family caregivers. The researchers have returned to the same areas surveyed in the PSSRU domiciliary care project of 1984–9 which reported in Resources Needs and Outcomes in Community-Based Care (Davies, Bebbington, Charnley *et al.*, 1990). They are finding evidence that the philosophy of reform has taken root insofar as expressed priorities are giving users a real chance to stay at home with very good care, and to enhance user empowerment. Encouragingly, resources appear to be related to needs to a much greater extent than in 1984–9. How the care manager perceives need, the extent to which this coincides with the views of the user and carer and the recognition of significant variables (in the study these were: cognitive impairment, depression, carer stress or bad user/carer relationship) will influence the type and quantity of resources provided. This research into community care for older people illustrates the inter-relationship between policy and practice. Clearly the care managers involved had absorbed into their practice the importance of targeting resources efficiently, and according to departmental policy. Nevertheless, the study also shows that the practice of social work, because it is concerned with complex and fluid relationships, can never be deterministic. It must always be sensitive to the particular needs of the user and/or carer.

### Learning disability services

The development of services for people with learning disabilities is a good indicator of the success of community care planning and practice. The history of services for people with learning disabilities is one of segregation and neglect (Means and Smith, 1994). The starting point for the change came as early as 1971 with the publication of the White Paper 'Better Services for the Mentally Handicapped' which sought to establish a '20-year programme' for the resettlement of mentally handicapped people from the large institutions into the community. The model proposed was the purpose-built local authority-funded hostel with an average of 25 beds. Progress was slow and the plan itself was overtaken by new concepts in working with the client group known by the late 1980s as 'people with learning disabilities'. A more respectful terminology was accompanied by the development of the idea of 'ordinary living' which encompassed a range of accommodation, but mostly in ordinary housing (stimulated by grants from the Housing Corporation for special needs accommodation), and small group homes. At the same time, the private residential sector expanded until its growth was checked by the Audit Commission report of 1986. Some specific resettlement projects were funded by the Department of Social Security and evaluated by Cambridge *et al.* (1994) as part of the Care in the Community Project. Interestingly, for this client group community care proved to be more expensive than hospital care. Factors indicative of successful projects were:

- a shared view of service objectives between the major public sector services, especially health, social services and housing;
- clear agency roles and responsibilities;

- an organisational capacity for strategic development;
- services designed around individuals and accumulated knowledge of resources and outcomes.

Five years on, the ideal of community participation had not been achieved and little progress made in extending social networks and social participation. Educational input had declined and statutory community care services were not readily available. Social work input had also declined. Lack of employment and reliance on state benefits contributed to the marginalisation of residents (Cambridge, 1994).

The picture that comes across is of a lack of forward planning; in particular, a failure aggressively to develop and provide services which would meet higher-level needs such as the need for social stimulation, friendship and personal development. This narrowness of vision was echoed in Mencap's (1995) survey of how community care was working at the level of individual assessments: 'Often assessments fall short of examining long-term needs and aspirations of people with learning disabilities and subsequent care packages severely limit the extent to which aspirations can be realised' (p. ii). This approach was exacerbated by the use of check list forms which concentrated on functional ability and the performance of activities of daily living, rather than people's own strengths and expectations. The conclusion to be drawn is that assessments of people with learning disabilities can be limited and stereotyped. Services subsequently provided may emphasise social exclusion rather than inclusion. For people with learning disabilities, the development of social networks based on ordinary life principles may offer the best opportunity of integration in the community.

## Physical disability services

Pilling (1992) describes the British experience of care management as an attempt to solve the problems of fragmentation and inflexibility for long-term user groups. She identifies three types of organisational arrangement within which care management can operate:

1. Independently of statutory services, with the care manager having no direct resources of his/her own, but acting as a 'service broker' to seek out and negotiate for the services that the user needs and wants (Brandon and Towell, 1989). Alternatively, the user of

services or their representative may act as their own care manager with individualised funding available from a funding agency.
2. The care manager has direct control over at least some resources; this is the type of model developed by the PSSRU at the University of Kent (Davies and Challis, 1986).
3. A multi-disciplinary team for the user group provides individualised care packages for some users; the Darlington scheme (Challis *et al.*, 1995) operated on this model.

The three models are based on different philosophies and, indeed, values. The first emphasises empowerment, the second emphasises the efficient allocation of resources, and the third sees care management as best linked with therapy or direct service provision (Pilling, 1992) In the second and third models power legitimately remains in professional hands. The disability movement would challenge this emphasis on professional assessment of need, in arguments for citizenship and rights to service (Oliver, 1996). In the design and delivery of services there may well be a difference in perspective between professionals and disabled people which embraces issues of choice and control (Kestenbaum, 1996). The social model of disability places independent living in the context of demands for human and civil rights; independence is created by having assistance when and how one requires it. The basic needs of independent living are:

- housing
- personal assistance
- transport
- access to the environment
- advocacy and training
- information and counselling
- equipment and technical assistance

These are the primary needs which, if satisfied, would give disabled people maximum possible access to mainstream opportunities and provision rather than leave them restricted to segregated and stigmatised 'care' (Kestenbaum, 1996). Thus the independent living movement challenges one of the basic assumptions of community care that 'care' itself is a worthwhile commodity to be bought and sold, mediated by an assessment of 'need'. The notion of community care itself is thus built upon an assumption that disabled people are to be dependent people; what Morris (1994) calls 'the custodial nature of caring' can, of itself, create institutionalisation within the community.

Disabled people's experience of community care (Lamb and Layzell, 1995) is one of disappointment; many respondents to this SCOPE survey felt that whether or not they receive services depends more on where they live and whether there is sufficient money in the budget, than on their needs. The introduction of charges for services and an inadequate level of service (particularly therapeutic health services such as physiotherapy and speech therapy) caused particular concern. Respondents were asked about their satisfaction with the social work service: 64 per cent of disabled people and 61 per cent of carers expressed satisfaction; figures were higher for disabled people living in supported accommodation rather than in the community. This may be compared with stated satisfaction with the service received from the GP: 89 per cent of disabled people and 84 per cent of carers are satisfied. This satisfaction appears to be linked to accessibility, confidentiality and continuity of care; carers who had been caring for a long time and those who cared for more hours each day were especially likely to say they were satisfied with their GP. However, there was some concern that treatment decisions by fund-holding GPs were being driven by financial considerations.

The research was undertaken before the Carers Act introduced separate assessments for carers, and two thirds of carers interviewed in the SCOPE research felt that incorrect assumptions were being made about the help that was needed, and that assessments did not take place regularly enough to take account of changing needs. This obviously raises issues about assessment and review that need to be addressed, both at managerial and individual level. Overall, the problem of matching resources to need was seen as a rationing device which challenged the professionalism of the front line worker:

> To some extent this has always been the case – open-ended budgets for health and social care have never existed. What has changed is where the decisions are made. The 1990 National Health Service and Community Care Act removed some of the freedom that traditionally clinicians and 'front-line' practitioners have had, and has given greater authority to purchasers. Those who control the budgets therefore have much greater power to decide who gets what services. (Lamb and Layzell, 1995, p. 38)

## People with multiple impairments

Developing adequate and effective services for people with multiple impairments is a major challenge for care management and highlights important issues in long term work. An SSI review, 'Whose Life is it Anyway' (SSI, 1993d) of services for people with multiple impairments emphasised:

- the importance of goal-setting
- working in partnership
- multi-disciplinary working
- smooth transitions between child and adult services

Generally, there was found to be a focus on past events rather than future goals, or on the finding of solutions to present difficulties rather than on the enhancement of life potential. This had a particular impact on the conduct of reviews which were given low priority and lacked focus. A dynamic review process is of course dependent upon there being agreed parameters within which to measure progress and achievement. The professional must change from being the expert definer of need and rationer of service to being a resource which the disabled person may negotiate to use as he or she chooses.

Work with people with profound and multiple impairments is to be informed by O'Brian and Lyle's (1987) 'Five Service Principles' which are supportive of normalisation. These are:

- community presence
- participation
- choice
- competence
- respect

Community presence militates against segregated services with people with multiple handicaps being enabled to experience a wide range of normal activities in natural community settings such as schools, shops, recreational centres and churches. Community participation involves active support for natural relationships with families, neighbours and co-workers. Services must provide enough information and support for people to make positive choices and to communicate interests and preferences in small everyday matters as well as in important issues such as who where to live and what type of work to do. Information-giving is thus placed at a premium.

Multi-disciplinary working is essential for people with multiple disabilities. If multi-disciplinary working is absent, care plans tend to focus on the particular discipline or specialism of the practitioner. Contact with both health and social services may generally be perceived as irregular, infrequent and crisis-driven. Deterioration can happen quickly if support is withdrawn or not available. Continuity of service is therefore important, particularly to meet new developmental needs.

**Transition services**

The interface between child and adult services is not always smooth so as to facilitate transitions and ensure a seamless service for users. The service needs of disabled young people aged 14–25 for so-called 'transition services' were considered by the SSI in 'Growing Up and Moving On' (SSI, 1996c). The OPCS survey of Disability in Britain (1988/9) showed that one in forty young people aged 16–25 have one or more functional impairments. Sixteen thousand of these young people leave school every year; leaving school is an important point of transition and a prime opportunity for inter-agency planning to take place. Promoting equality of opportunity will be a primary concern since it is known (Hirst and Baldwin, 1994) that disabled young people are comparatively less likely than those without disabilities to gain personal, social or economic independence. This is not surprising given that there is no tradition in the UK of promoting inclusive employment policies for those with disabilities and special educational needs, and structural changes in the economy from the early 1970s onwards have led to the permanent disappearance of much appropriate work.

Workshops organised nationally by the SSI to look at transition services (SSI, 1996d) produced both a management and a user agenda. The management agenda was to do with minimising disparity in services by producing complimentary and cross-referenced children's services plans and community care plans to address the specific needs of disabled young people and their families during transition. The conclusion was that cross-agency arrangements should be put into place to collate information, transfer responsibility, assess and plan. Representatives of disabled young adults and their families should be routinely involved in policy-making. The user agenda, however, was for disability equality training within agencies to promote understanding of user perspectives. Support and funding would be given to user-run groups and self-advocacy schemes. At an individual level, understanding of the potentially conflicting views of parents and their disabled children was seen as vital to enable each young person to grow up. Users thus emphasise the importance of having a forum for discussion with assessors and service providers. They also emphasise the importance of traditional social work skills in negotiation and mediation within families.

The legislative framework for promoting smooth transitions for school leavers is in principle already in place. Sections 5 and 6 of the Disabled Persons Act 1986 require schools to consult with social services departments when children who are statemented with special educational needs reach the first annual review after their fourteenth birthday. This enables the social services department to identify which of those children it will regard as 'disabled' within the meaning of s.29 National Assistance Act 1948 for whom further assessment will be necessary. Such assessments should begin, at the latest, within eight months of the child's expected school leaving date (normally 19). Not included within this system are school-leavers who are disabled but who do not have special educational needs. Health authorities and local authorities have a limited duty to assist education authorities in the exercise of their functions under s. 322 of the Education Act 1996 Part IV (dealing with special educational needs).

Section 322 (a) applies to health authorities which are required to assist local education authorities in the exercise of their functions unless 'having regard to the resources available to them for the purpose of the exercise of their functions under the National Health Service Act 1977, it is not reasonable for them to comply with the request.' Local authorities (including social services departments) may refuse to comply with a request if it is 'not compatible with their own statutory or other duties and obligations or unduly prejudices the discharge of any of their functions' (s. 322 (b)). Other statutory duties and resources restrictions may thus limit the amount of co-operation which will be forthcoming.

'Searching for Service', an inspection of service responses made to the needs of disabled young adults and their carers (SSI/DoH, 1996a), sought to establish how, in the light of legislative changes, different authorities were identifying and responding to the needs of disabled young adults. It was found that no discrete policy framework existed specifically for this age group in any of the authorities; few disabled young adults or their representatives were involved in policy-making and there was no evidence of an integrated approach to information production or dissemination involving key local agencies. At a practice level, there were continuing risks of disabled young people being involved in multiple – and sometimes overlapping – assessment processes; innovation was hampered by relatively late involvement by social services departments and an absence of day services specifically for young people. Significant use was made of further education college provision, though an absence of vocational training could be interpreted as confirming Tomlinson and Colquhoun's (1995) assertion (p. 193) that 'in an economy with an oversupply of labour, special education can itself become a mechanism for legitimating non-employment.'

Responding efficiently and sensitively to the needs of young people with disabilities is a particular challenge to local authorities. As a group, they significantly straddle administrative boundaries between health, education and social services departments; it is very important therefore that local agencies have agreements about mutual referral and assessment procedures. Commonly, referral forms are designed with older people in mind and may not reflect the 'routes into service' taken by young people from residential and educational provision. The SSI found little evidence of a systematic review of access to, or experience of, services; this is a particular cause for concern likely to perpetuate unhelpful service traditions linked either to specific functional impairments or to institution-based services for residential or day-care. Further education has received a boost from funding for 'Schedule 2' courses under the Further and Higher Education Act 1992, though this may be at the expense of those with profound disabilities. Support services such as transport and equipment are also not well developed. Financial competition between colleges has also affected joint planning (NAICE, 1996).

## Older people with learning disabilities

Though LAC 92 (10) identified older people with a learning disability as a distinct service group, research undertaken by the SSI (SSI, 1997b) indicates that few authorities have fully developed plans to respond to the changing pattern of need. Increases in the number of people with learning disabilities in the community are attributed to:

- improved public health and medical care which increases life expectancy;
- the growing old of the post-war baby boom generation;
- the policy of closing long-stay hospitals.

The physical health problems of older people with learning disabilities are similar to those of the elderly population as a whole, but their mental health needs are different. Although the prevalence of mental disorder in people with learning disabilities decreases as they grow older the type of illness experienced is less likely to be a psychotic illness, and more likely to be a depressive or reactive anxiety state. A number of studies of older people with Downs Syndrome has also shown a greater likelihood of neurological changes similar to those seen in Alzheimer-type dementia. The contention of the SSI report is that a mix of services is needed to meet this range of needs. In particular, a wide range of day care services is seen to be desirable, recognising that individual preferences and needs are likely to change over relatively short periods of time. Automatic 'retirement' from Adult Training Centres at age 60 or 65 does not fit this pattern of flexibility of need. As 35 per cent of adults with a learning disability are resident in some sort of residential care, the question arises of the extent to which such accommodation should be seen as 'a home for life' notwithstanding physical or mental deterioration. The report simply recommends that commissioning bodies should provide a wide range of accommodation and ensure that as far as possible people are not requested to move homes to gain access to appropriate services. At a practical level, social workers with people with learning disabilities will need a wide range of knowledge and skills to span the developmental needs of individuals from adolescence through into old age.

## Sensory impairments

Social work services for people who are blind or deaf are often separated from the mainstream. The SSI (1997b) found that sensory impairment workers generally stood outside care management structures and were organisationally isolated. Research by Lovelock, Powell and Craggs (1995) into the social support needs of visually impaired people, however, emphasised the 'generic' as well as the 'specialist' understanding required particularly in the case of older people with sight-related needs who sought assessment for services under the Disabled Persons Act 1986 and the National Health Service and Community Care Act 1990. These needs may not be subsumed under the certification process involved through referral from a consultant ophthalmologist under the form BD8 procedure. This procedure is evidence of eligibility to be registered as blind or partially sighted.

The British Deaf Association's (1996) Report 'Visible Voices' concluded that deaf people's effective participation in local services was dependent upon proactive measures which included training in skill-building, assertiveness and confidence raising. The focus of such work should be Deaf Clubs which, while they have rarely attracted outside attention, are an important part of deaf culture. Agencies, for their part, need to set aside time and resources and energy to make participation a reality. Social services staff were identified as needing training about the deaf community, its culture and British Sign Language: the employment of deaf workers or the use of deaf facilitators or advocates was viewed very positively as a sign that the agency was approachable. CCETSW (1994) has developed a checklist of five necessary elements associated with training required to develop more appropriate community care service delivery for this group. These are:

- information
- techniques
- understanding
- workforce resource implications
- training specifications

A model of care management which was not sensitive to the particular needs of the deaf community, would manifestly be inappropriate.


## Substance misuse

Before the implementation of the National Health Service and Community Care Act 1990, services for substance misusers (chiefly drug and alcohol services) consisted mainly of residential detoxification and rehabilitation funded through social security payments, and hospital treatment as part of the NHS. Advice and counselling services were grant-aided by health and local authorities often through joint finance (SSI, 1994). The decision to include drug and alcohol misuse services within the remit of the National Health Service and Community Care Act 1990, and to transfer funding by this means was intended to give local authorities scope to commission a comprehensive needs-led network of services (LAC (93)2). Expertise, however, continues to be located primarily in health care services and in the voluntary sector.

Substance misuse is recognised ('The Health of the Nation', 1990) as a significant public health problem associated with social problems such as offending, homelessness, unemployment, family breakdown, domestic violence and child abuse. There are, however, inherent difficulties in the commissioning of substance misuse services (SSI, 1994) because of:

- stigma;
- the absence of accurate prevalence data, due particularly to a reluctance to disclose the illegality of drug use;
- the aetiology of substance misuse which may make intervention dependent upon readiness to change;
- delay in service response to changing patterns of misuse.

At an inter-agency level, decisions have to be made locally concerning:

- where substance misuse services are best placed within health and local authority structures;
- the introduction of a common understanding of terms and a common system for recording and processing data;
- the role of GP fundholders;
- the role of the Probation Service;
- agreement on minimum standards and an agreed definition of priorities.

This is a complex service area, at an early stage of development, in which social services departments are trying to define and establish their roles and place themselves at the centre of service planning and development. The expectation is that people who misuse alcohol and drugs should be receiving services of the same standard as other adults assessed through the framework of community care. The outcome of this first inspection by the SSI in 1994 was disappointing insofar as it showed that none of the five authorities inspected had a policy or strategy which was specific to people who misuse alcohol or drugs.

Indeed, there may have been a regression in that, compared to others, this particular service group was seen as undeserving. There was a lack of collaboration with other local authority services and, more worrying, a lack of collaboration and information sharing between children's and adult services within social services departments. There were no examples of formal arrangements to involve staff in voluntary agencies in the assessment process; an over-emphasis on the purchaser/provider split was cited as the main reason for this.

In most cases services were inaccessible to service users who often had to jump through a number of hoops and express high levels of motivation before gaining access to a service at all. The fact that there was no outreach and that services were reactive compounded this situation. The standards against which services were to be evaluated were set out as follows:

Standard 1:     A published policy reflecting the values on which it is based, current knowledge and statutory requirements

Standard 2:     A strategic plan which sets measurable objectives and a time-scale for implementation

Standard 3:     A purchasing plan

Standard 4:     Operational management with responsibility for the development of policies, procedures and guidance

Standard 5:     Assessment procedures established in collaboration with health, Probation and independent agencies

Standard 6:     Care management and care planning

Standard 7:     Flexible and creative services to meet the individual needs and preferences of service users. Standards for quality are specified, monitored and evaluated

Standard 8:     Appropriate outcome measures to gauge the effectiveness of services

Standard 9:     Inter-agency collaboration

Standard 10:    Equal opportunities in service provision

Standard 11:    An information strategy

Standard 12:    Record keeping which accords with legislation and guidance on access and confidentiality

The development of such standards of service provides a useful framework for the assessment not only of services for substance misusers, but for other complex services which have a multi-agency component.

Ronald Victor is a 45 year old man with a long history of drug and alcohol misuse. He has previous convictions and is currently nearing the end of a twelve-month prison sentence imposed for a number of public order offences and an assault on a police officer. His physical and mental health are both impaired and he is of no fixed abode.

If you were Ronald's probation officer, what sort of services might you be considering for Ronald and what use might you make of community care legislation?

## HIV and AIDS

People with HIV and AIDS present significant challenges to both social and health care agencies because of their complex and often rapidly changing needs, which demand close collaboration between agencies to assure that these are met in a timely and appropriate manner. (DoH, 1994d)

In contrast with services for substance misusers the Department of Health's (1994) study of community care implementation revealed a commitment to joint planning, significant involvement of voluntary agencies and a profile within community care plans was a feature of community care for people with HIV and AIDS. Population needs assessment was, however, underdeveloped, as was the establishment of appropriate outcome measures across agencies. Whilst HIV and AIDS training was well established in local authorities, training strategies in community care across different agencies and sectors were less satisfactory.

The survey found that there had been few comprehensive assessments of people with HIV and AIDS. At this operational level, integration with services for drug misusers, with children and families services, and with housing was less evident. An HIV/AIDS user consultation exercise for Norfolk Social Services (Davies, 1995) brings together experiences of living with HIV and AIDS in a rural area. It also looks at the experience of a hospital social worker in giving support not only to patients but also to other staff traumatised by their experiences. The job involves dealing with carers also, and is long-term because of the protracted nature of the illness. There is an emphasis on transferable skills in dealing with anger and loss, and counselling is seen as particularly appropriate where depression and anxiety accompany physical problems.

## Mental health services

Services for people with mental health problems reflect the two policy strands of closure of the large institutions and the development of services for people in the community. Until recently the legal structure within which work with people with mental health problems was undertaken, i.e. the Mental Health Act 1983 was focused upon admission to hospital and treatment in hospital, rather than services in the community. The number of people resident in psychiatric hospitals reached its peak in 1954 (with a population of 151 400); this reflected the high-water mark of a policy of segregation and asylum. Comparative figures for 1992 showed a drop in numbers to just over 60 000. Goodwin (1989) examines the reasons behind the policy of de-institutionalisation after 1954, and observes a mixture of social democratic egalitarianism and pragmatism. Policy developments since the 1950s have focused on the development of psychiatric units in district general hospitals, a growth in the number of community psychiatric nurses, and the development of domiciliary and day care services. The 'pharmacological revolution' (Jones, 1993), and especially the development of psychotropic drugs, has enabled people to be given medication to assist them to live in the community when previously they would have been detained in hospital. Care in hospital has thus become only one of a range of services available for people who are mentally ill. Most people will be treated by their GP and in fact may never be referred to the specialist psychiatric services. The pragmatic reasons for favouring care in the community are that it is seen as a cheaper option at a time of financial pressure, and that it legitimates the intrusive nature of some psychiatric services by locating them in the normal environment of the community (Goodwin, 1989). What the nature of alternative provision outside of the large institutions should be is not often clearly articulated. Responsibility for planning is at the present time divided between health and social services, and there is also independent sector input. Of more general concern is insufficient support for the concept of care and treatment as a right; this is particularly worrying when the closure of institutions (and earlier discharge from the beds that remain) means that there is a large group of people living in the community whose condition is chronic and long-term or whose need for contact with services is high.

What is meant by the term 'community care' for people with a mental disorder is explored by Bennett and Morris (1983). Their definition is fourfold:

1.  It means that the patient's local community and not the institution must provide the context for the treatment, rehabilitation, support and long term management of people who are mentally ill.
2.  Community care is not *per se* a rejection of hospital care; hospital services (including in-patient services) are seen as a component of a *network* of services providing care.
3.  An active approach to rehabilitation and support is presumed within the model.
4.  Changing the locus of care is insufficient on its own. Community care depends upon the existence of an accepting and enabling environment which does not reject the most severely ill.

Since 1990 the emphasis at the structural level has been on co-ordination and targeting of services. At the practice level it has been about ensuring that people do not fall through the net of services available. The Green Paper 'Developing Partnerships in Mental Health' (1997) reviews recent developments and makes proposals for change in the future. At the present time, health and social services authorities are required to set up joint planning groups to plan for and co-ordinate services (some of which may be jointly funded under powers given by s.28A National Health Service Act 1977). However, there is no requirement on health authorities and local authorities to produce joint mental health plans. The introduction of community care as a system has, however, given an opportunity to apply specific funding for mental health projects. The Mental Illness Specific Grant introduced by s. 50 National Health Service and Community Care Act 1990 and available from 1991 onwards has ring-fenced some additional funding for mental health services and its top-slice, the Target Fund, is directed at improving local authority provision for severely mentally ill people. The Homeless Mentally Ill Initiative and Rough Sleepers Initiative have also targeted particularly vulnerable groups, the latter in areas of the country with greater than average difficulties. The importance of collaboration in the housing field has been acknowledged by the publication of a joint Code of Guidance on Parts VI and VII of the Housing Act 1996: Allocation of Housing Accommodation and Homelessness, by the Department of the Environment and the Department of Health. The inter-dependency of systems is something that was acknowledged in the Department of Health study visits which preceded the Green Paper; these emphasised the importance of collaboration with a range of partners other than social services and health, including those working in the criminal justice system, housing, education and employment. The Green Paper goes on to discuss options for change in the mental health field. One option is to move to single authority responsibility with either health authorities *or* local authorities responsible for planning, commissioning and purchasing both mental health and social care. Another option is for the establishment of a New Mental Health and Social Care Authority outside existing health and local authority provision; such a body would attract ring-fenced funding and would be directly accountable to the Secretary of State. The intention is obviously to find a mechanism for planning and executing an integrated mental health service.

Paradoxically, developments in legislation and guidance since 1990 have demarcated health and social services responsibilities more clearly so far as care in the community is concerned. The prevailing trend has also been more towards control than care, particularly for the proportion of people (as high as 75 per cent in some estimates; Saunders, 1992) who after discharge from hospital have no continuing contact with either health or social services. The much-publicised deaths of Jonathan Zito and Ben Silcock have focused attention on protection both of the public and of people who are themselves vulnerable upon discharge from hospital. The introduction of the Care Programme Approach for those referred to the specialist psychiatric services predated Care Management within Social Services by two years; the Care Programme Approach being introduced by guidance in 1991 (DoH, 1990a). The systems are similar insofar as each envisages a named worker with key responsibility for co-ordinating a package of care, but the Care Programme Approach is health-led, and Care Management is local-authority led. Problems of co-ordination when individual patients/clients are known to both systems can therefore be presumed. Supervision registers for those identified as a risk to themselves or others were introduced for health in 1993. Supervised discharge for the statutory follow-up of patients detained under s. 3 of the Mental Health Act 1983 was introduced in 1996, with health authority responsibility for its implementation. At the same time, joint health and social services responsibility for the after-care of detained patients under s.117 The Mental Health Act 1983 continues. The Department of Health Community Care Monitoring Study (DoH, 1993a) found, perhaps not surprisingly, that there was 'considerable confusion' (para. 2.20) about the application of the Care Programme Approach, Care Management and s. 117. One fundamental difficulty was health and social services personnel gaining access to each other's resources. Social services resources might only be made available where care management was being supplied, which could lead to unnecessary duplication of professional assessment. Conversely, particularly in multi-disciplinary teams, care managers would be designated purchasers but would not be able to purchase provider services from community psychiatric nurses. Community nursing might be purchased directly by fund-holding GPs, and there was some evidence that fund-holding GPs were not willing to finance care programmes. A common inter-professional perspective on mental health equally could not be assumed.

**Implications of multi-agency working**

The implication of multi-agency working is that identifying and agreeing within and between agencies their roles, responsibilities and accountability for planned action and future decision-making is central to an integrated system of care provision. Different statutory mandates, systems of managerial control, and professional training need clarification before co-operative working can take place in the community. It is, however, wrong to assume that consensus should always be the goal in multidisciplinary working. As Coulshed and Orme (1998) make clear, there can be creative conflict where different professional perspectives come into play, which dissipates unhelpful myths and stereotypes about other professions work. Biggs (1997) also warns that too much consensus can be collusive against the service user who has nowhere to go if faced with an assessment or care plan with which he or she is unhappy. CCETSW/IAMHW (1989) have produced guidance on models of good practice in multidisciplinary teamwork, which focuses on mental health services. They emphasise:

- partnership – the ability to engage with colleagues, allocate tasks and give feedback,
- negotiation,

- networking – including disseminating information,
- communicating – verbally and on paper,
- reframing – seeing problems in a different way,
- confronting,
- flexibility, and
- monitoring and evaluation.

'In the community', however, is not the only place in which co-operative working should take place. If there is a tendency for care management to concern itself only with assessment and care planning and not with the appropriateness or quality of services subsequently provided, then this should be resisted. A referral on for day care or residential provision should not be seen as shifting the responsibility onto those services. Yet frequently day care and residential workers complain that they have been provided with inadequate information or an inadequate care plan by fieldworkers. They may also find themselves designated as key workers not just for the purposes of their own establishments, but for the purposes of monitoring or reviewing as a whole. This does not provide an objectively satisfactory way of feeding back suggestions for the improvement of services into the planning and assessment processes.

# Conclusion

Community care cannot be described in terms of one system despite common ideological roots and a single legislative framework. The development of services for older people, for people with mental health problems and for people with disabilities has been influenced by historical antecedents, demographic issues and the diverse concerns of professionals and service users. The knowledge base of community care has become so large that a return from specialisation to genericism in the delivery of services is probably unrealistic. The major infra-structure issues however have commonalties. The provision of social care cannot be isolated from health care, housing and financial support. In all of these areas major change has taken place, emphasising both the split between purchasers and providers of services, and in its wake, the new mixed economy of public and independent sector provision. Support from informal carers has been a basic tenet upon which community care has been built. Chiefly, however, this has been provided by families rather than communities. Individualism remains the basic model of service provision in community care.

Community social work has not been much developed, nor has anti-discriminatory practice developed to the point where it has significantly enhanced community support. Social work under community care has thus continued to focus on the specific needs of individuals, albeit in a family and community context. This has in turn meant that the traditional methods and values of social case work have retained a continuing validity within community care.

At the structural level the strength of community care has been that it has allowed strategic planning to take place, often on an inter-agency basis. The requirements in s. 46 of the National Health Service and Community Care Act 1990 that local authorities should produce community care plans has required agencies to be explicit about what services they can provide, what services are the responsibility of other agencies, and their criteria for accessing services according to different levels of need. This in turn makes the whole administrative decision-making process more transparent. It is envisaged that the introduction of Primary Care Groups within the National Health Service (DoH,

1998a) will lead to better co-ordination of health and social services around continuing care in the community for those with complex needs.

Achieving a consensus between agencies, and between agencies and service users, on the proper definition of need will be more controversial. An assessment of need is the gateway to service provision, but 'need' itself is a term with a shifting meaning according to changing political and economic circumstances. Service planning must also be responsive to needs which may not have previously been well articulated. The needs of carers, for example, have only recently found legislative expression in the Carers (Recognition and Services) Act 1995 which gives those who provide a substantial amount of care on a regular basis a right to an assessment of their needs separate from that of the service user. The *appropriateness* of traditional service provision also needs to be evaluated. Services for black communities, for example, are in need of fundamental reappraisal. The disability movement has also raised fundamental issues about the worthwhileness of 'care' as a commodity in its own right. In the field of housing in particular, the importance of fine-tuning mainstream services as well as making specialist provision has emphasised the 'ordinary life' principles of community care as integration within living and working communities. In a fundamental sense, this is what community care was intended to achieve: the ending of separate and segregated provision, and the enhancement instead of people's ability to live and develop within their own communities.

Ensuring a firm value base for the development of social work within community care is absolutely fundamental. The social worker, especially in the role of care manager, will be constrained by agency policies and procedures and necessarily so, but this does not absolve them from the professional imperative to respect the lifestyles and choices of the people with whom they work. Arguably, respecting difference can be facilitated within the system of community care. The emphasis on due process within a bureaucratic model enables advocacy to flourish and unarticulated value positions in service provision to be challenged. Moves towards proceduralism also challenge social workers to analyse their practice more precisely. The emphasis on monitoring and review within care management requires the criteria for progress or success to be fixed more clearly at the assessment stage. There is thus less scope for ill-focused, and arguably oppressive, intervention when the mandate for involvement has to be agreed by all concerned at the outset. Agreeing and delivering upon such a mandate also requires basic and enduring social work skills in communication, assessment, negotiation and reflection. The conclusion to be drawn is that social work *per se* continues to have a role within community care in terms of the knowledge, skills and values that it brings to the task.

So what of the future? The goals of community care are explicitly to restore and maintain independence by enabling people to live in the community, promote individual choice and self determination, clarify the responsibility of agencies and make practical support for carers a high priority. The White Paper (1989) which propounded these principles was entitled 'Community Care in the Next Decade and Beyond'. The agenda is undoubtedly an ambitious one; wide ranging in its scope, and fundamental to the very functioning of a welfare state. It would be extraordinary if the ramifications of such an agenda for community care and for social work could be fully explored within the space of one decade. The challenges it poses in terms of policy and practice are destined to continue into the next century and beyond.

The Blair Government of 1997 onwards is developing its own interpretation of community care and is reflecting critically upon the system it has inherited. The emphasis is upon social inclusion and a recognition that all people face personal and family crises to which social services should be able effectively to respond. All people therefore will have an interest in efficient and well co-ordinated services. The White Paper 'Modernising Social Services' (DoH, 1998b) emphasises three things: promoting independence, improving protection and raising standards. Improving joint working between health and social services and ensuring greater consistency in the availability and cost of services in different parts of the country are clearly stated policy aims. A better qualified workforce which will in turn be monitored through clearer and more objective inspection arrangements is seen as central to an improvement in standards. Client satisfaction surveys are also seen as important in the development of user-centred services. All of these ideas are central tenets of community care policy presented in social-democratic rather than New Right terms. There is less emphasis on market forces and the role of the independent sector, but 'best value' continues to be an important indicator of efficiency in performance. A feature of the new system is likely to be greater control by central government of local spending priorities through the use of special and specific grants, and the evaluation of service effectiveness against pre-set targets. This is particularly so in the mental health field and in relation to hospital discharge where funding is linked to the effectiveness of partnership arrangements between health and social services.

For the social work practitioner, the impact of 'Modernising Social Services' is likely to be a greater emphasis on professional and public accountability. Workforce standards will be monitored by a General Social Care Council with responsibility not only for social workers but for the million or more other staff who constitute the social care workforce. Regulation of care standards will, it appears, be taken away from local control and invested in eight Regional Commissions which will regulate not only residential care but domiciliary care and also local authority services, according to national standards. The protection of vulnerable children and adults from abuse and neglect will receive further consideration; for children this will also include developing life chances and specifically improving transitions from care to independent adult life. Overall, the emphasis will be on greater clarity and consistency in service provision, on supporting independence (possibly through an expansion of direct payments) and on the meeting of targets for efficiency improvements. All of this will be supported by increased funding at 3.1 per cent above the level of inflation over the three years from 1999–2000. Whether or not this will be sufficient to meet the demands placed on the service remains to be seen.

# Bibliography

Action on Elder Abuse (1996), *The Abuse of Older People at Home: information for workers*. London: AEA.

Adams, A. and Wilson, D. (1996), *Older People with Mental Health Difficulties: user preferences and housing options*. Age Concern, Scotland.

Adams, R. (1998), Social Work Processes, in Adams, R., Dominelli, L. and Payne, M. (eds) *Social Work: themes, issues and critical debates*. Basingstoke: Macmillan.

ADSS (1995), *Mistreatment of Older People: A Discussion Document*. Wolverhampton: ADSS.

ADSS (1991), *Adults at Risk: guidance for directors of social services*. Stockport: ADSS.

Age Concern (1994), *The Next Steps: lessons for the future of community care*. London: Age Concern.

Ahmad, W. and Atkin, K. (eds) (1996), *'Race' and Community Care*. Buckingham: Open University Press.

Ahulu, S. (1995), Discharge to the community of older patients from hospital, in *Nursing Times*, 12 July, vol. 91 no. 28.

Alaszewski, A. and Wun W.-L. (1994), Residential Services, in Malin, N. (ed.) *Implementing Community Care*. Buckingham: Open University Press.

Appleby, J. and Ham, C. (1995), *The Future of Health and Health Care Services: a report for Healthcare 2000*. Birmingham: The Health Services Management Centre, University of Birmingham.

Arber, S. and Gilbert, N. (1993), Men: the forgotten carers, in Walmsley, J., Reynolds, J., Shakespeare, P. and Woolfe, R. (eds) *Health, Welfare and Practice. Reflecting on Roles and Relationships*. London: Sage/Open University Press.

Arblaster, L., Conway, J., Foreman, A. and Hawtin, M. (1996), *Setting Us Up to Fail? A study of the inter-agency working to address housing, health and social care needs of people in general needs housing*. Bristol: The Policy Press.

Askham, J. and Thompson, C. (1990), *Dementia and Home Care*. London: Age Concern.

Association of Metropolitan Authorities (1995), *Guidance on Contracting for Domiciliary and Day Care Services*. London: AMA.

Association of Metropolitan Authorities (1995), *Who Gets Community Care*. London: AMA.

Association of Metropolitan Authorities (1994), *A Survey of Social Services Charging Policies* (1991–2) London: AMA.

Association of Metropolitan Authorities (1994), *Local Authorities and Health Services: the future role of local authorities in the provision of health services*. London AMA.

Atkin, K. and Rollings, J. (1993), *Community Care in Multi-Racial Britain; a critical review of the literature*. London: Social Policy Research Unit/ HMSO.

Atkinson, D. (1986), Engaging Competent Others: A Study of the Support Networks of People with Mental Handicap, in *British Journal of Social Work* vol. 16, Supplement, pp. 83–101.

Audit Commission (1986), *Making a Reality of Community Care*. London: HMSO.

Baldwin, S. and Lunt, N. (1996), *Charging Ahead: the development of local authority charging policies for community care*. York: Joseph Rowntree Foundation.

Bamford, T. (1990), *The Future of Social Work*. London: Macmillan.

Banks, S. (1995), *Ethics and Values in Social Work*. London: Macmillan.

Barclay Report (1982), *Social Workers: their role and tasks*. London: Bedford Square Press.

Barrett, D. (1996), Research, Theory and Practice: Misunderstanding Verbal Language During Community Care Assessments, in Phillips, J. and Penhale, B., *Reviewing Care Management for Older People*. London: Jessica Kingsley.

Barton, R. (1996), *Case Management in Community Mental Health Services*. Norwich: Social Work Monograph.

Bennett, F. (1996), *Highly Charged: policy issues surrounding charging for non-residential care*. York: Joseph Rowntree Foundation.

Bennett, D. and Morris, I. (1983) 'Deinstitutionalization in the U.K.' *International Journal of Mental Health*, no. ii.

Bernard, M. (ed.), (1987), *Developing Services for Elderly Mentally Infirm People: responses to the 'Rising Tide' initiative*. Stoke-on-Trent: Beth Johnson Foundation.

Best, D. (1994), *Purchasing and Contracting Skills*. London: CCETSW.

Bewley, C. and Glendinning, C. (1994), *Involving Disabled People in Community Care Planning*. York: Joseph Rowntree Foundation.

Biestek, F. (1957), *The Casework Relationship*. London: Unwin.

Biggs, S. (1997), Social Policy as Elder Abuse, in Decalmer, P. and Glendenning, F. (eds.) *The Mistreatment of Elderly People*. London: Sage.

Biggs, S. (1991), Community care, case management and the psychodynamic perspective, in *Journal of Social Work Practice*, 5(1), pp. 71–81.

Bion, W. R. (1967), Notes on memory and desire, *Psychoanalytic Forum*, 2, pp. 272–3.

Bird, J. and Davies, M. (1996), *Supervision Registers: an exploratory study*. Norwich: Social Work Management Monographs, UEA.

Bland, R. (ed.) (1996), *Developing Services for Older People and their Families*. London: Jessica Kingsley.

BMA (1994), *Survey on the Implementation of the Community Care Reforms*. London: BMA.

BMA/Law Society (1995), *Assessment of Mental Capacity: guidance for doctors and lawyers*. London: BMA.

Bond, J. (1989), *Evaluation of Continuing Care Accommodation for Elderly People*. Newcastle: University of Newcastle-upon-Tyne Health Care Research Unit.

Bornat, J., Pereira, C., Pilgrim, D. and Williams, F. (eds) (1993), *Community Care: a reader*. Buckingham: Open University Press.

Bradley, G. and Manthorpe, J. (1995), The Dilemmas of Financial Assessment: professional and ethical difficulties, in *Practice*, vol. 7, no. 4.

Brand, E., King, M., Lapsley, I. and Llewellyn, S. (1995), *The Costs and Quality of Care for People with Disabilities*. Edinburgh: The Scottish Office.

Brandon, D. and Towell, N. (1989), *Free to Choose: an introduction to service brokerage*. London: Good Impressions Publishing Ltd.

Braye, S. and Preston-Shoot, M. (1998), Social Work and the Law, in Adams, R., Dominelli, L. and Payne, M. (eds) *Social Work: themes, issues and critical debates*. Basingstoke, Macmillan.

Braye, S. and Preston-Shoot, M. (1995), *Empowering Practice in Social Care*. Buckingham: Open University Press.

British Deaf Association (1996), *Visible Voices*. London: BDA.

British Quality Association, Social Care Agencies Committee (1994), *Notes for the Application of BS5750 to the Continuing Nursing Care Sector* Birmingham: BQA.

British Quality Association, Social Care Agencies Committee (1987), *Guidance on the Interpretation of BS5750 with reference to Social Care Agencies* Birmingham: BQA.

Brown, H. and Turks, V. (1992), *Defining Sexual Abuse as it Affects Adults with Learning Disabilities*. Mental Handicap 20, pp. 44–55.

Bulmer, M. (1987), *The Social Basis of Community Care*. London: Allen and Unwin.

Burgner, T. (1996), *The Regulation and Inspection of Social Services*. London: DoH.

Burke, B. and Harrison, P. (1998), Anti-oppressive Practice, in Adams, R., Dominelli, L. and Payne, M. (eds) *Social Work: themes, issues and critical debates*. Basingstoke: Macmillan.

Burnard, P. (1989), *Counselling Skills for Health Professionals*. London: Chapman and Hall.

Cambridge, P., Hayes, L., Knapp, M. with Gould, E. and Fenyo, A. (1994), *Care in the Community Five Years On*. Aldershot: Arena.

Cameron, E., Badger, F. and Evers, H. (1996), Ethnicity and Care Management, in Phillips, J. and Penhale, B. (eds) *Reviewing Care Management for Older People*. London: Jessica Kingsley.

Carlisle, J. (1996), *The Housing Needs of Ex Prisoners*. York: Joseph Rowntree Foundation.

CCETSW (1990), *Quality Work with Older People*. London: CCETSW.

CCETSW (1994), *Back from the Wellhouse*. London: CCETSW.

CCETSW (1995), *Assuring Quality in the Diploma in Social Work Rules and Requirements for the DipSW* (Paper 30) London: CCETSW.

CCETSW (1996), Adult Services: Particular Pathways to the Diploma in Social Work. Dip. SW Series no. 2. London: CCETSW.

CCETSW/IAMHW (1989), *Multidisciplinary Teamwork: models of good practice*. London: CCETSW.

Centre for Policy on Ageing (1984), *Home Life: a code of practice for residential care*. London: CPA.

Centre for Policy on Ageing (1996), *A Better Home Life*. London: CPA.

Challis, D. (1992), Community Care of Elderly People: bringing together scarcity and choice, needs and costs, in *Financial Accountability and Management*, 8, 2, 77–95.

Challis, D. and Davies, B. (1986), *Case Management in Community Care: an evaluated experiment in the home care of the elderly*. Aldershot: Gower.

Challis, D., Darton, R., Johnson, L., Stone, M. and Traske, D. (1995), *Care Management and Health Care of Older People: the Darlington community care project*. Aldershot: Arena.

Cheetham, J., Fuller, R., McIvor, G. and Petch, A. (1992), *Evaluating Social Work Effectiveness*. Buckingham: Open University Press.

Chetwynd, M. Ritchie, J., Reith, L. and Howard, M. (1996), *The Cost of Care: the impact of charging policy on the lives of disabled people*. Bristol: Policy Press.

Clements, L. (1996), *Community Care and the Law*. London: LAG.

Clifford, D. J. (1994), Towards Anti-oppressive Social Work Method, *Practice* 6(3).

Collins, J. (1996) *Housing, Support and the Rights of People with Learning Difficulties*. York: Joseph Rowntree Foundation.

Common, R. and Flynn, N. (1992), *Contracting for Care*. York: Joseph Rowntree Foundation.

Connolly, J. (1996), Scaling the Wall, *Community Care* 11–17 July (1996) pp. 26–8.

Cooper, R. and Watson, L. (1992), Housing and the Homely Environment, in *Housing*, July/August, p. 42.

Coulshed, V. (1991), *Social Work Practice: an introduction* (2nd ed.). London: Macmillan.

Coulshed, V. and Orme, J. (1998), *Social Work Practice: An Introduction*. Basingstoke: Macmillan.

Cowan, D. (1995), Community Care and Homelessness: R. v. Wirral Metropolitan Borough Council, ex parte B, in *Modern Law Review*, vol. 58, March (1995) pp. 256–61.

Cragg, S. (1996), Community Care Update, *Legal Action* September (1996) pp. 16–18.

Croft, S. and Beresford, P. (1990), *From Paternalism to Participation. involving people in social services*. London: Open Services Project.

Dalley, C. (1988), *Ideologies of Caring*. London: Macmillan.

Dalrymple, J. and Burke, B. (1995), *Anti-Oppressive Practice: social care and the law*. Buckingham: Open University Press.

Davies, B. and Challis, D. (1986), *Matching Resources to Needs in Community Care: an evaluated demonstration of a long term care model*. Aldershot: Gower.

Davies, B. P., Bebbington, A. C., Charnley, H. with Baines, B., Ferlie, E. B., Hughes, M. and Twigg, J. (1990), *Resources, Needs and Outcomes in Community Based Care*. Aldershot: Avebury.

Davies, M. and Connolly, J. (1995a), The Social Worker's Role in the Hospital: seen through the eyes of other professionals, in *Health and Social Care in the Community*.

Davies, M. and Connolly, J. (1995b), Hospital Social Work and Discharge Planning: an exploratory study in East Anglia, in *Health and Social Care in the Community*, vol. 3(6), pp. 363–71.

Davies, M. (ed.) (1997), *The Blackwell Companion to Social Work*. Oxford: Blackwell.

Davies, M. (1994), *The Essential Social Worker* (3rd ed.) Aldershot: Arena.

Davies, R. (1995), I Wanted a Pink Coffin, *HIV/AIDS year consultation exercise for Norfolk Social Services*. Norwich: Norfolk County Council Social Services Department.

Dawson, C. (1995), *Report of the Independent Living Project (Norfolk)*. York: Joseph Rowntree Foundation.

Day, P., Klein, R. and Redmayne, S. (1996), *Why Regulate? Regulating Residential Care for Elderly People*. Bristol: The Policy Press.

Decalmer, P. and Glendenning, F. (eds.) (1997), *The Mistreatment of Elderly People*. London: Sage.

Devore, W. and Schlesinger, E. G. (1991), *Ethnic Sensitive Social Work Practice* (3rd ed.) New York: Macmillan.

Diba, A. (1996) *Meeting the Cost of Continuing Care: public views and perceptions*. York: Joseph Rowntree Foundation.

Dimond, B. (1997), *Legal Aspects of Care in the Community*. Basingstoke: Macmillan.

Doel, M. and Shardlow, S. (1998), *The New Social Work Practice*. Aldershot: Arena.

DoH (1989a), *Working for Patients* (Cm 555). London: HMSO.

DoH (1989b), *The Care of Children: principles and practice in regulations and guidance*. London: HMSO.

DoH (1989c), *Caring for People: community care in the next decade and beyond*. (Cm. 849). London: HMSO.

DoH (1990a), *Community Care in the Next Decade and Beyond. Policy Guidance*. London: HMSO.

DoH (1990b), *The Health of the Nation*. London: DoH.

DoH (1992), *Committed to Quality: quality assurance in social services departments*. London: HMSO.

DoH (1993a), *Monitoring and Development: assessment special study*. A Joint SSI/NMHSE Study of Assessment Procedures in five Local Authority Areas. London: DoH.

DoH (1993b), *Diversification and the Independent Residential Care Sector*. London: HMSO.

DoH (1994b), *Implementing Caring for People: role of the G.P. and primary healthcare team*. London: DoH.

DoH (1994c), *Hospital Discharge Workbook*. London DoH.

DoH (1994d), *Implementing Caring for People: community care for people with HIV and AIDS*. London: DoH.

DoH (1995a), *Building Bridges: a guide to arrangements for inter-agency working for the care and protection of severely disabled people*. London: DoH.

DoH (1995a), *The 'F' factor: reasons why some older people choose residential care*. London: DoH.

DoH (1995b), Moving Forward: a consultation document on the regulation and inspection of social services. London: DoH.

DoH (1996), *Carers (Recognition and Services) Act 1995: Policy Guidance and Practice Guide*. London: DoH.

DoH (1998a), *The New National Health Service: Modern and Dependable*. London: DoH.

DoH (1998b), *Modernising Social Services*. London: DoH.

Dominelli, L. (1998), Anti-oppressive Practice in Context, in Adams, R., Dominelli, L. and Payne, M. (eds) *Social Work: themes, issues and critical debates*. Basingstoke, Macmillan.

Dowling, M. (1998), An Evaluation of Social Work Practice in Relation to Poverty Issues: do social workers' attitudes and actions correspond? in Cheetham, J. and Kazi, M. (eds) *The Working of Social Work*. London: Jessica Kingsley.

Doyal, L. and Gough, I. (1990), *A Theory of Human Need*. London: Macmillan.

Eastman, M. (ed.) (1994), *Old Age Abuse: A New Perspective* (2nd ed.). London: Chapman and Hall.

Egan, G. (1990), *The Skilled Helper* (4th ed.). Pacific Grove CA: Brooks/Cole.

Ellis, K. (1993), *Squaring the Circle: user and carer participation in needs assessment and community care*. University of Birmingham: Joseph Rowntree Foundation.

Evandrou, M. (1997), Social Care Today and Beyond 2020, in Evandrou, M. (ed.) *Baby Boomers: Ageing in the 21st Century*. London: Age Concern.

Evandrou, M. (ed.) (1997), *Baby Boomers: ageing in the 21st century*. London: Age Concern.

Fillit, H., Howe, J. L., Fulop, G., Sach, C., Sell, L., Siegel, P., Miller, M. and Butler, R. N. (1992), Hospital Social Stays in the Frail Elderly and their Relationship to the Intensity of Social Work Intervention, in *Social Work in Health Care* (1992), vol. 18(1), pp. 1–22.

Finch, J. (1989), *Kinship Obligations and Social Change*. Cambridge: Policy Press.

Finch, J. and Mason, J. (1993), *Negotiating Family Responsibilities*. London: Routledge.

Finkelstein, V. (1993), Disability: a social challenge or an administrative responsibility, in Swain, J., Finkelstein, V., French, S. and Oliver, M. *Disabling Barriers – Enabling Environments*. London: Sage.

Fisher, M. (1990), Care management and Social Work: Clients with Dementia, *Practice*, 4(4), pp. 229–41.

Gester, L. (1991), *Quality at the Front Line*. Bristol: School of Advanced Urban Studies, University of Bristol.

Giller, H. and Tutt, N. (1995), Pass the Parcel, in *Community Care*, 18–24 May (1995).

Goldberg, E. M. and Warburton, R. W. (1979), *Ends and Means in Social Work*. London: George Allen and Unwin.

Goldsmith, M. (1996), *Hearing the Voice of People with Dementia*. London: Jessica Kingsley.

Goodwin, S. (1989), Community Care for the Mentally Ill in England and Wales: myths, assumptions and reality, in *Journal of Social Policy*, vol. 18, part 1, pp. 27–52.

Goss, S. and Miller, C. (1995) *From Margin to Mainstream: developing user- and carer-centred community care*. York: Joseph Rowntree Foundation.

Goudie, F. and Alcott, D. (1994), Perspectives in training: assessment and intervention, in Eastman, M (ed.) ((1994)) (2nd ed.) *Old Age Abuse: a new perspective*. London: Chapman and Hall.

Green Paper (1997), *Developing Partnerships in Mental Health*. London: DoH.

Griffiths, S. (1997), *Housing Benefit and Supported Housing: the impact of recent changes*. York: Joseph Rowntree Foundation.

Griffiths, S. (1995), *Supporting Community Care: the contribution of housing benefit*. London: NISW.

Griffiths, Sir Roy, (1988), *Community Care: agenda for action*. London: HMSO.

Guillemard, A.-M. (1993), *Old Age and the Welfare State*. London: Sage.

Hadley, R. and McGrath, M. (1984), *When Services are Local – The Normanton Experience*. London: Allen and Unwin.

Hallett, C. and Birchall, E. (1992), *Co-ordination in Child Protection*. London: HMSO.

Hancock, R. (1998) *Can Housing Wealth Alleviate Poverty Among Britain's Older Population?* Bristol: Fiscal Studies Institute.

Harden, J. (1992), *The Contracting State*. Buckingham: Open University Press.

Harding, T. and Beresford, P. (1996), *The Standards we Expect: what service users and carers want from social services workers*. London: NISW.

Hatch, S. (ed.) *Volunteers: patterns, meaning and motives*. Berkhamsted: The Volunteer Centre.

Health Advisory Service (1983), *The Rising Tide: developing services for mental illness in old age*. London: HMSO.

Health Committee (1996) *Long Term Care: Future Provision and Funding*. Third Report, vol. I, HC 59–1. The Stationery Office Ltd.

Henwood (1992), *Through a Glass Darkly: community care and elderly people*. London: King's Fund Institute.

Heywood, F. and Smart, G. (1996), *Trends in Funding Adaptations*. Bristol: Policy Press.

Higgins, J. (1989), Defining Community Care: realities and myths, *Social Policy and Administration*, vol. 23, no. 1, pp. 3–16.

Hirschman, A. (1970), *Exit, Voice and Loyalty: responses to decline in firms, organisations and states*. Harvard: Harvard University Press.

Hirst, M. and Baldwin, S. (1994), *Unequal Opportunities: growing up disabled*. London: HMSO.

Hoggett, B. (1989), The Elderly Mentally Infirm: procedures for civil commitment and guardianship, in Eekalaar, J. and Pearl, D. (eds), *An Ageing World.* Oxford: Clarendon Press.

Home Office (1995), *Making a difference.* London: HMSO.

Homer, A. C. and Gilleard, C. (1990), Abuse of Elderly People by their Carers, *British Medical Journal,* 301, pp. 1359–62.

Howe, D. (1996), Values in Social Work, paper presented to the East Anglian Practice Teachers' Group. Norwich: UEA.

Hoyes, L., Jeffers, S., Lart, T., Means, R. and Taylor, M. (1993), *User Empowerment and the Reform of Community Care.* Bristol: School for Advanced Urban Studies.

Hudson, J., Watson, L. and Allan, G. (1996), *Moving Obstacles: housing choices and community care.* Bristol: Policy Press.

Hughes, B. (1995), *Older People and Community Care.* Buckingham: Open University Press.

Hughes, B. (1993), A Model for the Comprehensive Assessment of Older People and the Carers, in *British Journal of Social Work,* 23, pp. 345–64.

Huxley, P. (1990) *Effective Community Mental Health Services.* London: Avebury.

Huxley (1991), Effective Case Management for Mentally Ill People: the relevance of recent evidence from the USA for case management services in the UK, in *Social Work and Social Services Review,* 2(3), pp. 192–203.

Huxley, P. (1993), Care Management and Care Management in Community Care, 3, *Journal of Social Work,* 23, pp. 365–81.

Jack, R. (1995), *Empowerment In Community Care.* London: Chapman and Hall.

Jack, R. (ed.) (1998), *Residential versus Community Care.* London: Macmillan.

Joint Advisory Group of Domiciliary Care Associations (1992), *Standards for Registration for Domiciliary Care*: JAGDCA.

Jones, K. (1993), *Asylums and After.* Edinburgh: The Athlone Press.

Jones, S. and Joss, R. (1995), Models of Professionalism, in Yelloly, M. and Henkel, M. (1995) *Learning and Teaching in Social Work: Towards Reflective Practice.* London: Jessica Kingsley.

Jordan, B. (1995), Are the New Right policies sustainable? "Back to Basics" and public choice, in *Journal of Social Policy,* 24(3), pp. 363–84.

Jordan, B. (1996), *A Theory of Poverty and Social Exclusion.* Cambridge: Policy Press.

Jordan, B. (1997), Social Work and Society, in Davies, M. (ed.) *The Blackwell Companion to Social Work.* Oxford: Blackwell.

Joseph Rowntree Foundation Inquiry (1996), *Meeting the Costs of Community Care.* York: Joseph Rowntree Foundation.

Kestenbaum, A. (1996), *Independent Living: A Review.* York: Joseph Rowntree Foundation.

Kestenbaum, A. (1993), *Taking Care in the Market: a study of agency homecare.* RADAR and DIG.

Kohli, R. (1996), Values in Practice, Paper presented to the East Anglian Practice Teachers' Group. Norwich: UEA.

Lamb, B. and Layzell, S. (1995), *Disabled in Britain: counting on community care*. London: Scope.

Langan, J. and Means, R. (1996), Financial Management and Elderly People with Dementia in the UK, in *Ageing in Society*, 16(3): 287–315.

Langan, J. and Means, R. (1994), *Money Matters in Later Life: financial management and elderly people in Kirklees*. Oxford: Anchor Housing Association.

Lapsley, I. (1996), *Markets and Choices: contracts for care*. ESRC Library and Information Service.

Lapsley, I., Llewellyn, S. and Mitchell, F. (1994), *Cost Management in the Public Sector*. London: Longman.

Law Commission (1995), *Mental Incapacity: summary of recommendations*. Consultation Paper no. 231. London: HMSO.

Le Grand, J. and Bartlett, W (eds) (1993), *Quasi-Markets and Social Policy*. Basingstoke: Macmillan.

Letts, P. (1998), *Managing Other People's Property*. London: Age Concern.

Levin, E., Sinclair, I. and Gorbach, P. (1989), *Families, Service and Confusion in Old Age*. Aldershot: Gower.

Lewis, J. (1997), Community Care, in Evandrou, M. (ed.) *Baby Boomers: ageing in the 21st century*. London: Age Concern.

Lewis, J. and Glennerster, H. (1996), *Implementing the New Community Care*. Buckingham: Open University Press.

Lipsky, M. (1980), *Street Level Bureaucracy*. New York: Russell Sage.

Lowelock, R. and Powell, J. with Craggs, S. (1995) *Assessing the Social Support Needs of Visually Impaired People*. York: Joseph Rowntree Foundation.

Lyons, K., La Valle, I. and Gramwood, C. (1995) 'Career Patterns of Qualified Social Workers; Discussion of a Recent Survey. *British Journal of Social Work*, 25, pp. 173–90.

Lynch, G. and Pope, B. (1990), Involving Clients and Staff in the Development of a Quality Assurance System: Social Services and Quality Assurance, Manchester: Social Information Systems.

Macdonald, C. and Myers, F. (1995) *Assessment and Care Management: the practitioner speaks*. University of Stirling: Social Work Research Centre.

Macdonald, S. (1991), *All Equal under the Act?* London: REU/NISW.

Mackintosh, S. and Leather, P. (eds) (1992), *Home Improvement under the New Regime*. Occasional Paper 38. Bristol: School of Advanced Urban Studies.

Mackintosh, S., Means, R. and Leather, P. (1990), *Housing in Later Life*. School of Advanced Urban Studies Study 4. Bristol: School of Advanced Urban Studies.

Malin, N. (ed.) (1994), *Implementing Community Care*. Buckingham: Open University Press.

Malpas, P. and Means, R. (eds) (1993), *Implementing Housing Policy*. Milton Keynes: Open University Press.

Mares, P. (1996), *Business Skills for Care Management: a guide to costing, contracting and negotiating*. London: Age Concern.

Marsh, P. and Fisher, M. (1992), *Good Intentions: developing partnership in social services*. York: Joseph Rowntree Foundation.

Mattison, J. and Sinclair, I. (1979), *Mate and Stalemate*. London: Institute of Marital Studies.

Mayo, J. (1994), *Communities and Caring: the mixed economy of welfare*. New York: St. Martin's Press.

McCreadie, C. (1996), *Elder Abuse: Update on Research*. London: Age Concern.

McDonald, A. (1997), *Challenging Local Authority Decisions*. Birmingham: Venture Press.

McDonald, A. (1993), Elder Abuse and Neglect – The Legal Framework, in *Journal of Elder Abuse and Neglect*, vol. 5, no. 2, pp. 81–96.

McDonald, A. and Taylor, M. (1995), *The Law and the Elderly*. London: Sweet and Maxwell.

McDonald, A. and Taylor, M. (1994), Access to Health Care Services and Information in Residential Care, in *Elders: The Journal of Care and Practice*, vol. 3, no. 4, pp. 41–52.

McLeod, E. (1996), *Working for Equality in Health*. London: Routledge.

McPherson, B. (1988), In Whose Best Interests? in *Social Work Today*. 22 September.

McWilliams, C. L., Brown, J. B., Carmichael, J. L. and Lehman, J. M. (1994), A New Perspective on Threatened Autonomy in Elderly Persons – the Disempowering Process, in *Social Science and Medicine*, vol. 38(2), pp. 327–38.

Means, M. (1997), Housing Options in 2020: a suitable home for all? in Evandrou, M. (ed.) *Baby Boomers: ageing in the 21st century*. London: Age Concern.

Means, R. and Smith, R. (1994), *Community Care: Policy and Practice*. Basingstoke: Macmillan.

Mencap (1995), *Community Care: Britain's other lottery*. London: Mencap.

Morris, J. (1993a), Us and Them? Feminist research and community care, in Bornat, J., Pereira, C., Pilgrim, D. and William, F. *Community Care: a reader*. Buckingham: Open University Press.

Morris, J. (1993b), Gender and Disability, in Swain, J. Finkelstein, V., French, S. and Oliver, M. (eds) *Disabling Barriers – Enabling Environments*. London: Sage/Open University Press.

Morris, J. (1994), Community Care or Independent Living? in *Critical Social Policy*, no. 40, pp. 25–45.

NACRO (1996), *Keeping Your Home: information for prisoners on getting housing costs paid*. London: NACRO.

National Consumer Council (1995), *Charging Consumers for Social Services: local authority policy and practice*. London: NCC.

National Federation of Housing Associations (1995), *Managing Vulnerability: the challenge for managers of independent housing*. NFHA.

National Institute of Adult Continuing Education (1996), *Still a Chance to Learn?* Leicester: NAICE.

Neill, J. and Williams, J. (1992), *Leaving Hospital: elderly people and their discharge to community care*. London: HMSO.

Neill, J., Sinclair, I., Gorbach, P. and Williams, J. (1988), *A Need for Care? elderly applicants for local authority homes.* Aldershot: Avebury.
Nocon, A. and Qureshi, H. (1996), *Outcomes of Community Care for Users and Carers: a Social Services perspective.* Buckingham: Open University Press.
Norman, A. (1980), *Rights and Risks.* London: National Corporation for the Care of Old People.
Norman, A. (1991), *Triple Jeopardy: growing old in a second homeland.* London: Nation Corporation for the Care of Old People.
O'Brian, J, and Lyle C. (1987), *Framework for Accomplishment.* Atlanta, Georgia: Responsive Systems Associates.
Ogg, J. and Bennett, G. (1992), Elder Abuse in Britain, in *British Medical Journal*, 305, pp. 998–9.
Oliver, P.J.P. (1991), 'The social care directive: development of a quality of life profile for use in community services for the mentally ill. *Social Work and Social Services Review*, 3 (1), pp. 5–45.
Oliver, M. (1996), *Understanding Disability: from theory to practice.* Basingstoke: Macmillan.
OPCS (1988/9), *OPCS Surveys of Disability in Great Britain*, vols 1, 3, 4. London: HMSO.
Øvretveit, J. (1993), *Co-ordinating Community Care: multidisciplinary teams and care management.* Buckingham: Open University Press.
Øvretveit, J., Mathias, P. and Thompson, T. (eds) (1997) *Interprofessional Working for Health and Social Care.* London: Macmillan.
Parker, G. (1989), *With Due Care and Attention: a review of research on informal care.* London: Family Policy Studies Centre.
Parker, G. (1993), *With This Body: caring and disability in marriage.* Buckingham: Open University Press.
Payne, M. (1995), *Social Work and Community Care.* Basingstoke: Macmillan.
Payne, M. (1998), Social work theories and reflective practice, in Adams, R., Dominelli, L. and Payne, M. (eds) *Social Work: themes, issues and critical debates.* Basingstoke: Macmillan.
Peace, S., Kellaher, N. and Willcocks, D. (1997), *Re-evaluating residential care.* Buckingham: Open University Press.
Petch, A. (1994) *Assessment and Care Management in Scotland: an overview.* University of Stirling: Social Work Research Centre.
Petch, A. (1996), Delivering community care: initial implementation of care management in Scotland. Edinburgh: Stationery Office.
Petch, A. (1997) 'Community Care', in Davies, M. (ed.) *The Blackwell Companion to Social Work* London: Blackwell.
Personal Social Services Research Unit (1996) *Bulletin* University of Kent: PSSRU.
Pfeffer, N. and Coote, A. (1991), *Is Quality Good for You?* Social Policy Paper no. 5. London: Institute of Public Policy Research.
Phillips, J. (1990), *The Process of Admission into Private Residential Care.* London: Avebury.
Phillips, J. (1996), Reviewing the Literature on Care Management, in Phillips, J. and Penhale, B. (eds) *Reviewing Care Management for Older People.* London: Jessica Kingsley.

Pietroni, M. (1995), The Nature and Aims of Professional Education for Social Workers: a post-modern perspective, in Yelloly, M. and Henkel, M. (1995), *Learning and Teaching in Social Work: towards reflective practice*. London: Jessica Kingsley.

Pilling, D. (1992), *Approaches to Community Care for People with Disabilities*. London: Jessica Kingsley.

Price Waterhouse/DoH (1991), *Implementing Community Care: purchaser, commissioner and provider roles*. London: HMSO.

Qureshi, H. Challis, D. J. and Davies, B. P. (1983), Motivation and Reward of Helpers in the Kent Community Care Scheme, in Hatch, S. (ed.) *Volunteers: patterns, meaning and motives*. Berkhamsted: The Volunteer Centre.

Qureshi, H., and Walker, A. (1989), *The Caring Relationship: elderly people and their families*. London: Macmillan.

RADAR (1992), *Disabled People Have Rights*. London: Radar.

Radia, K. (1996), *Ignored, Silenced, Neglected: housing and mental health care needs of Asian people*. York: Joseph Rowntree Foundation.

Raiff, N. R. and Shore, B. K. (1993), *Advanced Case Management: new strategies for the nineties*. California: SAGE Publications.

Rees, S. (1991), *Achieving Power, Practice and Policy in Social Welfare*. North Sydney: Allen and Unwin.

Reigate, N. (1995), *The Social Worker as Care Manager*. Norwich: UEA Monographs.

Reigate, N. (1997), Networking, in Davies, M. (ed.) *The Blackwell Companion to Social Work*. Oxford: Blackwell.

Renshaw, J. (1988), Care in the Community: individual care planning and case management, in *British Journal of Social Work*, 18 (Supplement), pp. 79–105.

Robertson, S. (1995), *Fed and Watered: the views of older people on need, assessment and care management*. Age Concern: Scotland.

Rogers, C. (1967), *On becoming a person: a therapist's view of psychotherapy*. London: Constable.

Royal College of Nursing (1992), *A Scandal Waiting to Happen: elderly people and nursing care in residential and nursing homes*. London: RCN.

Russell, L. (1995) *Mixed Fortunes: the funding of the local voluntary sector*. York: Joseph Rowntree Foundation.

Sainsbury, E. (1975), *Social Work with Families*. London: Routledge and Kegan Paul.

Sainsbury, R., Hirst, M. and Lawton, D. (1995), *Evaluation of Disability Living Allowance and Attendance Allowance*. London: SPRU.

Saunders, D. (1992) Dimensions of Community Mental Health Care. London: Avebury.

Schön, D. (1993), *The Reflective Practitioner*. New York: Basic Books.

Scottish Federation of Housing Associations (1995), *Medical Priority in Housing Allocation: Briefing Paper no. 17*. SFHA.

Seed, P. (1988) *Day Care at the Crossroads*. Tunbridge Wells: Costello.

Seed, P. (1990), *Introducing Network Analysis in Social Work*. London: Jessica Kingsley.

Shardlow, S. (1998), Values, Ethics and Social Work, in Adams, R., Dominelli,

L. and Payne, M. (eds) *Social Work: themes, issues and critical debates.* Basingstoke: Macmillan.

Shemmings, D. (1991), *Client Access to Records: participation in social work.* Aldershot: Arena.

Sheppard, M. (1995), *Care Management and the New Social Work: a critical analysis.* Whiting and Birch Ltd./SCA (Education) Co-Publication.

Simiç, P. (1996), What's in a Word? From Social 'Worker' To Care 'Manager', in *Practice* vol. 7 no. 3 pp. 5–18.

Sinclair, I., Parker, R., Leat, D. and Williams, J. (1990), *The Kaleidoscope of Care.* London: HMSO.

Smale, G. and Tuson, G. with Biehal, N. and Marsh, P. (1993), *Empowerment, Assessment, Care Management and the Skilled Worker.* London: NISW/HMSO.

Smith, P. and Thomas, N. (1993), *Contracts and Competition in Public Services.* Paper presented at the Association of Directors of Services, National Research Conference, Bristol.

Social Services Committee (1985), *Second Report: Community Care.* H. of C. Paper 13–1, Session 1984–5. London: HMSO.

Specht, H. and Vickery, A. (eds) (1977), *Integrating Social Work Methods.* London: Allen and Unwin.

SSI (1987), *From Home Help to Home Care.* London: DoH.

SSI (1989), *Homes are for Living In.* London: HMSO.

SSI (1992), *Social Services for Hospital Patients III. Users and Carer Perspectives.* London: DoH.

SSI (1993a), *Guidance on Standards in Short-term Breaks.* London: HMSO.

SSI (1993b), *No Longer Afraid: the safeguard of elderly people in domestic settings: practice guidelines.* London: HMSO.

SSI (1993c), *Inspection of Assessment and Care Management Arrangements in Social Services Departments.* Interim Overview Report. London: DoH.

SSI (1993d), *'Whose Life is it Anyway?' A Report of an Inspection of Services for People with Multiple Impairments.* London: DoH.

SSI (1994), *Substance Misuse: commissioning community care.* London: DoH.

SSI (1995a), *Developing Quality Standards for Home Support Services.* London.: DoH.

SSI (1995b), *Assessing Older People with Dementia Living in the Community.* London: DoH.

SSI (1995c), *Social Services Department Inspection Units – third overview report of an inspection of the work of inspection units in nineteen local authorities.* London: DoH.

SSI (1996a), *Working Alongside Volunteers: promoting the role of volunteers in community care.* London: DoH.

SSI (1996b), *Young carers: making a start.* London: DoH.

SSI (1996c), *'Growing Up and Moving On'.* Report of a SSI Project on transition services for disabled young people. London: DoH.

SSI (1996d), *'Growing Up and Moving On'.* Report of SSI Workshops on transition services for disabled young people. London: DoH.

SSI (1996e), *The Inspection of Complaints Procedures in Local Authority Social Service Departments. 3rd Overview Report.* London: DoH.

SSI (1997a), *A Service on the Edge. Inspection of Services for Death and Hard of Hearing People*. London: DoH.
SSI (1997b), *Older People with Learning Disabilities*. London: DoH.
SSI (1998), '*They Look After Their Own, Don't They?' Inspection of Community Care Services for Black and Ethnic Minority Older People*. London: DoH.
SSI/DoH (1991a), *Care Management and Assessment: Practitioners' Guide*. London: HMSO.
SSI/DoH (1991b), *Care Management and Assessment: Managers' Guide*. London: HMSO.
SSI/DoH (1993), *The Inspection of the Complaints Procedures in Local Authority Social Services Departments*. London: DoH.
SSI/DoH (1996a), *Searching for Service – An Inspection of Service Responses made to the Needs of Disabled Young Adults and their Carers*. London: DoH.
SSI/DoH (1996b), *Overview of the National Inspection of Social Services Department Arrangements for the Assessment and Delivery of Home Care Services*. London: DoH.
Stalker, K. (1994) *Implementing Community Care in Scotland: early snapshots*. University of Stirling: Social Work Research Centre.
SSI/DoH (1996c), *Inspection of Social Services for People who Misuse Alcohol and Drugs*. London: DoH.
Stalker, K. (ed.) (1996), *Developments in Short-Term Care: breaks and opportunities*. London: Jessica Kingsley.
Strauss, A. L. (1964) *Psychiatric Institutions and Ideoligies*. New York: Free Press of Glencoe.
Stevenson, O. (1996), *Elder Protection in the Community: what can we learn from child protection?* London: DoH.
Stevenson, O. and Parsloe, P. (1993), *Community Care and Empowerment*. York: Joseph Rowntree Foundation.
Stewart, G. and Stewart, J. (1993), *Social Work and Housing*. London: Macmillan.
SWSI (1995), *Time Well Spent: A Report on Day Services for People with Mental Illness*. Edinburgh: HMSO.
Taylor, M., Langan, J. and Hoggett, P. (1995), *Developing Diversity: voluntary and private organisations in community care*. Aldershot: Arena.
Thoburn, J. (1986), Quality Control in Child Care, *British Journal of Social Work*, 16, pp. 543–56.
Thompson, N. (1995), *Age and Dignity: working with older people*. Aldershot: Arena.
Thompson, N. (1993), *Anti-Discriminatory Practice*. London: Macmillan.
Thompson, S. and Thompson, N. (1993), *Perspectives on Ageing*. Norwich: UEA Social Work Monographs.
Tinker, A. (1989), *An Evaluation of Very Sheltered Housing*. London: HMSO.
Tinker, A., McCreadie, C., Wright, F. and Salvage, A. V. (1994), *The Care of Frail Elderly People in the U.K.* London: HMSO.
Tomlinson, S. and Colquhoun, R. (1995), The Political Economy of Special Educational Needs in Britain, in *Disability and Society*, 10, 2, pp. 191–202.

Townsend, P. (1981), The structural dependency of the elderly: a creation in the twentieth century, *Ageing in Society*, 1(1) pp. 5–28.

Townsend, P. and Davidson, N. (1992) *Inequalities in Health: the Black report*. London: Penguin.

Turk, V. and Brown, H. (1992) Sexual Abuse and Adults with Learning Disabilities: preliminary communication of survey results, *Mental Handicap*, vol. 20, June, pp. 56–8.

Twigg, J. (1989), Models of Carers: how do social care agencies conceptualise their relationship with informal carers, in *Journal of Social Policy*, 18, pp. 53–66.

Vickery, A. 1976, A Unitary Approach to Social Work with the Mentally Disordered, in Olsen, M.R. (ed.) *Differential Approaches in Social Work with the Mentally Disordered*. Birmingham: BASW.

Victor, C. (1991), *Health and Health Care in Later Life*. Buckingham: Open University Press.

Wagner, G. (1988), *Residential Care. A Positive Choice*. London: HMSO.

Warburton, W. (1989), *Entering Residential Care: a survey of the literature*. London: DoH.

Watson, L. and Cooper, R. (1992), *Housing with Care*. York: Joseph Rowntree Foundation.

Wihner, M. (1992) *Quality Work with Older People: developing models of good practice*. London: CCETSW.

Willcocks, D., Peace, S. and Kellaher, N. (1987), *Private Lives in Public Places*. London: Tavistock.

Yelloly, M. and Henkel, M. (1995), *Learning and Teaching in Social Work: towards reflective practice*. London: Jessica Kingsley.

# Index

264

*Index*